Microsoft

Microsoft
Visual Basic®
Design
Patterns

William Stamatakis

PUBLISHED BY
Microsoft Press
A Division of Microsoft Corporation
One Microsoft Way
Redmond, Washington 98052-6399

Library of Congress Cataloging-in-Publication Data
Stamatakis, William.
 Microsoft Visual Basic Design Patterns / William Stamatakis.
    p.   cm.
  Includes index.
  ISBN 1-57231-957-7
  1. Microsoft Visual BASIC.   2. BASIC (Computer program language)   I. Title.

 QA76.73.B3 S815   2000
 005.26'8--dc21   00-020235

Printed and bound in the United States of America.

1 2 3 4 5 6 7 8 9   QMQM   5 4 3 2 1 0

Distributed in Canada by Penguin Books Canada Limited.

A CIP catalogue record for this book is available from the British Library.

Microsoft Press books are available through booksellers and distributors worldwide. For further information about international editions, contact your local Microsoft Corporation office or contact Microsoft Press International directly at fax (425) 936-7329. Visit our Web site at mspress.microsoft.com. Send comments to *mspinput@microsoft.com*.

Acquisitions Editor: Ben Ryan
Project Editor: John Pierce
Technical Editor: Jean Ross

This book is dedicated to my darling wife, Elva, who has given me nothing but love and support throughout this endeavor. Thanks for hanging in there.

Love always,
Bill

CONTENTS

C H A P T E R   S I X

Object By Value   **105**

C H A P T E R   S E V E N

Smart Proxy   **123**

CHAPTER ELEVEN

Repository **173**

CHAPTER TWELVE

State **189**

CHAPTER THIRTEEN

Event Service **207**

PART III: APPENDIXES

APPENDIX A

Object Notation **227**

APPENDIX B

Working with Interfaces and Classes **235**

ACKNOWLEDGMENTS

I first want to thank the authors of the book *Design Patterns*: Erich Gamma, Richard Helm, Ralph Johnson, and John Vlissides. Object-oriented programming principles are relatively new to Microsoft Visual Basic, and their evolution still has a ways to go. Your book, which takes object-oriented programming to new levels, inspired me to share with the Visual Basic community the concepts you developed primarily for C++ programmers. Because of the enhancements that have occurred in each subsequent version of Visual Basic, I think Visual Basic programmers are now ready to embrace object-oriented programming and the use of design patterns as implementation tools.

I next want to thank all the folks at Microsoft Press who made this book a reality. Many thanks to Ben Ryan for contacting me and lobbying for Microsoft Press to publish my unprecedented subject matter for Visual Basic. I'm a programmer who writes, more than a writer who programs, so I'm truly grateful to all those involved in the editing process who have turned my somewhat coherent words into a remarkably readable book. These people include Wendy Zucker, Jean Ross, Mary Barnard, Sally Stickney, and John Pierce. John, thanks for seeing the project through until the end. Jean, thanks so much for your due diligence in confirming the technical accuracy of the sample applications, which I think are a major benefit of this book.

I'd also like to thank Steven Lieblich for his extraordinary confidence in my abilities and for the tremendous opportunity he has given me to put my ideas into practice—ideas that have paid high dividends on many levels. Real-world experience is the affirmation that has allowed me to write this book.

In addition, I'd like to express my deepest thanks and gratitude to my mother, Aurea, who provided me with a solid foundation that has enabled me to achieve my aspirations.

Finally, I want to thank my wife, Elva, and our sons, Maxwell and Ethan, who bring such love and joy into my life. Your love and support have helped me cultivate the positive energy required to follow through on my ambitions. What I do, I do for you.

USING THE COMPANION CD

The CD included with this book contains complete sample files for all the design patterns discussed in this book. The CD also includes a fully searchable electronic version of the book.

Installing the Sample Files

All the files for the sample applications discussed in this book are located in the Samples folder. You can browse the samples from the CD, or you can install them onto your hard disk to run them and to use them with your own applications.

> NOTE: If you're unable to browse the files in the Samples folder, you might have an older CD driver that doesn't support long file names. If this is the case, to browse the files you must install the samples files on your hard disk by running the setup program.

If you have the autorun feature in Microsoft Windows enabled, you'll see a splash screen when you insert the CD into the CD-ROM drive that will provide you with setup options. To start this screen manually, run StartCD from the root directory of the CD. Installing the sample files requires approximately 4 MB of disk space. If you have trouble running any of the sample files, refer to the "Sample Application" section of the corresponding design pattern or to the Readme.txt file in the root directory of the CD.

To uninstall the sample files, open Add/Remove Programs in Control Panel, select VB Design Patterns Samples, and click Add/Remove. (In Windows 2000, click Change/Remove.)

Running the Sample Files

When you install the sample files, they are copied by default to your hard disk to a folder named VBDesign. The samples are in folders named according to the design pattern they implement. Most of the samples for this book require the use of DLL and EXE files, and sometimes IDL and TLB files. Some samples contain their own Setup program, whereas others must be set up manually before you can run them. Manually setting up the sample files requires that you register the DLLs and TLBs for the sample. Register DLLs by typing *regsvr32 filename.dll* at a command prompt. Always register the DLL files that are located in the Release folder of the appropriate project. An alternative to running regsvr32 is to open the projects and recompile them. The creation of a new DLL file will automatically register the DLL. Register TLBs by typing *regtlib filename.tlb*.

> **NOTE:** You can unregister a DLL by typing *regsvr32 /u filename.dll* at a command prompt, and you can unregister a TLB by typing *regtlib /u filename.tlb*.

System Requirements

The following is a list of system requirements necessary to run the sample files contained on this CD:

- Microsoft Windows 2000, Microsoft Windows NT 4.0 Service Pack 4 or higher, Microsoft Windows 98, or Microsoft Windows 95
- Microsoft Visual Basic 6.0 Service Pack 3
- Microsoft Excel 97 or later (Not required for all samples.)
- Microsoft Access 97 or later (Not required for all samples.)
- Microsoft ActiveX Data Objects 2.1 or later (Not required for all samples.)

E-book

This CD contains an electronic version of the book. This e-book allows you to view the book text on screen and to search the contents. For information on installing and using the e-book, see the Readme.txt file in the Ebook folder.

Support

Every effort has been made to ensure the accuracy of this book and the contents of the companion CD. Microsoft provides corrections for books through the World Wide Web at the following address:

http://mspress.microsoft.com/support/

If you have comments, questions, or ideas regarding this book or the companion CD, please send them to Microsoft using either of the following methods:

Postal Mail:
    Microsoft Press
    Attn: Microsoft Visual Basic Design Patterns Editor
    One Microsoft Way
    Redmond, WA 98052-6399
E-mail:
    MSPINPUT@MICROSOFT.COM

Please note that product support is not offered through the above mail addresses. For support information regarding Microsoft Visual Basic, see the Microsoft Visual Studio Web site at http://msdn.microsoft.com/vstudio. You can also call Standard Support at (425) 635-7011 weekdays between 6 a.m. and 6 p.m. Pacific time, or you can search Microsoft's Support Online at *http://support.microsoft.com/support.*

OBJECT BASICS

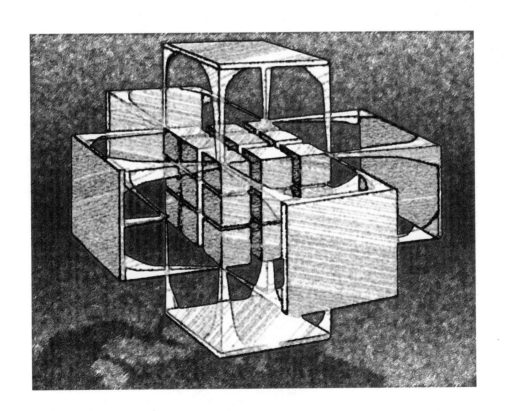

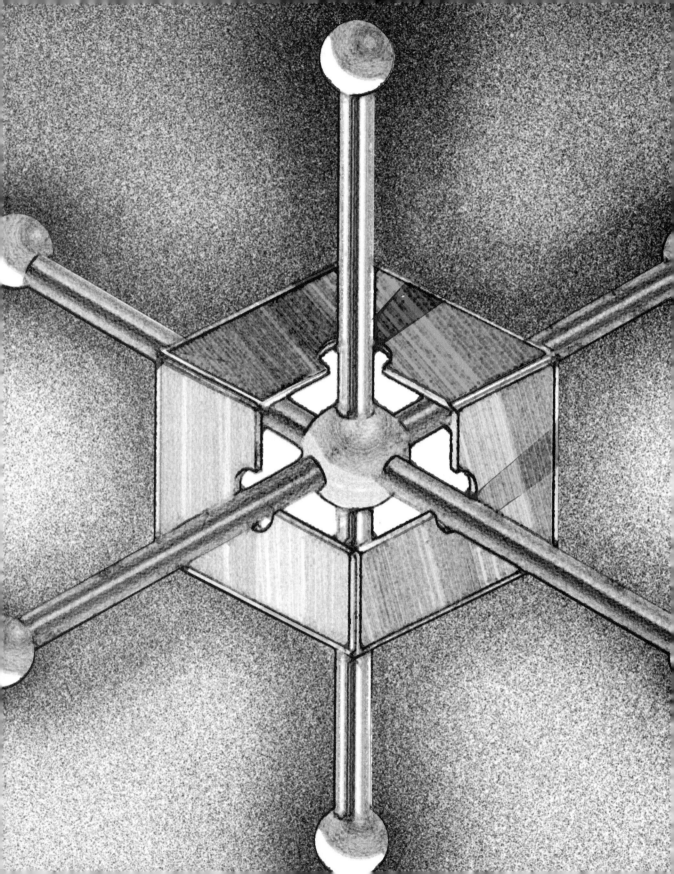

Introduction to Design Patterns

It is often said by programmers, managers, and end users alike that most applications written in Microsoft Visual Basic are easy to start but hard to finish. The truth is that this problem crops up in all programming languages if the design of the system is an afterthought to the implementation. What motivates this approach is that with practically no programming experience, you could build a Microsoft Windows application in Visual Basic by making use of its vast feature set, such as the Form window, Menu Editor, data-aware controls, and so forth. Using the mouse more than using the keyboard, you could build a Windows application that interacts with a database, which is amazing. As a result, many Visual Basic applications start out as prototypes with a heavy emphasis on the user interface. Many of these prototypes evolve into production systems as functionality is added. The line between prototype and polished application becomes fuzzy. Production systems created from prototypes in this fashion usually do not scale to acceptable production quality.

Novice programmers tend to concentrate on the features of Visual Basic, such as the visual aspects, third-party controls, or the language itself. Understanding how to use these features is crucial, but that knowledge is counterproductive if a system design has not been developed. Without a system design, a programmer discovers problems as they occur, and provides a solution each time without insight about the ramifications. Expert programmers, on the other hand, start with a design. This means they have done some analysis of the problem domain and have devised solutions for all the issues they have identified.

Designing Visual Basic object-oriented systems is not simple, but the payoff far outweighs the difficulty. If correctly designed, an object-oriented system is scalable, extensible, and reusable. Design patterns help expert object-oriented programmers reach that goal.

The purpose of this book is to help you design and code better-quality object-oriented systems in Visual Basic by making effective use of design patterns.

What Is a Design Pattern?

A *design pattern* is a predefined solution to a recurring object-oriented design problem. The design pattern defines a relationship between collaborating interfaces, classes, and objects, each with a unique role that helps solve the problem. An *interface* defines a group of property and method signatures. A *class* defines an implementation of the interfaces it supports. An *object* is constructed based on a class; therefore, an object supports the interfaces implemented by its class. Furthermore, interaction with an object is possible only through the interfaces exposed by that object. Object-oriented systems are based on objects. Clearly, then, design patterns are an abstraction of a solution to a problem in a specified context. Objects constructed based on classes defined by a design pattern are instances of the design pattern solution.

Using Design Patterns to Solve Design Problems

Designing object-oriented systems can be challenging. As an architect, you must break down a system into objects based on the information you gathered primarily during the analysis phase. You can derive certain generalizations from the objects you identify that make it possible for you to define classes for each unique object in your system. You can then produce a class diagram using any standard notation you favor, such as Object Modeling Technique (OMT), Unified Modeling Language (UML), and so on. (For more information on object notation, see Appendix A.) This class diagram is a self-documenting, accurate generalization of how your system is structured.

You can use one of several approaches to break down a system into objects. One approach is to identify the nouns and the verbs in the system: the nouns are the objects, and the verbs are the object methods. Another approach is to mirror your design to that of the business process. In this case, each process is an object, and each process flow is the action performed on an object; therefore, process flows are object methods.

Many questions will arise as you break down a system into objects. For instance, to what granularity should you break down the process? Suppose you have identified a process that requires information in a system to be cleared by the legal department. We'll call this the Legal process. This process might be complicated enough to warrant the implementation of several smaller internal processes. Should each internal process be an object in your system, or should they be methods of one Legal object type?

Objects package data and functions. By default, data is private to an object. Interfaces of an object are an abstraction of the object's representation. Conversely, an object's data is encapsulated to the point where the data is not exposed by the object's interface. Exposing the internal representation of an object increases its vulnerability to its consumers. As a result of this exposure, you lose the benefit of encapsulation. The amount of encapsulation determines an object's independence—more independence means you have more flexibility to modify the object to improve its implementation or to change its behavior without regard for any adverse effects on its consumers. The decisions you make regarding granularity and encapsulation will determine the extent to which the benefits of the object-oriented methodology, such as reusability, scalability, extensibility, and so on, are realized in your system.

If you're not realizing these benefits, you have problems in your system design. These problems are most likely a result of your attempt to mirror your design from a functional perspective or a process-flow perspective. To fully gain reusability, scalability, and so forth, you must extend your thinking to include ideas that will produce solutions that address these benefits. These solutions are abstractions of ideas that can be reapplied to systems that are completely diverse in nature. There is no greater form of reusability.

Expert object-oriented programmers and architects are proficient because they can design systems within a specified context, yet they can identify problems in the design and reapply solutions devised from experience. "Design patterns" is the official term that articulates these solutions, and the concept was more formally introduced in *Design Patterns* by Gamma, et al (Addison-Wesley, 1994). That book raised awareness in the object-oriented programming community about how to devise solutions that result in system reuse, scalability, and extensibility, and has inspired me to write this book. I strongly recommend you read Gamma's book.

Design patterns formally document the object-oriented design solutions—whether they are organic or were previously undocumented or inaccessible—known by many experts. Thus, the design patterns presented in this book are not new solutions, but rather are popular and proven solutions that have been implemented by expert object-oriented programmers. One intention of this book is to make these solutions easily accessible to the Visual Basic object-oriented programmer.

For example, if you wanted to reuse the functionality of legacy procedural code or dynamically extend the functionality of existing classes located in a class library, you could employ the Adapter design pattern, as shown in Chapter 4. What if you wanted to persist the state of an object to a data source, such as a Microsoft SQL Server database, an ASCII text file, or a Microsoft Excel workbook? Regardless of the data source or the context of the system, the Repository design pattern would be an appropriate solution. (See Chapter 11.) These kinds of problems frequently manifest themselves in object-oriented designs in varying contexts to which design pattern solutions can be applied.

Who Should Read This Book?

Programmers and system architects who have an intermediate or higher level of knowledge of Visual Basic object-oriented programming will find this book beneficial because it provides object-oriented design solutions that solve system design problems. Ultimately, problems in system design translate to failure in system implementation. In many cases, if you're going to produce optimal performance and reliability, you must rewrite the system rather than simply implement a quick fix.

Any expert will tell you that designing systems is an iterative process. The first design is usually not the answer to all possible system scenarios for such reasons as time constraints for system deliverables, the constantly changing list of end-user requirements, and limitations of the current technologies. Programmers and architects who are faced with these challenges will learn to construct designs that can evolve with the least amount of disruption.

Contents Overview

This book is made up of three sections. The goal of the first section is to lay the foundation for understanding and appreciating the design patterns discussed in the chapters of the second section. The appendixes in the third section cover topics you'll need to be familiar with to use this book effectively.

Part I: Object Basics

This section provides an overview of the hows and whys of Visual Basic object-oriented programming, which is made possible by COM (the magic behind the curtains). You do not have to be an expert on COM, but you should have a solid understanding of certain aspects of it that will affect the performance and the behavior of your Visual Basic application. This section raises the curtains by explaining specific features of COM and COM's impact on Visual Basic.

Part II: Design Patterns Directory

This section comprises several chapters, each dedicated to explaining a specific design pattern. To help you understand and select effectively the appropriate design pattern for your scenarios, chapters in this section adhere to the following structure:

- ■ **Purpose**   States the intent of the design pattern.

- ■ **Utilization**   Describes the design problems that warrant the use of the design pattern.

- **Scenario**   Describes a situation that motivates the need to use the design pattern.

- **Object Model**   Presents the layout of the design pattern using standard object notation, such as an OMT class diagram; the object model illustrates the design pattern solution in diagram form.

- **Roles**   Describes the roles of each object in the design pattern.

- **Relationships**   Describes the interactions of all objects in the design pattern.

- **Ramifications**   Describes the benefits and drawbacks of using the design pattern.

- **Implementation**   Explains how to implement the design pattern in Visual Basic.

- **Sample Application**   Provides a complete working implementation of the design pattern along with an in-depth analysis.

- **COMments**   All the design patterns described in this book can be implemented in Visual Basic to take advantage of the technologies offered in COM and ActiveX. Therefore, when appropriate, I'll provide further insight on these effects, based on the implementation of the design pattern specified.

- **Related Patterns**   Refers briefly to other related design patterns described in the book.

Because all design pattern chapters are identically structured, selecting the appropriate pattern for a given problem is a logical process, as described in the following section.

Part III: Appendixes

This section has two appendixes. Appendix A describes the object notation used in the illustrations in this book. Appendix B briefly discusses some of the issues involved in working with interfaces and classes, such as defining COM interfaces and classes in Visual Basic, freezing an interface contract using features in the Visual Basic intergrated development environment (IDE) and using the COM interface definition language (IDL), and supporting Automation in Microsoft ActiveX components created in Visual Basic for the benefit of scripting languages such as Microsoft Visual Basic, Scripting Edition (VBScript) and Microsoft JScript.

Selecting a Design Pattern

To select a design pattern, you should first know what problem you are trying to resolve. By reading the "Purpose" section of the design pattern chapters, you can identify a few design patterns that might provide the required solution. Next, read the "Utilization" section of each chapter you have chosen. This section provides brief, explicit instances that illustrate when that particular design pattern should be utilized. (This defines your design problem.)

At this point, you can compare the "Utilization" sections between chapters to help you make an intelligent choice. If you still want more information, read the "Scenario" section of each selected chapter, which provides a concrete example of implementing the design pattern in question. When you select your design pattern, read the entire chapter to appreciate fully how the design pattern solves your problem from design to implementation. Finally, explore the sample applications on the companion CD at the back of this book—they bring to life the solution you hope to duplicate.

In some cases, your design problem might not clearly match any one design pattern; it might require a hybrid solution of more than one design pattern, which is completely acceptable. In finding a solution, you might even discover or create a pattern not covered in this book. Maybe the scope of your problem is too broad. Refining the scope by restructuring your design can help significantly in finding your solution. Remember there is no one-size-fits-all solution to designing the perfect object-oriented system, if there is such a thing. You just get better at it with experience—and with the help of this book.

You don't have to read this book from front to back to benefit from the material presented. Feel free to skip around. If you consider yourself an expert Visual Basic object-oriented programmer, you can skim through the next two chapters and spend most of your time in Part II. If you consider yourself fluent in the language features that support the fundamentals of object-oriented programming, but you are wary of COM threading models, go straight to Chapter 3, "COM Threading Models." My point is that this book is not a how-to guide in which each chapter is a prerequisite to the chapter that follows; rather, each chapter is independent and has its own story to tell.

CHAPTER TWO

Programming Objects

Using Microsoft COM and Microsoft ActiveX as its underlying technology, Microsoft Visual Basic has made the leap from a procedural language to an object-oriented programming language. Understanding how COM and ActiveX contribute to Visual Basic to make this leap possible will provide you with further insight and appreciation for why objects behave the way they do. Don't despair if you don't fully comprehend the implications of COM and ActiveX— most experts on the subject agree that it takes about six months of continuous effort before this information starts to sink in. Regardless of how well you understand COM and ActiveX, Visual Basic does an excellent job of concealing this layer.

While it's intriguing to understand the "why" of object-oriented programming, it's imperative to understand the "how." Given that premise, I will explain how Visual Basic supports principles of object-oriented programming using the current language feature set. Next I will cover some aspects of object construction and destruction that you must understand in order to produce well-refined object-oriented systems. Finally, I will attempt to demystify the use of object variables by providing some insight into how objects behave and how they are manipulated in Visual Basic.

Is Visual Basic Object Oriented?

Yes. Although object-oriented purists might disagree, I found that Visual Basic met the definition of an object-oriented language as of version 5. I will admit, however, that there is definitely room for improvement. In this chapter, I will identify where Visual Basic comes up short and suggest the language features that Microsoft could add to make Visual Basic more robust. In addition, I will provide workarounds to these limitations where possible.

Visual Basic is object oriented because it supports the three fundamental principles of object-oriented methodology: encapsulation, inheritance, and polymorphism. Let's take a closer look at each principle in the following sections.

Encapsulation

Encapsulation is often referred to as "information hiding." It is the ability of a class object to restrict client access to that class object's internal representation (data and functions). The following sections provide an in-depth description of four methods by which you can enforce encapsulation: private class members, private static class members, friends, and private helper class objects.

Private Class Members

Encapsulation is accomplished by defining member variables and functions of a class as private. You can assume that class member functions (also known as methods) defined as public internally manipulate private member variables and functions. In object-oriented terms, the public methods of a class are an abstraction of the class's private representation. The result is that the private representation is encapsulated.

The advantage of encapsulation is that you can reimplement the class to contain different types of private member variables and functions, and you can update the implementation of the public methods as required (provided that the function signatures of the public methods don't change). For example, you might find that changing the type of a private member variable from a Collection to an array will significantly increase the performance for a given type of object. Because the Collection variable is private to the class, you can redefine its type and update the implementation of the public methods that use the variable without breaking client collaboration.

Client/Server Object Relationships

A client is an application, object, or component that requests a service from another object. The object receiving the request exposes available services via its public methods. Hence, this object is the server in this relationship because it is providing a service. An object can be a server to one object and a client of another object simultaneously, which models the real world. For example, you (the reader) are a client of mine (the author), and I am providing you this information service. In turn, I am a client of other authors who have published books that I have used during the research stages of this book.

Private Static Class Members

A standard class feature that supports encapsulation in most object-oriented languages is the ability to define static class members. Static member variables and functions are members of the class rather than members of class objects. A static member is created once for the class and is global to all instances of that class. Static members can be defined as private, so encapsulation is enforceable. Static members allow you to reduce the overhead required to maintain separate instances of members that can be shared by all class objects. Helper functions (described later in the section "Private Helper Class Objects") are excellent candidates to be declared as static, because they are private, implementation-specific functions that further modularize the internals of the class by enhancing code readability, reuse, and maintainability within the confines of the class implementation. A static member is also the perfect mechanism for sharing data between objects of the same class—it does not fall into a program's global namespace, so naming conflicts between other variables or functions defined outside its class will not occur.

The static class member feature is not directly supported in Visual Basic. Each instance of a Visual Basic class gets a separate copy of the class's members. I think Microsoft should, without a doubt, add this feature to Visual Basic. In any case, let me illustrate an alternative that provides the equivalent effect, albeit with certain limitations.

Public functions and variables defined in Visual Basic modules that are included in an ActiveX component project (such as a DLL, an EXE, and so forth) are global within that ActiveX component project but are private to external clients of the component. So, if your intention is to package related classes in a class library or to build a framework of collaborating class objects, you could receive similar results to static declarations by distributing your library or framework as an ActiveX component. Yes, all objects of classes defined within the project have access to these public variables, but if programmers maintain their professional etiquette, programmers of other classes in the same project will not violate the intended use of public variables or functions for their own benefit. I know I'm making a rather weak argument for using this ActiveX alternative to static declarations, but the ability to use class modules in this capacity does allow me to turn my object-oriented purist head the other way. In spite of this limitation of global access within a project, the issue of not being able to declare static methods is mostly solved because class overhead is reduced, information can be shared between class objects in the same component, and the public variables and functions are encapsulated by the component. The clients of the ActiveX component, therefore, are not aware of the existence of these public variables and functions.

Friends

Most of us maintain a certain facade that we expose to the public at large, which we can refer to as our public interface. (In the world of programming, an *interface* is a group of functions—more on this in the section "Types of Inheritance.") People's perceptions and interactions are determined by what they expose; other information is kept private and is not accessible through the public interface. In this manner, class objects are an exact model of the real world. All that is known about a type of object is exposed through its public properties, methods, and events. What is not known about a type of object is defined as private.

We all know that we're not supposed to keep too much personal information bottled up inside, so we confide in a friend and give them access to our private information. The same scenario is true for objects. One type of object can be a friend to another type. In fact, as in human friendships, the trust might be only one way. Each party (type of object) in the relationship individually decides whether to accept the other as a friend.

Each object-oriented programming language implements friends somewhat differently, but ultimately, each language provides the same result—the ability to access the private members of a class object by invoking a friend function. Personally, I favor the C++ implementation.

A friend in C++ terminology is a nonmember of a class (meaning it doesn't have access to nonpublic members of the class unless they are friends) that has access to another class's nonpublic members. (We say nonpublic rather than private here because unlike Visual Basic, C++ supports different levels of privacy.) C++ friends can be stand-alone functions, member functions of another class, or an entire class. Making an entire class a friend of another class is a shortcut to separately defining all class functions as friends of another class. It's clear that friends are public—the implementation of a friend function makes it possible to access the private members of another class object.

Visual Basic's implementation of friends is similar to its quasi-implementation of static class members. Friends, like static members, make sense only in an ActiveX component project because all classes within a component are friendly. You are therefore faced with the dilemma of open access to class members. Again, some professional etiquette will be necessary, or you'll have to include in an ActiveX component project only those classes and class members that should be friends, which might prove to be impractical.

Unlike in C++, friends in Visual Basic are class members that are publicly accessible to all classes of objects in the ActiveX component but that are not accessible to external clients of the component. As a result, friends in Visual Basic are not compiled as part of a class's public interface in a type library. Both early binding and late binding techniques of accessing friends from a client will result in error. For example, assume that *AnnualIncome* is a friend property of the class Person, which is defined in the PersonalFinances ActiveX DLL, and that you wrote the following client code:

```
Dim thePerson1 As Object
Dim thePerson2 As PersonalFinances.Person
Dim amount As Double

' Using late binding
Set thePerson1 = CreateObject("PersonalFinances.Person")
' Run-time error
amount = thePerson1.AnnualIncome

' Using early binding
Set thePerson2 As New PersonalFinances.Person
' Compile-time error
amount = thePerson2.AnnualIncome
```

Because the client code above is not within the context of the PersonalFinances ActiveX component, it cannot reference the friend property *AnnualIncome* of the Person class. A client of the ActiveX component can access only the public members of class objects defined within the component. That being the constraint, the approach I would take as the component developer would be to define other classes in the component that by default are friends of the Person class. For example, within my component I could define a FinanceCoordinator class that has a public method for retrieving a member of the Person class, and an Accountant class that has a public method for determining whether a given person's annual income falls within a particular range. The client code could then read as follows:

```
Dim theFinCoord As PersonalFinances.FinanceCoordinator
Dim thePerson As PersonalFinances.Person
Dim theAccountant As PersonalFinances.Accountant

Set theFinCoord = New PersonalFinances.FinanceCoordinator
Set thePerson = theFinCoord.GetPerson("John Smith")
Set theAccountant = theFinCoord.GetAvailableAccountant

If theAccountant.ClientSalaryRange(thePerson, OVER_50K) Then
    ' Give the loan to the candidate.
    ⋮
Else
    ' Deny the loan to the candidate.
    ⋮
End If
```

The point I'm trying to convey here is that a friend is someone who has access to private information about you. To translate, member functions of one class object have access to private members of a different class object. The *theAccountant* object of type Accountant is a friend of the *thePerson* object of type Person. Because the previous code extract belongs to a client that is not in the PersonalFinances ActiveX component, the client is not a friend of the Person class, so it cannot ask the *thePerson* object what its annual income is. Indirectly, however, the client can find out the information it needs by interacting with the *theAccountant* object. Visual Basic does not implement friends as I described at the beginning of this section in our discussion of C++ friends. Friends in Visual Basic are simply properties or methods of a class that are public within an ActiveX component and private outside the ActiveX component. Here is a code extract of what you might expect to find in the PersonalFinances ActiveX component project.

```
''''''''''''''''''''''''''''''''''''''''''''''''''''''''
' Project:     PersonalFinances (ActiveX DLL)
' Class Name:  Person
'
Private m_AnnualIncome As Double
    ⋮
Friend Property Get AnnualIncome() As Double
    AnnualIncome = m_AnnualIncome
End Property


''''''''''''''''''''''''''''''''''''''''''''''''''''''''
' Project:     PersonalFinances (ActiveX DLL)
' Class Name:  Accountant
'
    ⋮
Public Enum SalaryRange
    UNDER_20K
    BETWEEN_20K_AND_50K
    OVER_50K
End Enum

Public Function ClientSalaryRange(Psn As Person, _
  SR As SalaryRange) As Boolean
    Select Case SR
    Case UNDER_20K
        ClientSalaryRange = Psn.AnnualIncome < 20000
    Case BETWEEN_20K_AND_50K
        ClientSalaryRange = (Psn.AnnualIncome > 20000 And _
                             Psn.AnnualIncome < 50000)
```

```
    Case OVER_50K
        ClientSalaryRange = Psn.AnnualIncome > 50000
    End Select
End Function
```

As illustrated in this code extract, *AnnualIncome* is a friend property defined in the Person class that returns the value of the privately defined *m_AnnualIncome* member variable. Defining this property as a friend makes it accessible to the Accountant class that is defined within the same component. The Accountant class contains the *ClientSalaryRange* public method (member function) that determines whether a given Person object's salary falls within the specified range by referencing the *AnnualIncome* friend property. Now let's say I added another class, named StockBroker, to the component project. StockBroker class objects will also be friends of Person class objects, which gives the StockBroker class objects access to the *AnnualIncome* friend property. A client of this component cannot access the *AnnualIncome* friend class members, but it can access public methods such as *ClientSalaryRange*.

While enforcing encapsulation, friend relationships allow the collaboration of two or more class objects that would otherwise be impossible based on the information made available through their public interfaces. Even objects of the same class (type) cannot access each other's private members. Friends allow this type of encapsulation so that you can determine such information as whether two objects of the same class are in the same state. In this case, the client code could resemble the following:

```
Dim p1 As Portfolio
Dim p2 As Portfolio

Set p1 = New Portfolio
Set p2 = New Portfolio

' Process portfolios.
⋮
' Compare portfolios.
If p1.Equals(p2) Then
⋮
End If
' It is commutative; therefore, you could also
' get the same result from this code.
If p2.Equals(p1) Then
⋮
End If
```

A friend relationship is a clever concept to employ, but I suggest you use it sparingly. Although friends do not violate laws of encapsulation between class objects in an ActiveX component and clients of the component, if they're used as intended, friends can be a direct violation of encapsulation between class objects within an ActiveX component. As a result of creating friends, a direct dependency between class objects is created, making it difficult to change the private implementation of a class without adverse effects.

Private Helper Class Objects

As mentioned, helper functions are private member functions of a class that add significant value to the implementation of a class by modularizing code that can be reused by other elements of the implementation. Also, implementation code is easier to maintain and is more readable as a result. Why not take the helper function concept a step further by creating helper classes designed to support the implementation of another class?

The goal is to create a helper class object that is intended to be used solely within the context of a single class implementation, so the helper class should be defined as private within the single class that it supports. Ideally, Visual Basic would allow you to define nested classes similar to the following code:

```
Class TelephoneService

Private:
Class FiberOptics
    Public:
    Function ConfigureWireProtocol(...) As Boolean
        ' Configuration code
    End Function
End Class

Static m_FiberOpt As FiberOptics = New FiberOptics

Public:
Sub MakeACall(...)
    ' Do some stuff and call the FiberOptics
    ' helper class object to further facilitate
    ' this implementation.
    ⋮
    retcode = m_FiberOpt.ConfigureWireProtocol(...)
    ⋮
End Sub
End Class
```

The TelephoneService class is scoped globally. Therefore, a client process can instantiate objects of type TelephoneService, followed by calls to the publicly defined method *MakeACall*. Notice, however, that the FiberOptics class is private to the TelephoneService class. This implies that FiberOptics is a helper class designed to support exclusively the implementation of the TelephoneService class. Following the FiberOptics class definition, I defined and initialized a static TelephoneService class member variable named *m_FiberOpt* of type FiberOptics. The *m_FiberOpt* variable is a member of the TelephoneService class rather than a member of TelephoneService class objects. Hence, it is created once, and then is globally available to all TelephoneService class objects. But since it is private to the class, it is inaccessible from a client of a TelephoneService class object.

In short, a helper class is similar to a helper function in that it should be defined as private to the class it supports. Also, an object of the helper class type should be defined as private to the class it supports. Consequently, encapsulation is fully enforced, which allows developers to enhance the implementation of a class that now includes helper class objects without concern for breaking collaboration with clients. Because a helper class is for use exclusively with a single class, changing its public interface requires changes only in the implementation of the class it supports, which is the only user dependent on its interface. Code changes in this situation are easily maintainable.

Unfortunately, Visual Basic does not support the concept of helper classes or static class members as just described. In fact, the code extract in the previous example is not legal Visual Basic code—my intention is to show you what it could be. Visual Basic does not support the idea of nested classes. For that matter, you cannot define multiple classes in the same file in Visual Basic. As you know, there is a class module type in Visual Basic that uses the same editor as the standard and form modules. The *Class...End Class* syntax in the example also is not legal. The most reliable way to determine whether you are looking at the code of a class, a form, or a standard module is to view the Properties window. You will see in the Properties window object box the name of the module in bold, followed by the type of module in normal font style. A class module type is ClassModule. (See Figure 2-1.)

Similar to private static class members and friends, you can define private helper classes despite the missing language features, provided you are working within an ActiveX component project. As shown in the scenarios given earlier, you can define classes that are public to all classes in the component but that are private to clients of the component. To enforce this scope, use the Properties window to set the Instancing property value of a class module to Private. (See Figure 2-1.)

Module name   Module type

Figure 2-1.
*Use the Properties window for changing the Instancing property value of
a given class module.*

The following code extract, rewritten from the previous code extract—this
time in legal Visual Basic syntax—produces results equivalent to what we would
have hoped for from our illegal syntax. Keep in mind that this is possible only
in an ActiveX component project:

```
' Project:     TelephoneSvr (ActiveX DLL)
' Class Name: TelephoneService
' Note:   Component class accessible by clients of
'         the component.
'
'         This class's Instancing property value is
'         set to MultiUse, which is the default of
'         an ActiveX DLL component project.
⋮

Public Sub MakeACall(...)
' Quasi-static class member variable g_FiberOpt
' is defined as public in a standard module in
' this component project. It therefore has a
' global scope within the component, but is
' inaccessible to clients of the component.
If g_FiberOpt Is Nothing Then
    Set g_FiberOpt = New FiberOptics
End If
```

```
' Do some stuff and call the FiberOptics
' helper class object to further facilitate
' this implementation.
  ⋮
retcode = g_FiberOpt.ConfigureWireProtocol(...)
  ⋮
End Sub


'''''''''''''''''''''''''''''''''''''''''''''''''''''
' Project:    TelephoneSvr (ActiveX DLL)
' Class Name: FiberOptics
' Note:  Helper class of the TelephoneSvr ActiveX
'          component, designed to exclusively support
'          the TelephoneService class implementation.
'
'          This class's Instancing property value is
'          set to Private via the Properties window.
  ⋮
Public Function ConfigureWireProtocol(...) As Boolean
      ' Configuration code
End Function
```

From the point of view of an object-oriented purist, the code above illustrates that private helper class objects are possible in Visual Basic; however, the code's implementation falls short because, like static class members and friends, all classes within a component have access to helper classes. So the scope is the ActiveX component instead of the class, which results in a violation of encapsulation within the component. You cannot guarantee that a single class implementation is the only client of a specific helper class. Changing the interface of a helper class in any way could lead to a code maintenance nightmare if numerous classes in a component reference the same helper class. In place of the missing language features, those who develop a component should remember to maintain good object-oriented etiquette. On the other hand, clients of the component are unaware of the existence of helper classes, so encapsulation is enforceable on the client level, making this feature worthy of implementation despite its shortcomings.

By now you have probably noticed a recurring theme. Visual Basic effectively supports even the most advanced features of object-oriented programming, provided you are developing an ActiveX component of some sort. Hence, it seems almost an accident that Visual Basic's support for object-oriented programming works the way it does. Keep reading—I will eventually share some insights that will affirm that impression.

Inheritance

When you create an object-oriented programming solution, you hope to gain reusability as an end result. Instead of reinventing the wheel every time in the context of a new system, you should make classes of objects available for reuse. At times, however, having access to the public properties, methods, and events of a class isn't enough for effective reuse, so you have to make a few choices. First, you could simply redefine a private class member as public so that another class could obtain the interaction it needs. Second, you could establish friendships between classes in an ActiveX component by defining class properties and methods as friendly (using the keyword *Friend*). A friend preserves encapsulation by providing other, friendly classes with access to its private members. Third, a class could inherit the characteristics of other classes.

Concrete and Abstract Classes

A *class* is another name for a type of something. With respect to object-oriented concepts, that "something" is an object. A class defines the characteristics of an object, which include its structure and behavior. Objects are constructed based on a class (or type). Said another way, an object is an instance of a class.

Classes can either be concrete or abstract. A *concrete class* defines something that is tangible. Hence, an object can be constructed based on this class. For example, a Porsche Carrera object can be constructed based on an Automobile class, because Automobile defines the characteristics of something concrete.

An *abstract class*, on the other hand, defines a concept that in and of itself can not be materialized unless applied to something concrete. For example, color, shape, and sound are abstract terms. Conceptually you know what they are because someone pointed out a concrete object that exhibited those characteristics. If I were to say to you, "Give me a square," the first question you would probably ask me is, "A square what?" Objects, therefore, cannot be constructed based on an abstract type. Concrete classes can, however, inherit the characteristics of an abstract class. For example, an Automobile class could inherit color, shape, and sound from an abstract class. Now, based on the Automobile

Types of Inheritance

Inheritance is the act of deriving one class from another. Public inheritance implies that the descendant class is a subclass or subtype of its ancestor class. For example, if class Poodle and class Wolf derive from class Canine, they are both types of Canine. This is referred to as an "is a" relationship (as in, a Wolf "is a" Canine).

Nonpublic inheritance implies that the descendant class is not a subclass of its ancestor, but that it only inherits its characteristics. For example, if you create a Map collection class, you might want to privately inherit from an Array class. Your reasoning might be that a Map collection is not a type of Array, but the Array class has some storage functionality that you would like to reuse in your Map class. This type of inheritance enforces encapsulation and is similar to the composition of one class object being a private member of another. This is referred to as a "has a" relationship (as in, a Map "has an" Array).

---

class, you can construct a silver Porsche Carrera object that produces a deep throttling sound.

Visual Basic supports the concept of an abstract class in ActiveX component projects only. Provided you have at least one class in the component project that is creatable by an external client, you can create an abstract class by adding a new class module to the ActiveX component project. Next you can add public properties and methods with no implementation. You do this by changing the class's Instancing property value to PublicNotCreatable in the Properties window. Clients external to this component cannot create instances of this class by using the *New* keyword or the *CreateObject* function. However, classes defined within the context of the client can derive concrete classes from the abstract interface.

Be aware that classes within the component can create instances of this class and pass references to it back to an external client, which violates the intended abstract nature of the class. I consider this to be one of the many indications that this feature is really there for reasons determined by the underlying ActiveX/COM technology, which I will shed some light on in the following chapter. It is only by accident that a class defined as PublicNotCreatable serves as a means by which to enforce object-oriented principles.

Inheritance can be further categorized into two major forms: implementation inheritance and interface inheritance. *Implementation inheritance* supports the concept of a class hierarchy, where one class can derive from another class, potentially inheriting the structure and behavior of all its ancestors. The changes from the ancestor to the descendant are limited only by the capacity of the current technology. A descendant class might choose to override the behavior of certain public methods of its ancestor and leave others untouched. This form of inheritance might also permit access to nonpublic class members of an ancestor to its descendants. Unfortunately, Visual Basic currently does not support implementation inheritance.

Interface inheritance is the ability of one class to inherit the interface of another. An interface is a group of class property and method signatures declared as public. In Visual Basic, class properties and methods are defined inline, so the term "signature" might seem a bit confusing to a Visual Basic programmer. A property or method signature is the name of the property or method, followed by a list of parameters and a return type, if applicable. The signature does not include implementation code.

Visual Basic supports multiple-interface inheritance. Regardless of whether a class is abstract or concrete, one class can inherit the interfaces of many other classes.

The *Implements* Keyword

At the top of a class module, add the keyword *Implements*, followed by the name of the interface the class is implementing. The keyword *Implements* accurately describes what a class is about to do—provide implementation for the properties and methods for the interface from which it is deriving. To derive a class from multiple interfaces, add an *Implements* entry for each interface on a separate line in the class module. Keep in mind that the deriving class must implement every property and method of the specific interface. If your intention is to implement part of an interface, at a minimum you must select the remaining methods from the Procedure drop-down list in the top right-hand corner of the class module editor (as shown in Figure 2-2) to put an empty implementation of the method into the class module. I see this type of implementation as bad programming practice. If you are not implementing an entire interface, you should probably not derive your class from it. Interfaces are considered binding contracts, because a client that expects a specific interface is guaranteed that the object it intends to reference fully supports all properties and methods defined in that interface. Here is a code extract of what you might expect to find in a Visual Basic program.

```
'  ·  ·  ·  ·  ·  ·  ·  ·  ·  ·  ·  ·  ·  ·  ·  ·  ·  ·  ·  ·  ·  ·  ·  ·  ·  ·  ·  ·  ·  ·  ·  ·  ·  ·  ·  ·  ·  ·  ·  ·  ·  ·  ·  ·  ·  ·  ·  ·
' Project:    CanineExhibitSvr (ActiveX DLL)
' Class Name: Canine
' Note:  Interface that defines characteristics
'        of the canine species.
'
'        Notice there is no implementation defined in this
'        class module, just public properties and methods
'        with empty bodies.
'
'        This class's Instancing property value is set to
'        PublicNotCreatable via the Properties window.
'
'        Note: At least one class in an ActiveX component
'              project must have an Instancing property
'              value that allows it to be publicly creatable.
⋮
'
' Properties
'
⋮
'
' Methods
'
Public Sub Bark()
End Sub

Public Sub Eat()
End Sub

Public Sub Run()
End Sub

'  ·  ·  ·  ·  ·  ·  ·  ·  ·  ·  ·  ·  ·  ·  ·  ·  ·  ·  ·  ·  ·  ·  ·  ·  ·  ·  ·  ·  ·  ·  ·  ·  ·  ·  ·  ·  ·  ·  ·  ·  ·  ·  ·  ·  ·  ·  ·  ·
' Project:    CanineExhibitSvr (ActiveX DLL)
' Class Name: Wolf
' Note:  Concrete class that inherits the Canine
'        interface.
'
'        Notice all interface methods are implemented.
'
'        This class's Instancing property value is set
'        to MultiUse via the Properties window.
'
' Concrete class Wolf inherits the Canine abstract interface.
Implements Canine
⋮
```

(continued)

```
'
' Implementation of the Canine interface
'
Private Sub Canine_Bark()
    ' Implementation code goes here.
End Sub

Private Sub Canine_Eat()
    ' Implementation code goes here.
End Sub

Private Sub Canine_Run()
    ' Implementation code goes here.
End Sub
```

> NOTE: The boldfaced code in this extract indicates that these are the implementations of the Canine interface when you use the keyword *Implements.*

An external client of the CanineExhibitSvr ActiveX component cannot create an instance of type Canine. But the external client could either define a new concrete class that derives from Canine or create an instance of the concrete class Wolf that exhibits all the characteristics of Canine.

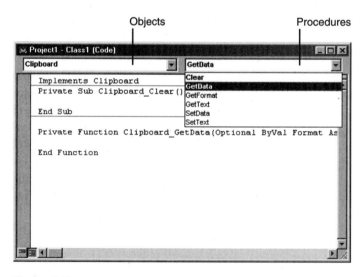

Figure 2-2.
You can use the Procedures drop-down list in the class module editor to implement each method in the class.

Implementation Inheritance

Although not supported by Visual Basic, implementation inheritance has benefits worth reiterating, and later in this section we look at how to gain those benefits in Visual Basic.

In implementation inheritance, when a class publicly inherits from another, the descendant class does or acts as the following:

- It is a subclass (or subtype) of its ancestor. This plays a key role in polymorphism, which is discussed in the next section.

- It not only inherits all the characteristics of its immediate ancestor but potentially those characteristics of all its ancestors in the descendant chain that came before it.

- It can override behavior for the methods defined in its ancestor.

- It can have access to nonpublic members of its ancestors when available.

Implementation inheritance has two significant drawbacks. The first is that if the programming language you are using supports multiple-implementation inheritance, as C++ does, it is likely that eventually you will derive a class from two or more other classes that have the same ancestor. This introduces an ambiguity that should be caught by the compiler. Essentially, the compiler is unable to anticipate your intended usage. For example, as the class diagram in Figure 2-3 illustrates, you might want to maintain separate ancestor instances. Notice that class A is an ancestor of classes B and C, both of which class D is derived from.

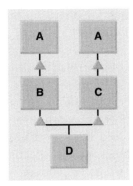

Figure 2-3.
An example of multiple-implementation inheritance showing that a class can be derived from classes that have the same ancestor.

Unless the programmer implements specific code changes, ambiguity will exist because it's not clear which class A ancestor should ultimately respond to an invocation initiated by class D. There are other programming changes that entail classes B and C sharing a single class A instance or that replace multiple inheritance with a combination of single inheritance and composition. The point is that it's not a trivial problem to solve. Since Visual Basic does not yet support implementation inheritance, let's just leave it as food for thought.

The second drawback of implementation inheritance is the amount of memory that a descendant class might require, depending on where the class falls in the class hierarchy. When a descendant class object is created, its entire ancestral line is created along with it. Otherwise, how else would a descendant reuse the functionality that it inherited from its ancestors? The compiler will not complain about the additional memory because, of course, memory use is not an error. So, it is up to the programmer to understand the effects of implementation inheritance on memory usage.

Interfaces in Visual Basic cannot derive from one another; therefore, it is impossible to create an ambiguous situation due to common ancestors. Also, the only overhead resulting from the derivation from an interface is in the derived class's implementation. You don't have to worry about a descendant chain of classes.

All the benefits of implementation inheritance can be gained in Visual Basic by using interface inheritance along with a few other innovative techniques. For example, in a PetshopSvr ActiveX component, I have created a GermanShepherd class that must derive from the concrete DomesticDog class. The DomesticDog class interface consists of three public methods: *Bark*, *Eat*, and *Run*. By default, I will accept the *Run* and *Eat* methods as implemented in DomesticDog, but I want to override its *Bark* method because a GermanShepherd object's bark has deeper undertones than the average DomesticDog object's bark.

The GermanShepherd class inherits the DomesticDog class interface through the use of the keyword *Implements*. Then the GermanShepherd class implementation of the DomesticDog interface's *Eat* and *Run* methods delegates their tasks to the private DomesticDog object member variable composed in the GermanShepherd class. However, the GermanShepherd class will override the *Bark* method of the DomesticDog class interface by providing its own implementation that does not delegate back to the private DomesticDog object member variable. The class diagram shown in Figure 2-4 is an accurate depiction of interface inheritance coupled with composition to gain results that are equivalent to implementation inheritance. The following is the Visual Basic source code you might expect to find in the PetshopSvr ActiveX component project.

```
''''''''''''''''''''''''''''''''''''''''''''''''''''
' Project:    PetshopSvr (ActiveX DLL)
' Class Name: DomesticDog
' Note:  Concrete class
⋮
'
' Properties
'
⋮
'
' Methods
'
Public Sub Bark()
    ' Implementation code goes here.
End Sub

Public Sub Eat()
    ' Implementation code goes here.
End Sub

Public Sub Run()
    ' Implementation code goes here.
End Sub

''''''''''''''''''''''''''''''''''''''''''''''''''''
' Project:    PetshopSvr (ActiveX DLL)
' Class Name: GermanShepherd
' Note:  Derived from the concrete class DomesticDog
'
'
' Inherit interface.
Implements DomesticDog
⋮
' Compose private DomesticDog object member variable.
Private m_domesticDog As DomesticDog

' When an instance of this GermanShepherd class is created,
' auto-construct an instance of DomesticDog and assign a
' reference to it to the private DomesticDog object
' member variable.
Private Sub Class_Initialize()
    Set m_domesticDog = New DomesticDog
End Sub
```

(continued)

```
' Implementation of the DomesticDog interface
'
Private Sub DomesticDog_Bark()
    ' GermanShepherd implementation that produces
    ' the bark required
    ⋮
End Sub

Private Sub DomesticDog_Eat()
    ' Delegate task to private DomesticDog object
    ' member variable.
    m_domesticDog.Eat
End Sub

Private Sub DomesticDog_Run()
    ' Delegate task to private DomesticDog object
    ' member variable.
    m_domesticDog.Run
End Sub
```

Interface inheritance is the only type of inheritance that is absolutely necessary for object-oriented programming in Visual Basic. Interfaces define an object's role in a system. The majority of the design patterns described in this book explain how to create interfaces implemented by classes that work together to solve a specific set of problems. I do provide full implementations of these interfaces; however, the point that will become evident is that the interface, more so than the class implementation, determines the scalability, reusability, and extensibility in a given system.

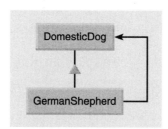

Figure 2-4.
Interface inheritance coupled with composition allows the German-Shepherd class to inherit the characteristics of the DomesticDog class.

Polymorphism

It is often said that an object variable in Visual Basic is actually an object reference to a type of object. This is not 100 percent accurate. A more precise definition would be that an object variable is a reference to a type of object that supports a specific interface. As described in the previous section on inheritance, one type (class) of object can support one or more interfaces. By using the keyword *Implements* followed by a valid interface name, a class can provide its own implementation for all properties and methods defined in an interface. Because an object is an instance of a specific class, it therefore supports the interfaces implemented by the class to which it conforms.

A Visual Basic class always has at least one interface that is referred to as its default interface. For the Visual Basic programmer, the default interface is the class itself. All public properties and methods defined in a class become part of its default interface.

Interfaces are not classes. Interfaces are unique identifiers for a group of property and method signatures. Classes define implementations for all properties and methods of an interface that they support. More than one class can support the same interface. Each class, however, will have its own unique implementation. On that note, Visual Basic supports two types of polymorphism, which I refer to as *smart polymorphism* and *oblivious polymorphism.*

Smart Polymorphism

Smart polymorphism occurs when you declare an object variable that can be assigned a reference to any type (class) of object that supports the interface the object expects. The resulting invocations of this object variable might produce different behavior depending on the object each invocation references. For example, say the following code fragment is defined in a project. The compiler will permit this code provided the project containing it either defines the Canine interface or references a type library that contains a definition for the Canine interface.

```
Sub StartBarking(Can As Canine)
    Can.Bark
End Sub
```

This subroutine is totally unaware of the type of object its *Can* parameter is referencing. But the compiler will guarantee that any type of object that is passed to the *StartBarking* subroutine will support the Canine interface, or else the compiler will produce an error. What the compiler is doing in this case is officially known as type checking. For example, if classes Poodle and Wolf both support the Canine interface, but class Iguana does not, the compiler will permit both Poodle and Wolf objects to be passed to the *StartBarking* subroutine, but it will raise an error when an Iguana object is passed. The following code fragment illustrates this:

```
' Declare object variables.
Dim myPoodle As Poodle
Dim myWolf As Wolf
Dim myIguana As Iguana

' Construct new instances.
Set myPoodle = New Poodle
Set myWolf = New Wolf
Set myIguana = New Iguana

StartBarking myPoodle   ' OK
StartBarking myWolf     ' OK
StartBarking myIguana   ' Failed: Type Mismatch
```

I call this smart polymorphism because the Visual Basic compiler is smart enough to notice at compile time whether a given class implements an interface expected by an object variable. Because the compiler can type check the object variables in the code fragment above, you can safely assume that the overhead for invoking a property or method will be miniscule. This low overhead results from the early binding technique that is used by the compiler because of how the object variables were declared.

Oblivious Polymorphism

Oblivious polymorphism occurs when you declare an object variable as type Object. Consequently, the object variable can reference any type of object without concern for the interfaces the object supports, so long as subsequent property or method invocations are supported by the default interface of that object. Because an interface contract is not defined, the compiler does no type checking at compile time for object variables of type Object. Therefore, the compiler is oblivious to whether the object variable is referencing an object that supports the properties or methods it is invoking. As a result, everything checks out OK by the compiler. Here's an example:

```
Sub StartBarking(Can As Object)
    Can.Bark
End Sub

⋮
```

```
' Declare object variables.
Dim myPoodle As Poodle
Dim myWolf As Wolf
Dim myIguana As Iguana

' Construct new instances.
Set myPoodle = New Poodle
Set myWolf = New Wolf
Set myIguana = New Iguana

StartBarking myPoodle    ' OK
StartBarking myWolf      ' OK
StartBarking myIguana    ' OK
```

At first glance, this type of polymorphism might seem more ideal than smart polymorphism, but it comes at a high price. Because the compiler does no type checking at compile time, it is highly feasible that errors will occur at run time. In the code extract above, all calls to the *StartBarking* method could potentially fail at run time, including the calls where the Poodle and Wolf objects are used, even if those objects inherit an interface that supports the *Bark* method. At run time, object variables of type Object can bind only to properties or methods of the interface they requested from the object they are referencing. In the code extract above, all interfaces requested by the *Can* parameter of the *StartBarking* subroutine are the default interfaces for each type of object. To further clarify my point, the code extract could be written as follows:

```
' Declare object variables.
Dim myPoodle As Object
Dim myWolf As Object
Dim myIguana As Object

' Construct new instances.
Set myPoodle = New Poodle
Set myWolf = New Wolf
Set myIguana = New Iguana

myPoodle.Bark
myWolf.Bark
myIguana.Bark
```

Each object variable of type Object will be assigned a reference to an object of type Poodle, Wolf, or Iguana. Each type of object returns its default interface. Because the compiler was oblivious at compile time, the system must compensate at run time by using significantly more overhead than the compiler because the system must locate and validate the *Bark* method to invoke it per the object variable's instructions. This is a late binding technique because the program must go through this validation process every time a method is invoked, regardless of whether it was called previously. For example, using the previous code extract, if you were to invoke the *Bark* method on the *myPoodle* object variable twice in a row, the overhead would be the same both times. This overhead can be a significant price to pay, especially if the object being invoked is not within the same thread or process it's being invoked from.

In summary, Visual Basic supports polymorphism using either an early binding technique (smart polymorphism) or a late binding technique (oblivious polymorphism). I highly recommend you use smart polymorphism whenever possible.

Object Construction and Destruction

An object is constructed based on its class type, or the class to which it conforms. It's good programming practice to always construct an object with a valid state, meaning the object contains all the information required to make it accessible to the application. Subsequent invocations might be futile if the object is not in a state in which it can positively respond. For instance, assume you want to open a savings account (the object) in a bank (the application). In order for the bank representative to successfully create the account, he or she is required to provide a valid bank account number, your name, address, and social security number to your account. If the account is opened without all the required information, it might become a nuisance to the computer system each time it tries to locate the account information, thereby bringing grief to both the bank and to you, the customer. For example, if the bank representative opened an account for you without a bank account number, how would the bank know where to put your deposits? You would, I'm sure, take your business elsewhere. The bank would also go out of business eventually, if it continued to run its operation in that manner. This scenario begs the question, "How can an object be constructed in an initially valid state?"

Classes have special methods that are called *constructors* in object-oriented terminology. A constructor is called during the construction process of an object. This is your opportunity to provide implementation code that initializes the state of the object during construction. If you do not explicitly use a specific constructor at object construction time, the default constructor is called. The default constructor accepts no parameters. If you do not define a default constructor in a class, the compiler will provide one that does nothing.

Most object-oriented languages permit classes to define multiple constructors. This gives the programmer the ability to construct an object of a given class in various valid states, depending on the situation. With the exception of the default constructor, a constructor can be defined to accept parameters. This will allow an object to be constructed in a valid state, that state being dependent on external factors that are passed at construction time. Similar to Visual Basic Sub procedures, constructors do not return anything.

Visual Basic supports only a default class constructor. To define a default constructor, open a class module in a Visual Basic project, and then select Class from the Object drop-down list in the code module editor. In the Procedure drop-down list, you'll find two event items: Initialize and Terminate. Selecting the Initialize event will create the event handler shown in Figure 2-5.

Figure 2-5.
Visual Basic uses the Initialize event as a constructor.

The subroutine *Class_Initialize* is the default constructor that is invoked when a Visual Basic class object is constructed. In the body of this subroutine, you can initialize private class members that represent the state of the object. Objects are constructed by using either the keyword *New* or the function *CreateObject*. If you declare an object variable and then try to use that object variable before you have used *New* or *CreateObject* to construct it, no compile-time errors will occur. However, at run time you will get an error because object variables are not objects, but rather are references to objects. Object variables by default are null, which is represented in Visual Basic by the keyword *Nothing*. In the following code extract, I've declared a SavingsAccount object variable, and then I've attempted to deposit $10 into the savings account. This code will compile, but at run time an error will be raised when the attempt to invoke the *Deposit* method occurs because the *mySavAcct* object variable refers to *Nothing*.

```
Dim mySavAcct As SavingsAccount
Dim nBalance As Long

' Compile time: OK
' Run time: Fail - mySavAcct refers to Nothing
nBalance = mySavAcct.Deposit(10)
```

This problem can be corrected by constructing an object in one of three ways: implicitly, using the keyword *New*; explicitly, using the keyword *New*; or explicitly, using the *CreateObject* function. The following sections take a closer look at each of these three methods.

Implicit Construction Using the Keyword *New*

By declaring an object variable as *New* followed by the type (class), Visual Basic will implicitly construct an object of the requested type and return a reference to the object variable upon the first invocation attempt. Following is a code extract in which I have modified the declaration of the *mySavAcct* object variable from the previous example to include the keyword *New*. This modification will automatically create an object and assign a reference to the object to the *mySavAcct* object variable when the first invocation attempt is made:

```
Dim mySavAcct As New SavingsAccount
Dim nBalance As Long

' Compile time:OK
' Run time:    OK - SavingsAccount object is auto-constructed and
'                   the reference is returned to mySavAcct.
'                   mySavAcct invokes the Deposit method of the
'                   SavingsAccount object that it references.
nBalance = mySavAcct.Deposit(10)
```

This approach will produce successful results every time. You never have to be concerned about an object variable that you declare referring to *Nothing*, because every time the object variable is invoked, Visual Basic checks whether it's set to *Nothing*. If the object variable is set to *Nothing*, Visual Basic constructs it. Despite this benefit of knowing the object variable will always reference something, I suggest you avoid using this method for a couple of reasons. First, you have to pay the price of overhead for every invocation performed on an object variable declared in this fashion because of the checking and constructing Visual Basic has to do. In the following code extract, three actions are performed on the SavingsAccount object referred to by the *mySavAcct* object variable. The comment above each invocation is an indication of what Visual Basic does that causes overhead:

```
Dim mySavAcct As New SavingsAccount
Dim nBalance As Double
Dim nInterestEarned As Double

' If mySavAcct Is Nothing Then
'     Set mySavAcct = New SavingsAccount
' End If
nBalance = mySavAcct.Deposit(10) ' Deposit cash.

' If mySavAcct Is Nothing Then
'     Set mySavAcct = New SavingsAccount
' End If
nInterestEarned = mySavAcct.IE  ' Check interest earned.

' If mySavAcct Is Nothing Then
'     Set mySavAcct = New SavingsAccount
' End If
mySavAcct.Owner.LName = "Jones" ' Update account owner's last
                                ' name to Jones.
```

A second important reason to avoid declaring an object variable as *New* is that it is impossible to check for the *Nothing* condition. Imagine a client that has an object variable that maintains a reference to a component object across machine boundaries. Accessing an object's properties or methods across boundaries to determine what action to take requires a lot of excess overhead if the choice of actions can be accomplished by checking for the *Nothing* condition. Checking for *Nothing* does not require the internals of Visual Basic to venture out of the client process.

Explicit Construction Using the Keyword *New*

To construct an object explicitly, first declare an object variable of a specific type. Then, in the body of the implementation, create a class object that represents the type declared by the object variable and return a reference to it. The syntax for doing so is as follows:

```
Dim mySavAcct As SavingsAccount

' Explicitly construct SavingsAccount object and return
' a reference to the object variable mySavAcct.
Set mySavAcct = New SavingsAccount

' OK at run time
nBalance = mySavAcct.Deposit(10)
```

Note that in an explicit construction, object variables are preceded with the keyword *Set*. Visual Basic requires that any time an object variable is being assigned a reference, it is preceded with *Set*. Although this syntax might seem awkward, it grows on you. Unlike the implicit construction approach, there is no additional overhead incurred because the compiler lets the programmer ensure that an object variable references a valid object. If not, the compiler will simply raise a run-time error.

Explicit Construction Using the *CreateObject* Function

A third alternative for constructing a Visual Basic object is to utilize the *CreateObject* function instead of the keyword *New*. *CreateObject* might be your only option if the object you want to construct resides in an ActiveX component that does not provide a type library. Consequently, you cannot declare an object variable of a specific type. You are forced to declare an object variable of either Object or Variant type. These days, it is extremely rare that a component does not have a type library. Keep in mind that you can still use *CreateObject* even with a type library.

CreateObject uses the COM object creation services for constructing COM objects. This implies that the Visual Basic programmer must have an understanding of COM in order to appreciate why *CreateObject* might be a desirable alternative over the keyword *New*. The *CreateObject* function creates a COM object and returns a reference to that object to an object variable by using a Set statement syntax similar to explicit construction using the keyword *New*. The syntax is as follows:

```
Set myObject = CreateObject("ActiveXComponent.Class")
```

ActiveXComponent is the name of the component that contains the desired class. *Class* is the name of the class from which the object is constructed. In COM terminology, this is referred to as a *programmatic identifier* (progID). When an ActiveX component is registered in Microsoft Windows, it adds a progID for each class defined in the component to the Windows Registry. (The Windows Registry is a system database that COM uses to manage ActiveX components.) You can think of the progID as the key in the database that allows COM to quickly locate ActiveX components and create instances of the classes requested by the *CreateObject* function.

The keyword *New* uses COM object creation services only when *New* is creating a COM object that is external to the project of which the object is a part. Therefore, the keyword *New* is faster for the creation of objects internal to a given project, because it has some private creation processes that are optimized for internal object creation. I will discuss in greater detail the subtleties of using the keyword *New* vs. the *CreateObject* function in Chapter 3, "COM Threading Models."

Explicit construction using the keyword *New* is the ideal way to create objects in Visual Basic for most situations. Use *CreateObject* only if you have no choice, such as in the case of a missing type library or when your intention is to take advantage of a COM feature that will otherwise be impossible. Avoid the implicit construction method at all costs—it is a hindrance because of the overhead incurred with every invocation, and because of the inability of the programmer to control the construction process of the class object referenced by an object variable.

No matter which of the three approaches you use, an object's default constructor is called, and this constructor is your only opportunity in Visual Basic to ensure that a class object is constructed in a valid state.

Self-Cleaning Objects

A well-behaved object should not only maintain a valid state while in existence, but it should also clean up after itself before it is destroyed. If encapsulation is exercised properly, only the object knows what parts of its representation need special attention before it destructs. Throughout Part Two of this book, you will find numerous design patterns that illustrate how different types of objects collaborate with one another to provide a solution to solve a specific problem domain. For design patterns to be successful, all objects of the pattern must play nicely together. If an object in a design pattern relationship is destroyed without regard to other dependent objects in the pattern, failure is imminent.

Classes define a special method known as a *destructor*. When a class object is in the process of being destroyed, it calls its destructor. The destructor method takes no parameters and returns nothing. A class can define only one destructor. This destructor method gives a class object an opportunity to do whatever house cleaning is necessary, such as notifying dependent objects of its departure. In general, a destructor should not be made accessible to clients of a class object, because calling a destructor should nullify the representation of an object, thus making its state invalid.

Visual Basic supports the concept of a destructor in the form of a Terminate event handler defined in a class module. In the Object drop-down list of the class module editor, select Class. Notice that the Procedure drop-down list contains two events: Initialize (which I've mentioned previously) and Terminate. When you select Terminate, Visual Basic automatically creates the following event handler skeleton, which it will call when an object of this particular class is destroyed. Put your cleanup code within the body of this method:

```
Private Sub Class_Terminate()

End Sub
```

Visual Basic objects cannot be destroyed explicitly. An object is destroyed when all references to it are released. As mentioned, object variables are not objects; rather, they hold on to references of objects. Therefore, the life of an object is controlled implicitly by object variables.

Object Variables Demystified

Object variables maintain references to objects. When an object variable goes out of scope, obtains a reference to another object, or is explicitly set to *Nothing*, the reference count of the object it was referencing decrements by one. The object is destroyed when the reference count of the object reaches zero. Objects in Visual Basic cannot be destroyed in any other way. This actually works in favor of the Visual Basic programmer, because it is impossible for an object variable to have a dangling reference caused by the destruction of the object it was referencing by another process.

An object's constructor is called only when the object is created. (Remember that objects are created by using the keyword *New* or the *CreateObject* function.) Here's an example:

```
Set myCat = New Cat ' The Cat constructor is called.
```

Additional references to an object are automatically assigned to new object variables when an existing object variable with a valid reference to an object is assigned to the new object variable by means of the Set statement. Said another way, the reference count of an object increments as the number of object variables that contain references to it increases:

```
' - Cat object created
' - Constructor called
' - Reference to Cat object returned to myCat1
' - Cat object reference count = 1
Set myCat1 = New Cat

' - Second reference to Cat object obtained by myCat2
' - Cat object reference count = 2
Set myCat2 = myCat1
```

Because object variables are references, and objects are destroyed only when their reference counts reach zero, careless management of object variables can cause undesired behavior in an application that might be difficult to resolve. Two dilemmas generally arise. First, it can be difficult to control the state of an object, because one client can change the state of an object without another client with a reference to the same object knowing. Second, because objects are deleted only when the last reference is released, circular referencing (referencing an object from another object and vice versa) could cause a deadlock—neither object's reference count will reach zero unless the programmer takes premeditated measures to avoid such a problem. The next section illustrates these dilemmas and the actions you can take to better evade them.

Object References

When more than one object variable has a reference to the same object, both have full rights to affect the state of the object via its public interfaces, as illustrated here:

```
Set mySavAcct = New SavingsAccount
mySavAcct.Deposit 25

Set anAccount = mySavAcct
anAccount.Withdraw 20

MsgBox mySavAcct.Balance   ' Message box will show $5.000.
```

This example shows clearly what has transpired, but imagine the difficulties in following the actions on an object when the tasks performed by the object variables *mySavAcct* and *anAccount* occur in different places.

A less obvious case is one in which you have created a class that has a read-only property. For example, the following code extract illustrates an object variable of type Person that has a read-only property called *Name*, which returns a string:

```
strName = Person.Name    ' OK
Person.Name = "Spike"    ' Error: property Name is read-only.
```

However, if the read-only property is of some object type, read-only access is easily violated. If you define a class property of some object type, the property will return a reference to an object based on your implementation, as shown in the following code extract.

```
' Class Foo
'
Private m_bars As Collection

Private Sub Class_Initialize()
    Set m_bars = New Collection
End Sub

    ⋮

Public Property Get Bars() As Collection
    Set Bars = m_bars
End Property

''''''''''''''''''''''''''''''''''''''''''''''''''''''''
' Client Code
'
Dim Foo1 As Foo
Dim myBars As Collection

Set Foo1 = New Foo

' Set a reference in myBars to the Bars
' collection returned from Foo1.
Set myBars = Foo1.Bars

' Add Peanut Butter to object variable myBars.
myBars.Add "Peanut Butter"

' Based on implementation in class Foo, the read-only
' property Bars is violated. The message box will display
' Peanut Butter.
MsgBox Foo1.Bars(1)
```

Because the implementation of the read-only property *Bars* in class Foo returns a reference to a Collection class object that it created privately, the object variable receiving that reference can change the contents of that Collection object. In this case, the read-only designation does not protect the state of the object *Foo1*. All it does is prevent *Foo1*'s *Bars* property value from referring to another Collection object:

```
' Compile-time Error: Invalid use of property
Set Foo1.Bars = New Collection
```

This behavior is inconsistent with intrinsic types. Visual Basic implicitly generates a copy of the property value for intrinsic types such as Long, String, and so forth; therefore, the receiving client can do whatever it pleases with its copy without affecting the property value of the originating object.

Object variables are never implicitly cloned by the Visual Basic compiler. To provide full read-only protection of a property of an object type, you must define your own cloning mechanism. To make the *Bars* property of the Foo class completely read-only, I have modified the code as follows:

```
' Class Foo
'
Private m_bars As Collection

Private Sub Class_Initialize()
    Set m_bars = New Collection
End Sub

  ⋮

Public Property Get Bars() As Collection
    Dim cloneBars As Collection
    Dim nIndex As Long

    ' Clone m_bars collection object.
    '
    ' Create clone collection.
    Set cloneBars = New Collection

    ' Add all items from m_bars collection to clone.
    For nIndex = 1 To m_bars.Count
        cloneBars.Add m_bars(nIndex), nIndex
    Next nIndex

    ' Return clone.
    Set Bars = cloneBars
End Property
```

Notice that a new Collection object is created, and a reference to it is stored to the object variable *cloneBars*. Then, in order to copy the contents of the property value *m_bars*, the entire collection is traversed, and each item is singly added to the *cloneBars* Collection object. Depending on the size of the collection, this can be an expensive price to pay for read-only property object values. Hence, you must evaluate the usage of object variables as read-only property values on a case-by-case basis.

Another misleading example of the same magnitude is passing objects by value to a function or subroutine. Here again, you would think the following code would allow you to modify an object passed by value without affecting the state of the object external to the function:

```
' Foo subroutine definition
Sub Foo(ByVal theBar As Bar)
    theBar.Flavor = "Oatmeal Raisin"
End Sub


'''''''''''''''''''''''''''''''''''
' Client code
'

Dim myBar As Bar

Set myBar = New Bar
myBar.Flavor = "Chocolate Chip"

Foo myBar

' You might think the message box will display
' myBar = Chocolate Chip because the myBar object
' is passed by value. But it will display
' myBar = Oatmeal Raisin because the object variable,
' not the object, is passed by value; hence, it is still
' referring to the same object.
'
MsgBox "myBar = " & myBar.Flavor
```

Remember, you work with object variables that are references to objects. Passing an object by value to a function does not protect the state of the object external to the function. The reason for this is that the object variable is passing by value, not the object. As a result, the compiler creates a hidden object variable that is assigned a reference to the same object as the passing parameter:

```
' The function typed in by the programmer...
Sub Foo(ByVal myBar As Bar)
    myBar.Flavor = "Oatmeal Raisin"
End Sub

' translates to the function generated by the Visual Basic compiler.
Sub Foo(ByRef myBar As Bar)
    Dim HiddenObject As New Bar
    Set HiddenObject = myBar
    HiddenObject.Flavor = "Oatmeal Raisin"
End Sub
```

Visual Basic is creating a new instance of the Bar object, only to have it released when a reference to the Bar object currently held by *myBar* is assigned to the *HiddenObject* object variable—and you know the rest. This overhead can be avoided by always passing object variables by reference.

Circular References

Circular references occur when two or more objects refer to one another. Because an object is not destroyed until the last reference to it is released, you can easily have a deadlock in Visual Basic. Keep in mind that it is the deadlock scenario you want to avoid, not circular referencing. In fact, some of the design patterns in this book intentionally use circular references to establish a specific relationship. For example, if you were to create a Manager design pattern, you would want the Manager object to maintain a one-to-many relationship with its Worker objects. This implies that the Manager object can contain a collection of many Worker object references, and each Worker object contains a reference to a single Manager object. Hence, it is clear that in order to have a one-to-many relationship in object-oriented terms, circular referencing might be unavoidable. (See Figure 2-6.) This further implies that in such a relationship, the Manager object cannot be destroyed while its Worker objects still exist. Conversely, Worker objects cannot be destroyed while their Manager object still exists.

To avoid deadlock, you could remove this one-to-many relationship. Doing so would defeat the purpose of this design pattern, however. The only true option is to design the Manager and Worker classes to expose methods that reflect an explicit understanding in their relationship. For example, prior to destroying a given Manager object, all dependent Worker objects must be notified. (Prior to destroying a Worker object, its Manager must be notified.) Notification should be in the form of a method call that results in the release of the object reference held by the object being notified. The object referenced by the notifier will be destroyed once the notifier releases its reference because it should contain the last remaining reference.

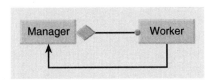

Figure 2-6.
This class diagram of the Manager design pattern illustrates circular referencing.

In short, circular referencing can be intentional. When this is the case, an architecture must be put in place that permits explicit notifications between objects in this relationship in order to break the circle and avoid deadlock. Deadlock occurs when objects in a relationship contain references to one another, and for that reason cannot be destroyed through standard means. Consequently, objects in this scenario will not be destroyed until the process in which they exist is destroyed. Because Visual Basic objects are based on COM technology, the process sometimes will not destruct until all its objects are destroyed. When this happens, you will have to destroy the process manually. This can be accomplished through the Task Manager in Microsoft Windows NT and Windows 2000 and through the Close Program dialog box (press Ctrl+Alt+Delete) in Microsoft Windows 95 and later. I'll leave it up to you to figure out how these operating system tools function. In fact, if you have noticed in the Task Manager that you have lingering Visual Basic component processes despite having verified that all references to objects the component contains have been released, your component is exhibiting symptoms of deadlock due to circular referencing.

Design patterns rely heavily on object collaboration. Understanding how to use object variables effectively will allow you to better appreciate the design pattern implementation techniques used throughout this book.

C H A P T E R   T H R E E

COM Threading Models

Microsoft Visual Basic has made its reputation as a well-insulated Microsoft Windows programming language. The Visual Basic programmer does not have to be concerned about many of the fundamental aspects of Windows programming, such as creating windows programmatically, understanding message queues, constructing the required Windows application message loop for retrieving messages from the application's message queue, and dispatching messages to the target window that contains a callback function for handling events intended for its window. At its lowest level, Windows programming is available to users in the form of a large set of C language functions packaged in various libraries known as the Windows application programming interface (API). Despite the benefits of C, programming Windows in this language requires implementation of all the items I mentioned above, which are of no concern to the Visual Basic programmer. If you need a reminder of what programming Windows involves, pick up a copy of *Programming Windows* by Charles Petzold (5th ed., Microsoft Press, 1999).

In short, programming Windows in C is an arduous task. Using Visual Basic to program Windows, on the other hand, is gratifying because results are almost instantaneous. As you know, the benefits do not stop there. If, for some reason, the core functionality available in Visual Basic does not meet your needs, you can extend an application by incorporating Windows API functions, by integrating external functions from third-party DLLs, or by embedding components that accomplish some amazing feats, such as 3-D charting, data binding, and so forth. Prior to Visual Basic 5, components could be developed only in C or C++. Therefore, it was the C/C++ developer's responsibility to build components that functioned properly in Visual Basic.

But times have changed—Visual Basic 5 leveled the playing field to the Visual Basic programmer's advantage. Now that Visual Basic is heavily peppered with Microsoft ActiveX-based and COM-based technologies, Visual Basic is no longer just a Windows graphical user interface (GUI) application programming language. Version 5 added a long list of enhancements—for example, the ability to create ActiveX controls, documents, and servers. Visual Basic 6 picked up the torch by including further enhancements that allow the programmer to create Internet-based components seamlessly. The point is that along with these new benefits, the responsibility shifts to the Visual Basic programmer to understand the various contexts in which components developed in Visual Basic can be applied.

All design patterns described in this book are implemented in the ActiveX and COM technologies furnished with Visual Basic. As I've mentioned, the reason for design patterns is to produce reusable solutions for recurring problems, so why limit those solutions to Visual Basic when you can take advantage of ActiveX as a vehicle for transporting these solutions to various programming languages, environments, and operating systems? The intention of this chapter is to make you aware of one of the features of COM that will help you develop these solutions: the threading aspects of COM on a Win32 operating system. Understanding how COM functions in this environment will help you comprehend the impact on system performance and behavior that results from the decisions you make when developing ActiveX components in Visual Basic. To this end, I will give you a brief overview of Win32 fundamentals. This overview is followed by a discussion on COM threading models, with in-depth coverage of the areas supported by Visual Basic and light coverage of the remaining areas. For a detailed discussion about COM, refer to the following books: *Essential COM* by Don Box (Addison-Wesley, 1998), and *Inside Distributed COM* by Guy Eddon and Henry Eddon (Microsoft Press, 1998).

Win32 Basics

Visual Basic has done an excellent job of hiding the fine details of how 32-bit Windows applications are truly structured, and rightfully so. Knowing these details defeats the purpose of programming in Visual Basic. Still, some information about threads had to be revealed in order to deliver ActiveX and COM to the Visual Basic developer. This information shows itself in the frame labeled Threading Model on the General tab of the Visual Basic IDE Project Properties dialog box. (See Figure 3-1.) Depending on the type of ActiveX project you select, certain options are enabled and others are disabled. I will cover these options in detail later in the chapter in the sections "Thread Management" and "The Cost of Living for Visual Basic Objects." First let me give you a brief overview of how 32-bit Windows applications are defined with respect to the operating system.

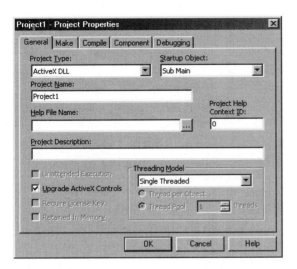

Figure 3-1.
Visual Basic 6 Project Properties dialog box.

A Windows application is defined in terms of a *process,* which is an instance of a running application. The process can own an address space of up to two gigabytes, consisting of memory and resources. Memory comprises the code and data of an application's EXE file and dependent DLLs. Resources consist of kernel objects such as thread, mutex, and file objects. Resources also include user objects such as windows, menus, brushes, and fonts. When a process terminates, all memory and resources it owns are reclaimed by the operating system.

Processes are dormant—a process must own a thread that will execute the code residing in the process's address space. In fact, when a process is initialized, the operating system automatically creates a single thread (known as the *primary thread*) that ultimately calls the application's *WinMain* function. This primary thread continues to execute until the *WinMain* function returns, which leads to the termination of the primary thread. Because it makes no sense for a process to exist without its primary thread, the process also will terminate at this point, relinquishing all memory and resources to the operating system.

A process can contain more than one thread, hence the term *multithreaded application.* All code execution within a thread is synchronous; however, you might sometimes want your application to execute different segments of its code asynchronously. For example, you might want your application to print reports while allowing the user to continue entering data via the user interface. In order for two tasks within an application to run simultaneously, you must create another thread. To do this, you need to call the Win32 API function *CreateThread.*

This function takes several parameters. Please refer to the Microsoft Platform SDK available at *msdn.microsoft.com/downloads/sdks/platform*) for a full disclosure of these parameters. More important, however, is that *CreateThread* requires the address of a function prototyped as follows:

```
DWORD WINAPI ThreadFunc( LPVOID )
```

This function—often referred to as the *ThreadFunc* function—accepts a single 32-bit pointer as an argument and returns a 32-bit exit code. When *CreateThread* is called, it creates a new thread that executes a given *ThreadFunc*. When *ThreadFunc* returns, the thread terminates. Visual Basic does not have inherent support for creating threads, except in the case of creating an out-of-process ActiveX EXE, which is configurable only by using the Project Properties dialog box as previously described. Nevertheless, provided you declare the appropriate Win32 API functions correctly in Visual Basic (see the Win32api.txt file on your Visual Basic 6 CD for examples of Win32 API declarations in Visual Basic), you can create threads by calling the *CreateThread* function as illustrated in the code extract below:

```
Sub DoSomeThing()
    ' Code executes
    ⋮
    ' Spawn a new thread that executes the code defined
    ' in function MyThreadFunc.
    CreateThread(..., ..., AddressOf MyThreadFunc, ..., ..., ...)
    ' Code here continues to execute without waiting for
    ' MyThreadFunc to return.
End Sub
```

This approach is somewhat unorthodox because, for various reasons, you can easily violate access to memory. For instance, the Visual Basic IDE is not thread-safe. Any attempt to debug an application will result in a general protection fault, which causes an involuntary termination of the application.

What makes a multithreaded application capable of executing code in different threads concurrently is the fact that Microsoft Windows 2000, Microsoft Windows NT, Microsoft Windows 98, and Microsoft Windows 95 are preemptive multitasking operating systems. In short, the operating system schedules time for all threads—not processes—to execute on the processor. The process's priority in conjunction with the priority level of the thread determines how frequently the operating system will schedule a given thread. If all threads have the same priority, the operating system gives each thread equal time in a round-robin fashion until all threads have terminated. In general, this time-slicing algorithm is so fast and efficient that it gives the illusion that multiple tasks are executing concurrently. Actually, only one task can execute at a time on a single-processor system. If, however, the computer has multiple processors, tasks can run concurrently because each processor can execute a separate thread.

Obviously, multithreaded applications can be very useful. Nonetheless, having an application with multiple threads introduces two possible problems: *race conditions* and *deadlocks*. A race condition occurs when the operating system gives control to a thread that changes the contents of memory that was being accessed by another thread. This leads to the corruption of unprotected memory shared by multiple threads and produces unpredictable, if not fatal, results. To avoid corrupting memory, Win32 allows you to synchronize thread access to a specific section of memory. The specific memory remains protected until the thread that initiated the protection releases it. For example, when the operating system gives control to Thread A, which wants to execute code in a section currently protected by Thread B, Thread A must wait until Thread B releases the protection before it can enter that code segment. Win32 primitives, including critical sections, mutexes, semaphores, and events, provide thread synchronization. Each primitive has unique features that favor one over the other in certain situations. More important, however, is that the primitives all help serialize access to memory shared by multiple threads.

The second problem, deadlock, is caused by serializing access to memory shared by multiple threads. A deadlock occurs when two or more threads are suspended while each waits on the other to release protection on a code segment. Deadlock is possible if a thread executes a block of code whose completion is contingent upon some other shared code segments, which the thread attempts to enter at the very point where it's needed. For example, Thread B has locked a segment of code that Thread A needs, which forces Thread A to wait. However, Thread B might very well be in a suspended state waiting to enter a code segment locked by Thread A, thus creating deadlock. To avoid the problem, a thread should establish protection (obtain locks) on all dependent shared code segments as a group at the beginning of the block of code. The thread remains in a suspended state until it can protect all dependent shared code segments using an "all or nothing" protection policy. This policy mandates that a thread cannot lock code segments as they become available unless *all* segments are available.

COM Apartments

COM objects manufactured on the Win32 platform cannot ignore the possibility of multiple threads attempting access, so you must take certain steps to ensure that COM objects are thread-safe. Lucky for us, Microsoft anticipated this requirement. Microsoft's COM implementation provides transparent support for thread-safe access to all COM objects. Multithreaded clients can safely access thread-oblivious COM object servers, and single-threaded clients can safely access multithreaded COM object servers. In fact, any variation of these two scenarios is guaranteed to work. Neither the client nor the server needs to consider the other's use of threads. COM has assumed responsibility by requiring all COM objects to belong to a specific category of thread safety. This category is formally referred to as an *apartment*.

COM defines two types of apartments: single-threaded apartments (STA) and multithreaded apartments (MTA). A process can contain zero or more STAs, but it can have only one MTA. A thread can enter only one apartment at a time, and the thread must explicitly leave an apartment before entering another. COM objects must reside in an apartment, and they can reside in only one apartment. An apartment can contain many COM objects. STAs, as their name suggests, allow only a single thread at a time to enter an apartment. All invocations made to COM objects in that apartment are synchronized through the apartment's Windows message loop; I'll cover this concept later in the section "Single-Threaded Apartments in an ActiveX EXE." Unlike their single-threaded counterparts, MTAs allow multiple threads to enter a single apartment. As a result, multiple threads can access the same COM object concurrently. COM does not provide synchronization for MTA; therefore, the programmer is responsible for serializing access to objects where needed by employing one or more of the Win32 primitives for synchronizing thread access. Neglecting to serialize access will eventually lead to catastrophic results.

All classes defined in a Visual Basic ActiveX component project are COM classes. Visual Basic provides no inherent support for MTA. It does, however, allow you to create multithreaded STA COM out-of-process servers, or COM in-process servers that are either thread-oblivious or that support STA. Although Visual Basic insulates the programmer from the details of COM programming, it does not protect COM components written in Visual Basic from the potential impact on performance and behavior when mixed with other COM clients and servers that support a particular COM threading model. On that note, let's peel back the Visual Basic layer and examine more closely the COM threading models it supports.

THREE: COM Threading Models

Single-Threaded Apartments in an ActiveX EXE

Multithreaded out-of-process COM components (ActiveX EXE projects, in Visual Basic terminology) allow concurrent access to multiple COM objects. A multithreaded COM server process can have multiple threads. In the STA model, only one thread can enter an apartment—each thread enters a unique apartment containing objects that it alone can access directly. Remember that an object can belong to only one apartment, and a thread in an STA can enter only one apartment. Once a thread enters an apartment, it owns the apartment: no other threads can enter. Therefore, a multithreaded STA out-of-process COM component allows concurrent access to multiple objects, but those objects must reside in separate apartments. The number of threads cannot exceed the number of objects. To achieve maximum concurrency, each object must live in its own apartment.

When a thread is created, it must enter an apartment before attempting to use COM. To do so, it must call one of the following three COM API functions from within its *ThreadFunc* function:

```
HRESULT CoInitialize(void * pvReserved );
HRESULT CoInitializeEx( void * pvReserved, DWORD dwCoInit );
HRESULT OleInitialize(void * pvReserved );
```

The first parameter in all three API functions is reserved by COM and must be set to NULL. To enter an STA, each thread must call *CoInitialize* or *OleInitialize*, or call *CoInitializeEx* with the *dwCoInit* parameter value set to COINIT_APARTMENTTHREADED. Before terminating, each thread that enters an apartment should explicitly exit the apartment by calling one of the following COM API functions. Failure to exit explicitly might delay the reclamation of resources by the operating system.

```
void CoUninitialize();
void OleUninitialize();
```

CoUninitialize must be called from each thread that entered an apartment by calling either *CoInitialize* or *CoInitializeEx*. *OleUninitialize* must be called from each thread that entered an apartment by calling *OleInitialize*.

A thread that enters an apartment has direct access to the COM objects that reside in that apartment. In an STA, only the original thread that created and entered the apartment is allowed to execute on objects in that apartment. All objects are thread-safe because there is only one thread of execution.

To allow incoming calls from other threads, each STA must contain a *GetMessage/DispatchMessage* loop in its *ThreadFunc* function. Incoming calls are put on the thread's message queue. When a thread enters an STA by calling one of the three COM API initialization functions mentioned above, COM creates a hidden window of the class OleMainThreadWndClass. The thread's message loop retrieves each incoming call message and then dispatches it to this hidden window. The window procedure of the hidden window then calls the associated interface method of the target object. Just as in the typical Windows application, each message is processed one at a time. While a thread is processing a message, all incoming calls are added to the queue and will remain there until the thread's message loop retrieves the message.

If a thread from one STA wants to access an object in another STA, the thread must obtain a proxy to that object. The interface of the proxy is semantically identical to that of the real object. The difference is that the proxy must delegate the request across thread boundaries to the real object in the other apartment. This process, called *marshaling*, is frequently referred to in cross-process interaction of COM objects. Marshaling also applies to cross-thread interaction of COM objects that reside in different apartments. It involves the transparent packaging and sending of a request from the client proxy in one apartment to the real object in another apartment.

COM objects that are instantiated based on classes written in Visual Basic use COM's universal marshaler. The universal marshaler is an inherent part of the Windows operating system setup and is located in oleaut32.dll. To gain the full benefit of COM using Visual Basic 6, a current version of oleaut32.dll must be installed. It can be obtained by installing Windows 98, Windows NT 4 with Service Pack 4 or later, Windows 2000, or any of the Microsoft Visual Studio 6 products. The universal marshaler does all the work of transporting requests. These requests might travel between apartments owned by different threads in the same process, across processes on the same machine, or across machine boundaries on a network.

The STA model affords thread affinity, but this affinity is not obtained without a price. As you can imagine, it is much more efficient to access an object through an object reference, which is a direct pointer to an address in memory, rather than marshaling across threads. Yet the ability to create a multithreaded COM server without having to deal with thread safety is appealing.

Creating an ActiveX EXE project in Visual Basic is synonymous to constructing a multithreaded STA COM out-of-process server. In keeping with its theme, Visual Basic has shielded the programmer from the gory details of COM.

No COM programming activity is necessary, but having been exposed to the COM layer will allow you to understand some of the previously inexplicable performance and behavioral issues of your Visual Basic applications.

Single-Threaded Apartments in a Standard EXE

Client applications that want to access COM components must select the type of COM threading model the application supports, because clients, like servers, can be multithreaded. And like servers, clients too must prevent race conditions and deadlocks. A client thread must enter an apartment before it can access a server-side COM object by calling *CoInitialize*, *CoInitializeEx*, or *OleInitialize*, as described for ActiveX EXE components. Prior to terminating, a thread should also explicitly leave the apartment by calling one of the associated uninitialize COM functions. Failure to do so might delay the reclamation of system resources by the operating system.

All the rules of COM that apply to server processes hold true for client processes. The only distinction between the two is the obvious one—servers create objects and serve them up to the clients that use them. Given this distinction, infrastructure differences exist between clients and servers that, as you can imagine, are a bit more complicated on the server side. Regardless, threads invoke behavior whether they exist in a client process or in a server process. Said another way, the concept of a client and a server is an implementation detail of COM. The operating system sees only processes and threads, which is why the rules of COM cannot discriminate between clients and servers.

It is feasible for a client to support MTA, STA, or a combination of one MTA and several STAs. Visual Basic 6 supports only STA clients that contain one thread and apartment where all references to COM objects reside. As I have mentioned earlier in this chapter, extending the thread support of a Visual Basic application is possible using the Windows API, though I do advise you to proceed with caution. An alternative is to create an ActiveX EXE project that contains forms. As mentioned, an ActiveX EXE can contain multiple threads, each of which enters a unique STA. It is not difficult to imagine a server being a client of another server. I will leave it to those of you interested in multithreaded COM clients to take this information as a hint on how to accomplish this in Visual Basic. For those of you who are not in immediate need of this functionality, it is a fairly safe bet to assume that support for threads will increase in future versions of Visual Basic. Eventually, no fancy workarounds will be necessary.

Threading Models for an ActiveX DLL

Unlike their ActiveX EXE counterparts, ActiveX DLLs are loaded into the client process's memory space. COM classes defined in an ActiveX DLL do not declare their support for a COM threading model by calling a variation of *CoInitialize*, because the client will have already done so. Instead, threading model support for each COM class that is creatable by a COM client is stored in the Windows Registry under the class's associated class identifier (CLSID), as shown in the following code extract:

```
[HCR\CLSID\{1E9E3F20-3E84-11D2-BDB4-00805F9BDA1C}\InprocServer32]
@="C:\MyActiveX.dll"
ThreadingModel="Apartment"
```

ActiveX DLLs support four types of threading models: Free, Apartment, Both, and thread-oblivious. Setting the ThreadingModel name value to *Free* indicates that an instance of the specified class can be created only in an MTA. When the ThreadingModel name value is set to *Apartment*, class instances can be created only in an STA. If the ThreadingModel name value is set to *Both*, the class instances can be created in either an MTA or an STA. Not setting the ThreadingModel name value implies to COM that the class is thread-oblivious.

Let us not forget that COM classes defined in an ActiveX DLL are instantiated within a COM client thread. This leads to some very interesting scenarios. If the threading model entered into by the client thread and the class the client wants to create are compatible, the instance of the class will be created in the client thread's apartment. This will give the client direct access to the instance, resulting in the best possible performance. If the client thread's apartment type is not compatible with the type defined for the class in the ActiveX DLL, COM will interpose and spawn another thread from the client process that enters an apartment supported by the class. A class instance is then created in that apartment, and a proxy to that instance is returned to the apartment of the thread that initiated the request. This guarantees thread safety, but performance is affected because the client thread that initiated the request does not have direct access to the object it created. Its requests are marshaled across thread boundaries.

COM even guarantees thread safety for thread-oblivious objects by spawning a main STA thread in which all thread-oblivious objects are created. If the client thread that initiated the request is not the main STA thread, it will receive a proxy to the object. Table 3-1 illustrates the actions taken by COM for all possible scenarios.

Table 3-1. ActiveX DLL Object Interactions with a Client Process

	Threading Model Defined for an ActiveX DLL Class		
Threading Model Entered Into by a Client Thread	STA	MTA	Thread-Oblivious
STA	Class instances are created in the client thread's apartment. The client thread has direct access to the class instance, which results in optimal performance.	COM spawns a thread that enters an MTA, creates a class instance in the MTA, and returns a proxy to the client thread's STA. Object requests are marshaled across thread boundaries. Performance due to marshaling can potentially degrade to unacceptable levels.	COM designates one of the client STA threads as the main STA. COM creates all oblivious class instances in the main STA. If the thread initiating the request resides in the main STA, it will have direct access to the class instance. If not, a proxy is returned from the main STA to the apartment of the client thread that made the request.
MTA	COM spawns a thread that enters an STA, creates a class instance in the STA, and returns a proxy to the client thread's MTA. Object requests are marshaled across thread boundaries. Performance due to marshaling can potentially degrade to unacceptable levels.	Class instances are created in the client thread's apartment. The client thread has direct access to the class instance, which results in optimal performance. The programmer, however, must make use of Win32 thread synchronization primitives to ensure class instances are thread-safe.	COM designates one of the client STA threads as the main STA. If no STAs exist, COM spawns a thread that enters an STA. This now becomes the main STA. COM creates all thread-oblivious class instances in the main STA and returns proxies to the MTA of the requesting client thread.

Visual Basic supports the creation of in-process COM components (ActiveX DLLs) that are either thread-oblivious or STA-bound. You can select a threading model for COM classes defined in Visual Basic from the drop-down list in the General tab of the Project Properties dialog box. (See Figure 3-1.) Select Single Threaded for thread-oblivious classes, or select Apartment Threaded for classes that support STA. The threading model selection applies to all classes creatable by a client process. Creatability is determined in Visual Basic by setting the *Instancing* property value of a class to MultiUse or GlobalMultiUse. (I'll talk more about *Instancing* property values later in this chapter, in the section "*Instancing* Property Value.") When you compile the ActiveX DLL, Visual Basic will automatically add a ThreadingModel name value to the Registry as described previously. Once again, Visual Basic takes care of the COM details and lets the programmer concentrate on developing object-oriented solutions.

In spite of this fact, the programmer is still exposed to unwelcome performance and behavioral issues that can be avoided to a certain extent if the programmer understands how to determine in which apartment a Visual Basic object will reside.

Apartment Living Options for Visual Basic Objects

Visual Basic objects are COM objects; therefore, they must live in an apartment. You do not have to make any native COM calls in Visual Basic code, but several features are available that determine which apartment an object will live in and how objects will interact with other objects and resources in the same apartment or across apartments. What follows is an explanation of these features.

Thread Management

When you create an ActiveX EXE project, you can select one of two approaches for managing threads and apartments on the General tab of the Project Properties dialog box. The server can either create a Thread Per Object, or it can maintain a Thread Pool.

Creating a thread per object allows each instance of a class with an *Instancing* property value of MultiUse to be created in its own thread that has entered a unique apartment. As I mentioned previously, this is the highest level of concurrency possible in a multithreaded STA COM out-of-process component.

Creating a thread pool allows each instance of a class with an *Instancing* property value of MultiUse to be created in an apartment of a thread from the thread pool. New threads are created until the maximum size limit set by you in the Project Properties dialog box is reached. At this point, each new instance is created in the apartment of the next available thread from the pool in a round-robin fashion. Consequently, multiple objects can live in the same apartment owned by a single thread.

Global Variables and Methods

Publicly defined variables, functions, and subroutines in Visual Basic modules are globally accessible to all objects of an ActiveX component that live in the same apartment. These variables, functions, and subroutines are completely inaccessible to objects that do not live in that apartment, even if they are a part of the same component or client process.

Friend Class Members

A friend is someone you trust; therefore, friends have access to information about you that the rest of us are not privileged to have. In Visual Basic, you can define properties and methods of a class with the keyword *Friend*. With respect to these friend properties and methods, an instance of a class is considered friendly (accessible) to all other objects that reside in the same apartment, but remains unfriendly (inaccessible) to objects that do not live in that apartment, even if they are a part of the same component or client process. Properties and methods defined as public in the same class as the friend properties and methods will remain accessible to all COM objects.

Instancing Property Value

A class's *Instancing* property value plays a significant role in determining the residence of a Visual Basic object. Several options for setting the *Instancing* property are listed below:

- **Private** Objects of this class are globally accessible to all objects of an ActiveX component that live in the same apartment. These objects are completely inaccessible to objects that do not live in that apartment, even if they are a part of the same component or client process.

- **PublicNotCreatable** Objects of this class are accessible from any apartment in the same component or client process, or across processes. However, only apartment members can create this object.

- **SingleUse** Clients can create instances of this class, but each new instance will launch a new component process that contains a thread and an STA in which this instance will reside. This option applies only to ActiveX EXEs.

■ **GlobalSingleUse** This option is the same as the SingleUse option, except the client does not need to explicitly instantiate this class. Visual Basic will automatically instantiate the class upon the first object request. In addition, you can call a property or method of this class without an object prefix, which is syntactically equivalent to calling a global method. This option applies only to ActiveX EXEs.

■ **MultiUse** Clients can create instances of this class. When the thread management selection in an ActiveX EXE is a thread per object, the component will spawn a new thread, enter a unique STA, create an instance of this class in the STA, and then return a proxy of the instance to the calling client. If the thread management selection is a thread pool, the component will do as just described until the maximum number of threads set by you have been created in the pool. At this point, further object creations will be added by the component process to a thread and an STA selected from the thread pool in a round-robin fashion. Unlike the SingleUse option, MultiUse will allow multiple instances of a class to reside in the same component process and, depending on the thread management configuration, the component could contain multiple STA threads, each containing one or more class instances. If the component is an ActiveX DLL, a client process can create an instance of this class. All class instances of an ActiveX DLL component will reside in an STA. The STA in which the instance resides is determined by the factors described in the section "Threading Models for an ActiveX DLL."

■ **GlobalMultiUse** Same as MultiUse, except GlobalMultiUse does not require an explicit instantiation of this class. Visual Basic will automatically instantiate it upon the first object request. In addition, you can call a property or method of this class without an object prefix, which is syntactically equivalent to calling a global method.

Using Keyword *New* vs. the *CreateObject* Function

Before you can use an object in Visual Basic, it must be explicitly constructed (with the exception of classes with *Instancing* property values of the Global variation). To construct an object, you can use either the keyword *New* or the *CreateObject* function. The following source code extract illustrates the usage of both:

```
Dim myEspressoMaker As New CoffeeLib.EspressoMaker
```

or

```
Set myEspressoMaker = New CoffeeLib.EspressoMaker
```

or

```
Set myEspressoMaker = CreateObject("CoffeeLib.EspressoMaker")
```

When a Visual Basic client of an ActiveX EXE component uses the keyword *New*, and depending on the thread management approach selected, a new thread might be spawned that enters a unique apartment, creates the object, and returns a proxy to the client. In an ActiveX EXE component, using the keyword *New* to construct an object will result in Visual Basic verifying that the type of object to be created is defined locally in the component. If the object is defined locally, Visual Basic will create the object in the apartment that initiated the request. This scenario can occur if a client has a proxy to an object in an existing apartment and then makes a request that will in turn preempt that apartment object to create an instance of another class defined in the component.

Using the *CreateObject* function from a Visual Basic client will have the same effect as using the keyword *New*. However, this is not the case in an ActiveX EXE. If you have selected a thread per object, or a thread pool that contains more than one thread, creating an object using *CreateObject* will result in Visual Basic bypassing the internal verification of whether the class is locally defined. Instead, *CreateObject* will create the object in another thread and apartment in the same component process and then return a proxy to the apartment that initiated the request.

The Cost of Living for Visual Basic Objects

You have found the apartment of your dreams, so now it's time to return to reality and find out how much it's going to cost you. Many factors will contribute to the cost, and if you don't conduct the proper research, you might run into some unwelcome surprises later on. For instance, consider just the location factor. The distance from your dream apartment to your place of employment is 50 miles. The distance from the apartment to a large international airport is only 5 miles. The rent might be affordable, but when you add in the transportation cost, the time spent in travel, and—maybe most important—the noise of airplanes between the hours of midnight and 4:00 A.M., you might decide it's not a price you're willing to pay.

Apartment hunting for Visual Basic objects is no different. You should fully research and understand the apartment-living options described above. The performance and behavior of COM objects is determined largely by whether collaborating objects reside in the same or different apartments.

Visual Basic objects are either thread-oblivious or support the STA model. STA allows the Visual Basic programmer to create thread-safe classes that can coexist in a multithreaded process. This process can be a multithreaded out-of-process component (ActiveX EXE written in Visual Basic) that serves up objects on multiple threads to numerous clients to prevent the processing of one client request from blocking the request of another client. In general, the intention of making Visual Basic objects support STA is to create an ActiveX server that scales when the usage volume increases. Furthermore, the process can be a client process written in C++ (such as Microsoft Internet Explorer) that spawns multiple threads, each invoking requests on class instances created from an in-process component (an ActiveX DLL written in Visual Basic).

Objects that live in the same STA are considered thread-safe because only the thread that owns the apartment can directly reference all objects in its apartment. This is the optimal situation because a direct reference implies that a thread refers to an address in memory where a given object is loaded. When a thread makes a request to an object in another STA, it cannot do so directly. All requests are marshaled across thread boundaries by proxy. There is significant overhead with this approach, but it exists to provide thread-safe access to COM objects. In addition, Visual Basic has some features of its own that further determine the behavior.

In Visual Basic, classes with an *Instancing* property value of Private, global variables, global functions and subroutines, and friend class properties and methods are accessible to all objects that reside in the same apartment. If another STA is created as a result of spawning a new thread, another instance of all globals will be created in that apartment. Objects in that apartment with friend members and private class instances are accessible only to other objects within the apartment.

Setting a Visual Basic class's *Instancing* property value to MultiUse indicates that a client of a given ActiveX component can create an instance of this class. This also results in the creation of an instance of this Visual Basic class within an STA. Depending on the threading model, each Visual Basic MultiUse class could potentially end up residing in its own thread and STA.

It should be clear to you as a component designer how the implementation of your component will function. For instance, if you've designed each class instance in the component to be completely self-reliant, feel free to set the

Instancing property value to MultiUse. If you intend minimal collaboration, be aware that objects residing in different apartments that interact with one another must marshal their requests across thread boundaries, which degrades performance. On the other hand, if your intention is to share information stored in global variables among multiple objects or to make use of the Friend declaration, you'll need a deeper understanding of COM threading apartment models.

For predictable results with optimal performance, set the *Instancing* property value to MultiUse for all classes in an STA ActiveX DLL component that employs globals and friends, and then use that DLL in a Visual Basic Standard EXE project. Using the same ActiveX DLL in Internet Explorer will result in unpredictable results, because the content of global variables is inconsistent between objects from the same component. Also, run-time errors will occur if an object with friend members is accessed by another object in the same component that is friendly when used in the Standard EXE project.

These errors might startle and frustrate you, but the reason they occur is because of incompatible apartment types between the client process and the ActiveX DLL component. In short, the Internet Explorer client process supports MTA, but the ActiveX DLL supports STA. Because the threading apartment models are incompatible, the COM objects instantiated from the ActiveX DLL cannot live in the same apartment as the client thread that initiated the request. COM therefore interposes by spawning a new thread in the client process that enters an STA, creates the object there, and then returns a proxy to the thread requesting service in the MTA. Each class with an *Instancing* property value of MultiUse in the ActiveX DLL will result in COM spawning a new thread and STA. Each apartment will contain a separate instance of globals. Objects residing in different apartments cannot share global references; friendships can exist only within an apartment. Visual Basic will raise a run-time error if an object attempts to access friend methods or properties of another object in a different apartment. If proper exception handling does not exist, the Internet Explorer client process will terminate.

To overcome this problem, here are three solutions that I've listed from least elegant to most elegant:

1. Avoid using globals and friends as a means for sharing information between objects.

2. Set the threading model for the ActiveX DLL to Single Threaded.

3. Use an Object Factory design pattern (as shown in Chapter 8), and set the threading model to Apartment Threaded.

Although the first solution is obvious, we often discount it. As programmers, we sometimes forget that not every problem requires an elaborate, sophisticated solution. Assuming the problem does require extra effort, you are left with solutions 2 and 3.

Solution 2 suggests making the COM objects created from your ActiveX DLL thread-oblivious. In another context, this would mean the objects created from this DLL are not thread-safe. In COM, all objects are thread-safe. Because the COM classes defined in this DLL support no threading model, COM will also intervene when a request is initiated from a thread in the Internet Explorer client process. In this case, however, COM will create all the thread-oblivious objects in Internet Explorer's main STA, and then return proxies to the client thread in the MTA. If no STA exists, COM will spawn a thread that enters an STA. This STA will now be the designated main STA for all subsequent thread-oblivious objects. Each class in the Single Threaded ActiveX DLL with an *Instancing* property of MultiUse will be instantiated in the main STA. As a result, a single instance of globals will be shared between all objects, and friend object members will be accessible to all objects in the apartment. Behavior will remain as expected, but performance will degrade significantly because of cross-thread marshaling and object-request blocking.

Multiple threads that have entered into the client's MTA could feasibly reference objects from the ActiveX DLL. For each reference, a proxy will be maintained in the MTA. Because all objects reside in the same thread and STA, Internet Explorer will behave more like a single-threaded application, because all object invocations are synchronized through the main STA thread (if the ActiveX DLL is a spreadsheet component, for example). Performance will diminish if a request from one MTA thread causes a lengthy spreadsheet recalculation. Other requests from other threads will be queued in the main STA message queue to be sequentially processed by the single thread that owns the apartment. These threads will be unable to execute further until their requests are processed.

Solution 3 is the most elegant approach. Implementing an Object Factory design pattern (Chapter 8) within an STA-defined ActiveX DLL gives the component designer the desired behavior with the best possible performance. An object factory defers object creation from the client code to a factory instance designed to manufacture the object requested by the client. In one factory class, you can define a create method for each class that you want to make available to a client. The factory class's *Instancing* property value should be the only one set to MultiUse. The *Instancing* property value of the remaining classes that have corresponding create methods in the factory should be set to PublicNotCreatable. Because the factory class is the only one labeled as MultiUse, COM will spawn a new thread and STA in the Internet Explorer client process only when an instance of the factory is created. All objects created by the factory instance will share the same apartment. Consequently, these objects will be able to share global references and maintain friendships. Performance will still be an issue to the extent that requests are submitted from other client threads, but sets of objects living in unique STAs can simultaneously execute tasks. For example, modifying the spreadsheet component in the example in solution 2 to support this model will allow one instance of the spreadsheet to recalculate without affecting the performance of another.

Conducting the proper system analysis that leads to the employment of various design patterns is not enough for a successful Visual Basic implementation. You must also understand COM technology well enough to make the appropriate cost-effective design decisions. Most chapters in Part Two include a section titled "COMments" that will emphasize significant consequences due to implementation decisions of the design pattern at hand.

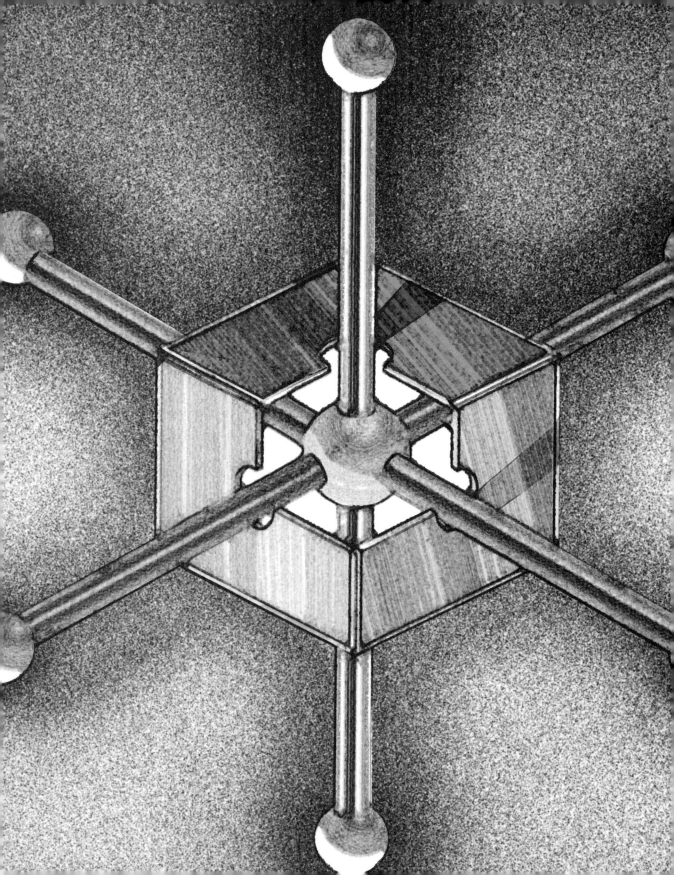

PART II

DESIGN PATTERNS DIRECTORY

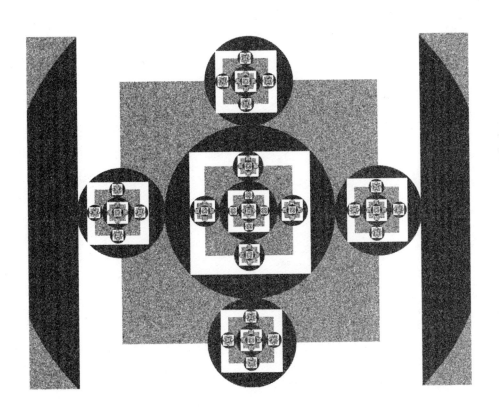

CHAPTER FOUR

Adapter

Wouldn't it be ideal to extend the functionality of an object or plug in to the existing services of a legacy system without any disruption to that system whatsoever? The Adapter design pattern described in this chapter allows you to accomplish just that by advocating loose coupling of a class's interface to its implementation.

> NOTE: Coupling is a measure of how closely related modules or classes are to each other. Loose coupling implies that the modules aren't restrictively interdependent.

Purpose

The Adapter design pattern provides a new interface to a class, object, or function that allows it to collaborate with other objects in a given domain.

Utilization

The Adapter design pattern is useful in the following circumstances:

- The application's architecture requires a specific interface, but the class you want to use is located in a compiled class library (such as a Microsoft Visual Basic in-process ActiveX DLL or a Microsoft Visual C++ out-of-process ActiveX server) and doesn't support the interface. Because you don't have access to the source code for the class library, adding a new interface to an existing class via inheritance is not an option.

- Implementing a new interface in an existing class proves to be impractical. A single class might be overloaded with the implementation of numerous interfaces in an attempt to improve the utility value gained by each caller. For example, if a class inherited from 100 different interfaces, and each unique caller utilized a single unique interface, the overhead incurred by the implementation of all these interfaces outweighs the utility value gained by each caller.

■ The functionality to support a specific interface is dispersed among many existing classes in a system. Instead of maintaining separate object references to each class instance needed, you could define a new class that exposes a single interface that internally maintains references to the required class instances. Not only do you simplify access to a set of objects, but you also encapsulate the logic that determines which objects to use when.

■ Plugging in to the functionality of existing non-object-oriented legacy code makes sense. It is often the case that a firm has already invested a considerable amount of time and money in developing services in legacy code. Using the Adapter design pattern to reference the legacy code might be more cost-effective than rewriting the code as an object-oriented solution.

■ The intention is to extend the functionality of an object without modifying its interface. This will result in a *transparent adapter* (explained in the next section).

Scenario

An adapter class abstracts classes, objects, or functions. Adapters are either transparent or opaque, depending on whether the class, object, or function (the adaptee) is accessible to the client.

With transparent adapters, the adaptee remains accessible to the client. Transparent adapters are mostly used for the following:

■ To enhance the functionality of a class or object by attaching various adapter classes

■ To attach to different implementations of an adaptee that is derived from an abstract interface

Opaque adapters encapsulate the access to the adaptee by making that interaction private to the adapter. The following sections show two of many possible scenarios for using an Adapter design pattern.

Scenario A: Opaque Object Adapter

You're building a Visual Basic toolkit class library, in which you would like to define a sorted map class (SMap) that derives from an abstract map interface (Map). (A *map* is a class that maps keys to items, or values.) The key is of type String, and the item could be of any type (Variant). Instead of building your map classes totally from scratch, you decide to delegate most of the work to the existing Visual Basic Collection class. You embed a private object reference to an instance of a Collection in SMap—SMap is the adapter class that abstracts the Collection object (the adaptee). Because this relationship is unknown to the clients of SMap, and because it involves abstracting an object instance, this is an Opaque Object Adapter design pattern. (See Figure 4-1.)

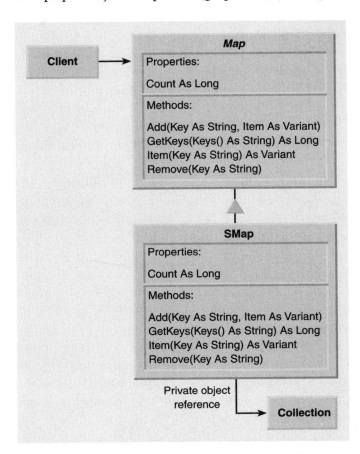

Figure 4-1.
The SMap collection class implemented as an Opaque Object Adapter.

Scenario B: Transparent Class Adapter

You would like to define a sorted map class similar to the one described above. However, instead of delegating the core tasks to an object instance, you decide to inherit the SMap class from the user-defined collection class, CCollection. Using this approach, you will have to be aware of certain constraints of the Visual Basic language. Your intent is to inherit the implementation of CCollection, but with classes in Visual Basic, only interface inheritance is possible, not implementation inheritance. Because implementation inheritance is not possible, an opaque adapter makes no sense—therefore, all class adapters are transparent. Hence, your intent should be to create a transparent SMap adapter where a client can reference it from both its Map interface and its CCollection interface. Figure 4-2 shows

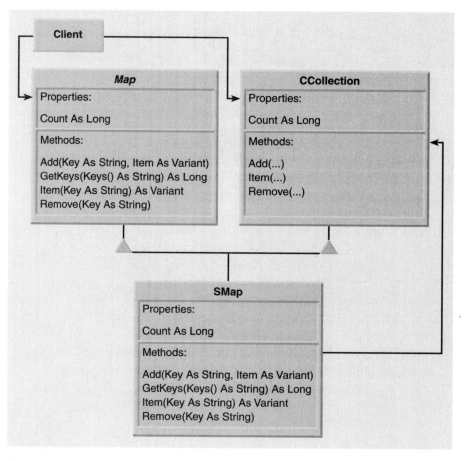

Figure 4-2.
The SMap collection class implemented as a Transparent Class Adapter.

that, in order to give the illusion of implementation inheritance in Visual Basic, a CCollection object reference is maintained in SMap. All invocations through the CCollection interface of SMap are passed on one-for-one to the CCollection object instance. Invocations through the Map interface of SMap are processed by the CCollection object instance to the extent deemed necessary by you, the programmer of the SMap adapter. Let me reiterate the fact that although the CCollection object instance might be private to SMap, this is still a Transparent Class Adapter design pattern by definition, because SMap publicly inherited the CCollection interface.

Object Model

The Adapter design pattern is a fairly straightforward concept to grasp. However, as you can see by reading through the scenarios, you can choose from alternative designs depending on whether your intention is to adapt a class, an object, or a function, and on whether you want the adapter to be transparent or opaque. (The benefits and drawbacks of these types of adapters will be explored further in the "Ramifications" section of this chapter.) With so many types of adapters, I think it's only fair to illustrate object models for a variety of possibilities. Figure 4-3 below, and Figures 4-4 and 4-5 on the following page, model class, object, and function adapters, respectively. Figures 4-3 and 4-4 are transparent adapters, while Figure 4-5 is an opaque adapter.

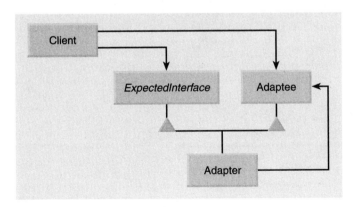

Figure 4-3.
Transparent Class Adapter.

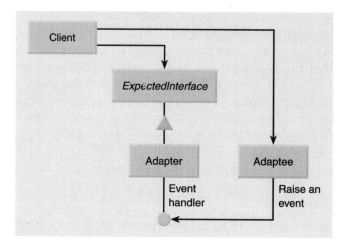

Figure 4-4.
Transparent Object Adapter (with events).

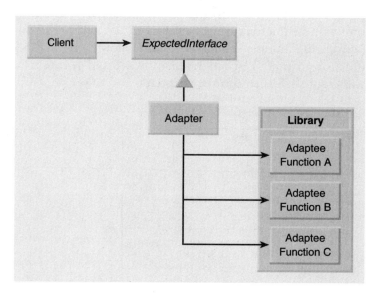

Figure 4-5.
Opaque Function Adapter.

Roles

The roles and functions of the elements of the Adapter design pattern, as well as how they relate to the elements in the scenarios discussed previously, are as follows:

- **Client**   Collaborates with all objects that implement the expected interface.

- **ExpectedInterface (Map)**   Defines the interface expected by the client.

- **Adapter (SMap)**   Serves as a bridge between a client that requires a specific interface (ExpectedInterface), and other classes, objects, and functions that contain the functionality desired but would otherwise be impossible to leverage because the interfaces they expose are incompatible with the interface the client expects.

- **Adaptee (Collection)**   Contains functionality that is useful to the calling client. An adaptee might be in the form of a class, object, or function. However, because the interface exposed by the adaptee is incompatible with the interface expected by the client, interaction is possible only indirectly through the adapter.

Relationships

As reflected in the three object models, the adapter class implements the interface (ExpectedInterface) expected by the client. Upon client invocation, the adapter class delegates the work to the adaptee. Furthermore, clients might have access to the adaptee if the adapter is transparent.

Ramifications

Existing functionality that has been proven to be reliable can be plugged in to new system architectures without compromise to that functionality. The Adapter design pattern defines a class that supports the interface expected by a client in a given domain. This class exhibits a loose coupling of interface and implementation and encapsulates the delegation of work to classes, objects, and functions that contain the desired functionality. This implementation of the functionality by the client would be otherwise unattainable when the interface expected by the client is incompatible with the interface exposed by the source of the functionality.

Class adapters are always transparent in Visual Basic because Visual Basic supports only public interface inheritance. This constraint has advantages and disadvantages, which are mentioned in the following sections.

Advantages of Visual Basic–Enforced Transparency of Class Adapters

A single adapter instance can serve the needs of clients that require the new interface and clients that use the interface exposed by the source.

Instead of disrupting the implementation of a class by modifying its interface or having it inherit new ones, you can extend its functionality by defining an adapter that inherits a new interface as well as the class's existing interface. Therefore, the client will deliberately maintain a reference to both interfaces from the same adapter instance. In reality, you cannot fully anticipate how an existing class will be extended to support the intentions of a client. Modifying an interface is a "no-no." An interface serves as a contract between a client and the object serving up that interface. Breaking the contract usually breaks the collaboration between the client and its server objects, which ultimately leads to system failure. Applying multiple inheritance to a designated class can be a good idea in many situations; however, you should reconsider excessive inheritance that is motivated by the constant iterative process of identifying new functionality. Also, you should take into account the scope of the utility value for supporting a new interface. An Adapter design pattern is a sensible alternative to a new interface.

If you refer back to the Transparent Class Adapter object model (see Figure 4-3), you will notice that the Adapter class inherits the interface of the adaptee (not its implementation), and that it also contains a reference to an object instance that supports the adaptee interface. The Adapter design pattern suggests a few advantageous implementation possibilities. If the reference to an object that supports the adaptee interface is private to the adapter, the adapter could define two possible implementations. The adapter could delegate one-for-one all invocations made through the adaptee interface directly to the object via its reference. Then again, because the adapter has inherited the interface of the adaptee, it could just as easily define new behavior for any function in the adaptee interface. If the reference to an object that supports the adaptee interface is publicly settable from the adapter, all implementations mentioned here are possible. In addition, the adapter could dynamically realize new behavior for the adaptee interface at run time by obtaining references to objects that are instances of unique classes that implement the adaptee interface.

Disadvantages of Visual Basic–Enforced Transparency of Class Adapters

You cannot privately inherit the implementation of the adaptee class, so the adaptee is exposed whether you like it or not. If your intention is to create an opaque adapter, you cannot implement a class adapter, and you must implement an Opaque Object Adapter design pattern.

Opaque adapters maintain private object references to adaptee instances, or private access to non-object-oriented adaptee functions. With this feature comes the full benefit of encapsulation. Because only the adapter is aware of the adaptee's existence, individual concrete adapter classes that implement the same abstract interface expected by the client each could adapt different objects or functions that would produce the preferred results.

Transparent object adapters have the same goals and provide the same benefits as transparent class adapters. However, sometimes it is not possible to inherit the interface of an adaptee. In Visual Basic, if you try to inherit the Collection interface you will get a compile-time error stating, "Bad interface for Implements." Microsoft Excel 97 was totally revamped to support Microsoft Visual Basic for Applications 5 technology, which implied you could do everything in Excel 97 that you could do in Visual Basic 5. Unfortunately, that isn't true. For example, you can create classes in Excel 97, but you cannot inherit interfaces from other classes. (This functionality was changed in Excel 2000.) In short, you need transparent object adapters for those times when inheritance is not possible.

Class adapters by default allow you to override the behavior of the adaptee. Object adapters cannot override the behavior of adaptee objects unless the adaptee makes the opportunity available. This opportunity comes in the form of events that must be defined in the adaptee class. These events can then be raised at will by the adaptee objects. Figure 4-4 illustrates a Transparent Object Adapter in which the adaptee object raises events and the adapter handles those events. The designer of a class must have the foresight to determine whether instances of the class should raise events to allow interested parties the opportunity to produce varying behaviors upon event notification.

Implementation

By now it should be clear that an Adapter design pattern is implemented either through multiple interface inheritance (Class Adapter) or by the creation of an object reference to the adaptee instance (Object Adapter and Function Adapter). To better appreciate the Adapter design pattern, let's go through the steps required to implement the Transparent Class Adapter as shown in the object model in Figure 4-3. Next, let's assume that the adaptee exists in an ActiveX DLL. (You create a reference to the DLL in your project by selecting References from the Project menu in Visual Basic.) In your project, you would create a class module and change the name to ExpectedInterface. The Expected-Interface class is abstract, so the functions defined in this class module will contain no implementation, as shown in the code extract below:

```
' Class Name:    ExpectedInterface
' Note:          This is the abstract interface expected
'                by the client and implemented by the
'                concrete Adapter class.

Option Explicit

Public Function Func1(sVal As String) As Boolean
End Function

Public Function Func2(iVal As Integer) As String
End Function
```

Now create another class module and change the name to Adapter, and then inherit both the ExpectedInterface class and the Adaptee class using the *Implements* keyword. Next, you must define a private object variable named *m_adaptee* of type Adaptee. In the *Adapter.Class_Initialize* event handler, construct an instance of the Adaptee class and store a reference to it in the *m_adaptee* private object variable. The Adaptee class is concrete; therefore, it contains implementation for all the functions of its interface. Regardless, classes in Visual Basic can inherit only the interface. Hence, in order to improvise for the lack of implementation inheritance, the *m_adaptee* variable is defined to provide the equivalent benefit. Finally, the Adapter class must implement all functions from both the ExpectedInterface interface and the Adaptee interface. You, the designer of the Adapter class, determine the extent to which work is delegated to the Adaptee instance. All work that results from invocations via the Adaptee interface should be delegated appropriately to the Adaptee instance. The following code extract is a possible implementation of the Adapter class:

```
' Class Name:    Adapter
' Note:          Concrete Adapter class inherits both the
'                ExpectedInterface interface and the Adaptee
'                interface and provides implementation
'                for all functions in both interfaces.

Option Explicit

' Interface expected by client
Implements ExpectedInterface
' Interface of concrete class being adapted
Implements Adaptee

' Visual Basic doesn't support implementation
' inheritance, so this Adaptee object variable is a
' workaround that provides the same result by simply
' delegating one-for-one all invocations via the Adaptee interface
' through this Adaptee object variable.
Private m_adaptee As Adaptee

' When an instance of this Adapter class is instantiated,
' the Initialize event handler gets called. This is the
' perfect time to instantiate the Adaptee. You are now
' guaranteeing that all invocations that delegate work
' to the Adaptee will occur without the client having to
' explicitly create an Adaptee. This type of arrangement
' is automatic with implementation inheritance, so it is
' only fair that you provide the same behavior.
Private Sub Class_Initialize()
    Set m_adaptee = New Adaptee
End Sub

' Implement all functions of the ExpectedInterface
' interface. Notice the delegation of work to the Adaptee
' via the m_adaptee object variable. Also notice that it is
' up to the programmer of this Adapter to delegate and
' interpret the results accordingly.

' ExpectedInterface.Func1
Private Function ExpectedInterface_Func1(sVal As String) As Boolean
    If m_adaptee.FuncB(sVal) > 37 Then
        ExpectedInterface_Func1 = True
    Else
        ExpectedInterface_Func1 = False
    End If
End Function
```

(continued)

77

```
' ExpectedInterface.Func2
Private Function ExpectedInterface_Func2(iVal As Integer) As String
    If m_adaptee.FuncA(CLng(iVal)) < 10.9 Then
        ExpectedInterface_Func2 = "Great Job!"
    Else
        ExpectedInterface_Func2 = "Needs Improvement."
    End If
End Function


' Implement all functions of the Adaptee interface.
' Notice the one-for-one delegation of work.


' Adaptee.FuncA
Private Function Adaptee_FuncA(lVal As Long) As Double
    Adaptee_FuncA = m_adaptee.FuncA(lVal)
End Function

' Adaptee.FuncB
Private Function Adaptee_FuncB(sVal As String) As Long
    Adaptee_FuncB = m_adaptee.FuncB(sVal)
End Function
```

The client code is completely oblivious to the processing details of the Adapter. Hence, writing the source code for the client is blatantly simple, as this code extract illustrates:

```
' Client code
'
' Declare object variable of type ExpectedInterface.
Dim ei As ExpectedInterface
    ⋮

' Instantiate Adapter that supports the ExpectedInterface
' interface.
Set ei = New Adapter
retcode = ei.Func1("45")
strMsg = ei.Func2(2)

MsgBox "Func1 returned " & retcode & vbCr & _
        "Func2 returned " & strMsg

' Remember, this is a Transparent Class Adapter design pattern;
' therefore, an interface to the Adaptee could be
' acquired easily using the following approach:
'
'Dim wr As Adaptee
'Set wr = ei
```

Sample Application

In an ActiveX DLL project named Adapters (located in the Adapter directory on the companion CD), I have implemented fully the SMap collection described in Scenario A of this chapter, which is an Opaque Object Adapter design pattern. What follows is a brief compilation of all participants in the sample application. Please refer to the companion CD for the full source code.

- Map, the interface expected by clients, is an abstract interface that defines how objects of any type are stored in a collection. It maps a key of type String to the object's location in the collection. So instead of traversing through a collection for the object required, you use the object's key for easy and instant retrieval. Because Map is an abstract interface, I created a class module named Map. Then I changed its *Instancing* property value to PublicNotCreatable, which means you will not be able to create instances of the Map type outside this project. You can declare object variables of type Map without receiving an error, but you will not be able to use the keyword *New* or the *CreateObject* function to create an instance. As the following code extract illustrates, the Map class module contains property and function definitions with no implementation (empty function bodies):

```
' Class Name:    Map
' Note:          This is an abstract interface from which
'                concrete classes will inherit.

Option Explicit

Property Get Count() As Long
End Property

Public Sub Add(Key As String, Item As Variant)
End Sub

Public Function GetKeys(Keys() As String) As Long
End Function

Public Function Item(Key As String) As Variant
End Function

Public Sub Remove(Key As String)
End Sub
```

■ SMap (Adapter) is a concrete Map class that implements the interface defined by Map. Said another way, SMap is a type of Map. SMap also has the added functionality of maintaining the collection in sorted order by key, hence the *S* prefix:

```
' Class Name:    SMap
' Note:          This is a concrete Map class.
'                It maintains a map collection
'                sorted in key order.

Option Explicit

' Inherits the Map interface
Implements Map
⋮
```

■ The important functionality contained in SMap is its maintenance of a private object variable that stores a reference to a Visual Basic Collection object. Most of the work necessary to maintain the sorted map collection is delegated to the Collection object via the reference stored in *m_collection*. Notice that all the functions derived from the Map interface—except for *GetKeys*—delegate all work to the *m_collection* object variable:

```
' Class Name:    SMap
⋮

Option Explicit

' Inherits the Map interface
Implements Map

Private m_collection As Collection
⋮

' Add
Private Sub Map_Add(Key As String, Item As Variant)
    m_collection.Add Key:=Key, Item:=Item
    ' Add key in sort order
    AddKey Key
End Sub

' Count
Private Property Get Map_Count() As Long
    Map_Count = m_collection.Count
End Property
```

```
' Item
Private Function Map_Item(Key As String) As Variant
    If VarType(m_collection.Item(Key)) = vbObject Then
        Set Map_Item = m_collection.Item(Key)
    Else
        Map_Item = m_collection.Item(Key)
    End If
End Function

' Remove
Private Sub Map_Remove(Key As String)
    m_collection.Remove Key
    m_keys.Remove Key
End Sub
```

This example clearly illustrates the major advantage of an Adapter design pattern, which is its ability to define a new type of object that makes effective use of existing system components.

NOTE: You can use the AdapterTester project, located in the Adapter\AdapterTester subdirectory on the companion CD, to test the Adapters DLL.

Related Patterns

The Bridge (Chapter 5), the Smart Proxy (Chapter 6), and the Event Service (Chapter 13) design patterns are all basically adapters, because they provide interfaces expected by clients that wrap different implementations that were otherwise incompatible (and not intended to be used by the client in question). However, each of these patterns is a solution for a specific problem domain and should be applied according to the problem it addresses.

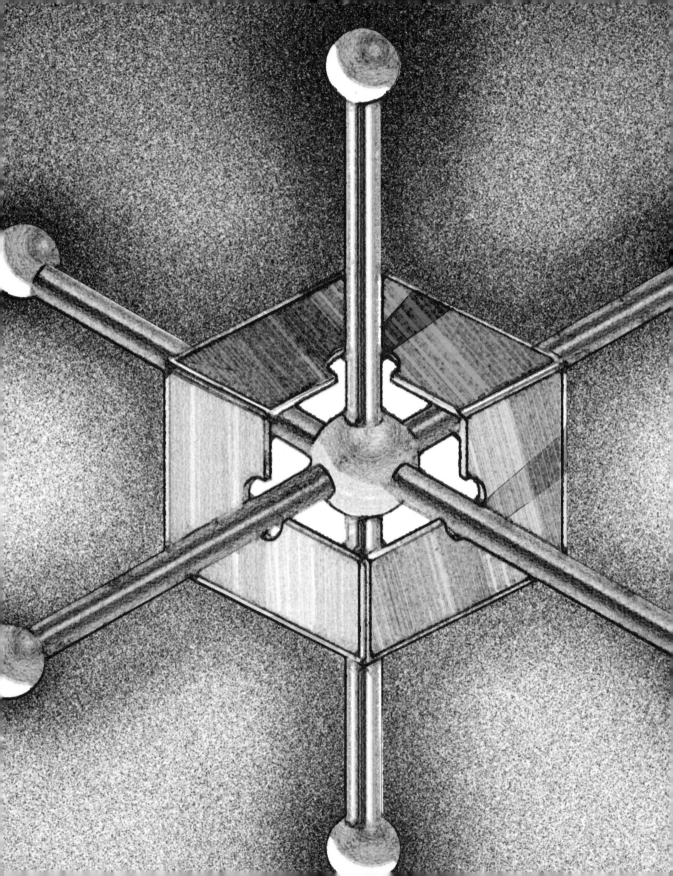

CHAPTER FIVE

Bridge

As defined in Chapter 2, interface inheritance is the means by which you obtain reusability in Microsoft Visual Basic. Different classes can inherit the same interface. Each class can then define a unique implementation for that interface. An object exposes the interfaces supported by the class the object is based on. Communication with an object is possible only through the interfaces it exposes.

For this reason, a Visual Basic object-oriented developer programs to an interface rather than to a class. As a result, an ideal system is said to exist when the *consumer code,* which initiates interaction with one or more interfaces, is written only once. The objects that are bound to the interfaces used by the consumer can easily be replaced by other objects of different classes, so long as those classes support the same interfaces. Binding to a different object results in different behavior of the consumer for the same interfaces, which leads to polymorphism. As you'll recall from Chapter 2, polymorphism is the ability to dynamically bind an interface to an object that supports it.

As you'll also recall from Chapter 2, reusing an interface requires you to use the keyword *Implements*, followed by the interface name, in a given class module. The class must then implement all the properties and methods defined in that interface. This is the conventional way to reuse an interface, but the Bridge design pattern accomplishes the same end while providing benefits not realized with interface inheritance.

Purpose

The Bridge design pattern breaks the direct and permanent link between the interface and the implementation formed by conventional language features, which results in the plug-and-play capability of either the interface or the implementation of the interface.

Utilization

The Bridge design pattern is useful in the following circumstances:

- **The client referencing an interface defined in an ActiveX component is written in a language that doesn't support inheritance.** For example, interfaces defined in an ActiveX DLL that has been written in Visual Basic cannot be used in Microsoft Excel 97 because Microsoft Excel 97 Visual Basic for Applications (VBA) does not support interface inheritance.

- **Statically binding an interface to a class is too restrictive.** For instance, you might want to do any of the following:

  - Implement only part of an interface.

  - Provide an implementation that is not restricted to one class module.

  - Dynamically assign an implementation to an object at run time.

  - Modify, extend, or replace an interface without having to retrofit those changes in all classes that inherit the interface.

  - Reuse a single implementation with multiple interfaces.

Scenario

Your MIS manager has come to the realization that all application systems developed and supported by your department should retain personal configurations for each user. The main reason for this idea is that not all users use a system in the same way. While providing a single approach to configuring all systems might be consistent, it might also be too rigid. Consequently, some users will love the system, some will hate it, and still others will have mixed feelings about it. When users are not pleased with a system, it sometimes reflects negatively on the department. If users have a choice, they might opt to not use the system at all. Hey, who said life was fair?

In an effort to minimize the possibility that this situation might occur, your manager pitches an idea of maintaining user profiles for system elements such as user interface (UI) settings (such as window positions, toolbar selections, and color settings), the name of the most recently used system host, and so forth. Your manager points out that no one system is similar to another in functionality, user interface, or infrastructure, so you really have two choices: you can either solve the problem on a system-by-system basis, or you can build a user profile framework that is reusable in all systems. In keeping with the primary theme of this book, which is how to create reusable solutions, you will opt for the latter alternative.

You will be building a User Profile Service framework—packaged in an ActiveX DLL—that creates and stores user profile objects and retrieves those objects upon request from a given user profile repository. (See Chapter 11, "Repository," for more on this type of design pattern.) The User Profile Service framework takes into account the list of possible attributes that could be stored in a user profile by defining one UserProfile class that is flexible enough to contain any number of attributes of any given type. In addition, the User Profile Service framework defines a UserProfileRepository interface, which provides a uniform interface for concrete implementations for creating, storing, and retrieving user profiles from Microsoft SQL Server and Microsoft Access. Your framework is extensible because a consumer of your framework can define its own concrete repository classes for other data sources, such as the Windows Registry and ASCII text files, by inheriting the UserProfileRepository interface in a class module.

Exposing the UserProfileRepository interface to consumers of your User Profile Service framework might seem sufficient for making your framework reusable and extensible. But you must not forget that your framework exists in an ActiveX component; therefore, the benefits of your framework are not limited to just Visual Basic consumers. Any programming language that supports ActiveX can profit in the same manner—however, not all programming languages are created equal.

For instance, let's assume you have applications in your department that are add-ins to Excel 97. (If you've upgraded to Excel 2000, you don't need to worry about this because Excel 2000 supports interface inheritance.) It's important to your manager that these applications retain user profiles. You're in luck because Excel 97 supports the use of ActiveX technologies, such as the ActiveX DLL where the User Profile Service framework resides. With the assistance of Excel's robust macro language technology (which was completely revamped based on VBA), you can easily write framework consumer code in Excel that is almost identical to the same code in Visual Basic. Excel VBA and Visual Basic are so similar that the untrained eye can barely differentiate between the two. In spite of this fact, Excel 97 VBA does not support interface inheritance, which by convention is the only way possible to extend the User Profile Service framework. Besides, you have discovered that these Excel 97 applications currently do not interact with SQL Server or Access. Adding this dependency to gain the benefits of retaining user profile settings is not an acceptable solution within the context of your situation. The desired solution is to implement a UserProfileRepository interface that retains user profile settings in an Excel 97 workbook.

Incorporating a Bridge design pattern in your User Profile Service framework will allow Excel 97 VBA programmers to extend your framework to support an Excel 97 workbook repository without any disruption to the framework code. As illustrated in the class diagram in Figure 5-1, the Bridge design pattern is implemented as a concrete class that inherits the UserProfileRepository interface, similar to the way in which the SQL Server and Access repository classes inherit an interface. The difference is that the implementation of the Bridge class does not persist user profiles to a data source like the other concrete repository classes do.

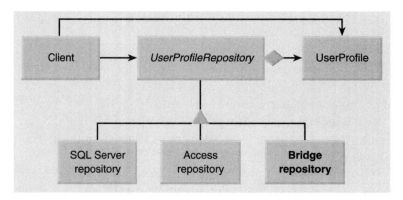

Figure 5-1.
Class diagram of the User Profile Service framework.

For each method defined in the UserProfileRepository interface, the Bridge class defines an analogous event that can be captured by event handlers defined in other classes. In this scenario, the consumer of these events is an Excel 97 workbook repository class defined in an Excel 97 add-in. (See Figure 5-2.) This particular implementation of the Bridge design pattern delegates method invocations from the UserProfileRepository interface to any class object that subscribes to the event.

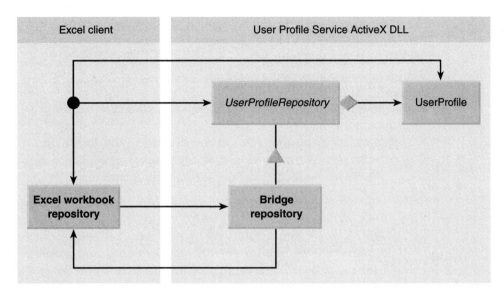

Figure 5-2.
Class diagram showing the relationship between the UserProfileRepository interface and the implementation of that interface defined in the Excel 97 workbook repository class.

Object Model

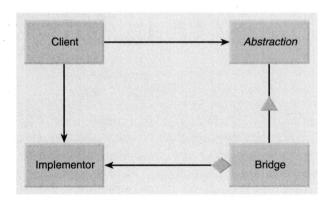

Roles

The roles and functions of the Bridge design pattern are as follows:

- **Abstraction (UserProfileRepository)**   Defines an abstract interface.

- **Bridge (BridgeRepository)**   Concrete class that implements the abstraction. Its implementation is unique because it defines a corresponding event for each method defined in the abstraction. Upon invocation of a method, the bridge raises the equivalent event that will be recognized by all subscribing implementors.

- **Implementor (ExcelWorkbookRepository)**   Concrete class that defines implementation intended for the abstraction. The implementor subscribes to events published by the bridge. When an event is raised, the implementor executes the appropriate implementation, which is defined in terms of an event handler function.

Relationships

The client application sends a request for an expected interface (abstraction), which is implemented by a bridge that the client application is referencing. The bridge then forwards that request by raising a corresponding event. One or more implementors can receive the event published by the bridge. When an implementor is notified, it executes its implementation of the event.

Ramifications

One advantage to using the Bridge design pattern is that ActiveX-enabled programming languages that do not support interface inheritance can now benefit from interface reuse.

Implementation inheritance, which is not supported by Visual Basic, provides reuse of implementations through a class hierarchy. A descendant class could potentially reuse implementations from all ancestor classes in its inheritance chain. Using the Bridge design pattern, you can accomplish the implementation reuse by having multiple implementor classes subscribe to the same event published by a single bridge. Each implementor class's event handler will be called as a result of a single client request.

The Bridge design pattern accomplishes the decoupling of an interface from its implementation, which results in the following benefits:

- In conventional interface inheritance, any changes made to the properties or methods of an interface directly affect all supporting classes, which requires you to recompile and redeploy those classes. In the Bridge design pattern, modifications made to an interface do not directly affect the implementors—only the bridge class needs to be updated. Keep in mind that changing property and method signatures of an interface in Visual Basic constitutes a binary incompatibility with the previous version of the interface. Behind the "curtains," COM considers this update a new interface, not a change to an existing one. Visual Basic internally asks COM to generate a new interface identifier (IID) that uniquely identifies this interface throughout the universe. As a result, early bound clients have to reference the new interface and recompile accordingly.

- Implementors can reside in a different ActiveX component from where the abstraction and the bridge and from where other implementors reside. Therefore:

  ❑ Modification of an implementation requires a recompile of only the component in which the implementor resides.

  ❑ New implementors can bind dynamically to a single interface by subscribing to events published by a given bridge.

  ❑ Implementation can be hidden from the clients of an interface.

These benefits are also realized through interface inheritance and through the COM and ActiveX technologies that are an inherent part of Visual Basic. By using polymorphism, an interface can bind dynamically at run time to an object that supports it. Interfaces are made available through type libraries, and different components can all reference the same type library. This ability allows the components to define and change their implementations at will and requires a recompile of only the changed component. The only thing missing is the granularity at which an interface can bind to an object.

The Bridge design pattern adds this granularity. Implementations for all properties and methods of an interface are no longer bound to one class module. In other words, the Bridge design pattern allows a client to have a reference to a single instance of a bridge object that supports the interface the client expects. Yet the implementation for each property and method of the expected interface can be dispersed among different class objects. As a result,

- Implementors can implement parts of an interface. Reusability shifts from the interface level to the functions and properties of the interface. Interfaces are viewed as contracts between the client and the object serving up the interface. In general, providing partial implementations of an interface is not good programming practice because it breaches the contract. A client expects references to all properties and methods of an interface to produce valid results.

- Confusion might arise as to where the state of an object should reside—should the state be dispersed among multiple implementors, or should it reside in the bridge?

To avoid these potentially unacceptable results, you should make certain design decisions before you implement the Bridge design pattern. For instance, if you intend to have multiple implementors to implement parts of an interface, the bridge should provide default behavior if no subscribing implementors exist. Also, you should have the state reside solely in the bridge.

Implementation

Now that you know what a Bridge design pattern looks like, let's take a look at how to implement this design solution in Visual Basic. As I said in this chapter's "Scenario" section, a Bridge design pattern fits well in the framework paradigm by making the framework extensible through inheritance and through the composition of implementor objects. Before you start implementing anything, you should already know where the different participants will reside, which all depends on your perspective as a designer.

The interface (abstraction) expected by the client and the concrete bridge class (along with other concrete classes) reside in the same ActiveX component as each other. The implementor resides in the client process's address space. You should feel free to slice and dice this configuration any way you see fit. Your decisions will determine the extent to which you can use the different participants interchangeably. The source code implementation remains the same despite any physical partitioning.

On that note, to implement the abstraction, you create a class module that defines an abstract interface. This is the interface expected by clients. Because the interface is abstract, the implication is that the interface has no implementation of its own. So, all you do is define properties and methods with empty function bodies (no implementation), as shown in the code below. To prevent clients from creating instances of this interface, set the interface's *Instancing* property value to PublicNotCreatable using the Properties window in the Visual Basic integrated development environment (IDE).

```
' Class Name:   Abstraction
' Note: This is an abstract interface expected by the client.
'       The Instancing property must be set to PublicNotCreatable.
Option Explicit

' Read-only property PropA returns a string value.
Public Property Get PropA() As String
End Property

' Method Func1 takes two Integer parameters and returns an Integer
' result.
Public Function Func1(ByVal X As Integer, ByVal Y As Integer) _
    As Integer
End Function
```

Next you want to define a concrete bridge class that inherits the abstract interface. The bridge class's implementation defines the events it associates with the properties and methods of the interface it inherited, which is the interface expected by the client. In response to requests made via this interface, the implementation fires a corresponding event, as shown here:

```
' Class Name:   Bridge
' Note: This is a concrete class that inherits the Abstraction
'       interface. Its purpose is to publish events that correspond
'       to requests made via the Abstraction interface that it
'       supports. Potential subscribers (implementors) can then
'       execute implementation upon notification.
'
Option Explicit

' Inherit the Abstraction interface.
Implements Abstraction
```

(continued)

```
' Define corresponding events for each property and method
' of the Abstraction interface.
'
Public Event PropA(ByRef GetVal As String)

Public Event Func1(ByVal X As Integer, _
                   ByVal Y As Integer, _
                   ByRef retVal As Integer)


' Bridge class concrete implementation for:
'
' Abstraction.PropA
Private Property Get Abstraction_PropA() As String
    ' Publish corresponding event PropA.
    RaiseEvent PropA(Abstraction_PropA)
End Property

' Abstraction.Func1
Private Function Abstraction_Func1(ByVal X As Integer, _
                                  ByVal Y As Integer) As Integer
    ' Publish corresponding event Func1.
    RaiseEvent Func1(X, Y, Abstraction_Func1)
End Function
```

Visual Basic events are prototyped as subroutines; therefore, event handlers cannot return values. But an interface like Abstraction will typically contain properties and methods that return values. No need to worry, though; you can return values by passing parameters by reference. The content of parameters passed by reference can be changed from within the subroutine or function. This is an alternative means to the same end.

The Abstraction interface defines a read-only property, *PropA*, and a function, *Func1*, that return a String and an Integer, respectively. In the code extract above, for the event definitions in the Bridge class that correspond with *PropA* and *Func1*, I have labeled a specific parameter as *ByRef* followed by a parameter name that indicates the intended use.

To return a value from a function, you simply assign the value to the function name from within the function. The process is the same to return a value from a property procedure. In the Bridge class implementation, events corresponding to the function and the property procedure are published by passing along the names of the class's property and function. Event publication is synchronous; therefore, the *RaiseEvent* function will not return until all subscribing implementors have executed. You can then rely on the implementor to assign values to parameters passed by reference. These parameters correspond to the return values of the properties and functions of the Abstraction interface that is implemented by the Bridge class. The values are then returned to the client that made the request.

> **N O T E :** The *RaiseEvent* function raises an event that has been declared within the same class module. Raising the event causes the event code to be executed.

After defining the Abstraction interface and the Bridge class, you need to define a concrete implementor class that provides an implementation for the Abstraction interface by subscribing to events published by a given bridge, as shown here:

```
' Class Name:    Implementor
' Note: This is a concrete class that indirectly implements all
'       properties and methods defined in the Abstraction interface.
'       It connects to the Abstraction interface by subscribing to
'       events published by a bridge that supports the interface for
'       which this implementation is intended.
'
'       Interface inheritance requires the class to implement all
'       properties and methods of the interface it inherits. An
'       implementor might provide partial implementation by
'       subscribing only to events of interest.
'
Option Explicit

' Declaring a Bridge object variable as follows will enable
' the Implementor object to subscribe to events published by the
' Bridge object to which it attaches.
Private WithEvents theBridge As Bridge

' Attach Implementor to Bridge. Doing so will allow the
' Implementor object to subscribe to events published by the Bridge
' object.
Public Sub Attach(Bridge_ As Bridge)
    Set theBridge = Bridge_
End Sub

' Detach Implementor from Bridge. This results in an implicit
' unsubscribe of all events published by the Bridge object.
Public Sub Detach()
    Set theBridge = Nothing
End Sub
```

(continued)

```
' Implicitly subscribe to the events Func1 and PropA published by
' the Bridge class by defining the following event handlers
' respectively.
'

' Implementor.ImplicitSubscribe(Publisher:=theBridge,
'                               Event:=Func1,
'                               EventHandler:=theBridge_Func1)
Private Sub theBridge_Func1(ByVal X As Integer, _
                           ByVal Y As Integer, _
                           retVal As Integer)
    retVal = X * Y
End Sub

' Implementor.ImplicitSubscribe(Publisher:=theBridge,
'                               Event:=PropA,
'                               EventHandler:=theBridge_PropA)
Private Sub theBridge_PropA(GetVal As String)
    GetVal = "Greetings from the Implementor object"
End Sub
```

The Implementor class must declare an object variable that will reference a Bridge object by using the keyword *WithEvents*. This will enable the Implementor object to subscribe to events published by a given Bridge object. If you were to type this code into a Visual Basic class module editor, you would notice an item named theBridge in the Object drop-down list in the editor. Selecting this item populates the Procedure drop-down list with the events published by the Bridge class.

When a client calls the *Implementor.Attach* method to obtain a reference to a Bridge object, an implicit subscription is registered with that instance of a Bridge. From a Visual Basic programmer's perspective, the comments above the Implementor class's event handlers in the preceding code loosely describe what Visual Basic does internally. Conceptually, this code is correct, but technically this is not legal Visual Basic code, nor is it completely accurate. Behind the scenes, Visual Basic applies COM's connectable-object technology. (See MSDN Library Visual Studio 6 online help for information on connectable objects.) As a Visual Basic programmer, you don't have to concern yourself with this level of detail. I mention it only to reiterate the fact that the magic of Visual Basic object-oriented programming depends heavily on COM.

Visual Basic automatically subscribes to events and will call the event handlers that are defined in the Implementor class module. If you don't want to subscribe to a specific event, don't define an event handler for it. Unsubscribing from events automatically occurs when the reference to the Bridge object publishing the events is released, as shown in the *Implementor.Detach* method in the preceding code. Also keep in mind that Visual Basic will automatically release the reference to the Bridge object when the Implementor object is destroyed. The *Implementor.Detach* method is useful when you want to unsubscribe from events, but keep a reference to the Implementor object around for future use in the client application. The important point is this: the client is responsible for maintaining references to both the Bridge and Implementor objects. Following is a code extract of a possible client implementation that clearly illustrates how to establish collaboration between all Bridge design pattern participants:

```
' This is a possible client (consumer) of the Bridge design pattern.
'
Option Explicit

Private Sub cmdClient_Click()
    Dim anAbstraction As Abstraction
    Dim aBridge As Bridge
    Dim anImplementor As Implementor
    Dim retVal As Integer
    Dim propVal As String

    ' Create an instance of a Bridge and
    ' assign a reference to the aBridge object variable.
    Set aBridge = New Bridge

    ' Using polymorphism, obtain an object reference
    ' to a Bridge object that supports the Abstraction interface.
    Set anAbstraction = aBridge

    ' Create an instance of an Implementor object and
    ' assign a reference to the anImplementor object variable.
    Set anImplementor = New Implementor

    ' Attach the Implementor object to the Bridge object. Doing so
    ' will allow the Implementor object to subscribe to events
    ' published by the Bridge object.
    anImplementor.Attach aBridge
```

(continued)

```
' Because the anAbstraction object variable is currently
' referencing an instance of a Bridge that supports the
' Abstraction interface, all requests made via this interface
' result in the publication of a corresponding event. This
' event is handled by the currently attached subscriber,
' which, based on the previous source code, is the Implementor
' object referenced by the anImplementor object variable.
'
' Client->Abstraction.PropA->Bridge.RaiseEvent(PropA)
' ->Implementor.theBridge_PropA
propVal = anAbstraction.PropA

' Client->Abstraction.Func1->Bridge.RaiseEvent(Func1)
' ->Implementor.theBridge_Func1
retVal = anAbstraction.Func1(5, 100)

' The following should appear in a message box:
'    anAbstraction.PropA = Greetings from the Implementor
'    anAbstraction.Func1(5,100) = 500
MsgBox "anAbstraction.PropA = " & propVal & vbCr & _
       "anAbstraction.Func1(5,100) = " & retVal
```

Sample Application

I'm drawing from the "Scenario" section of this chapter to provide a sample that includes a User Profile Service framework that resides in an ActiveX DLL, and an Excel client application that is a consumer of this framework. To recapitulate, this User Profile Service framework allows you to create user profile objects, as well as store and retrieve those objects to and from a repository (UserProfileRepository). What the Excel client does with this information is of no concern to the framework. The intended purpose of the framework is to provide a uniform approach to maintaining user profile settings of practically any variation. These settings are packaged in a UserProfile class object that is flexible enough to contain any amount of attributes of generally any type. The UserProfileRepository interface serves as a persistent object service for UserProfile objects.

Concrete classes inherit the UserProfileRepository interface, providing their own implementations that primarily involve storing and retrieving the state of a UserProfile object to and from a designated data source. A typical repository can store and retrieve settings to and from a SQL Server or Access database. A concrete repository class relies on interface inheritance to reuse the UserProfileRepository interface. As mentioned earlier, not all ActiveX-enabled programming languages support inheritance. Therefore, although such programming languages could be used to create client applications that are consumers of the User Profile Service framework, the languages could not be used without the inheritance language feature to extend the framework to support concrete repository classes.

Based on that premise, the User Profile Service framework sample I've included implements the Bridge design pattern, which essentially creates a bridge between the UserProfileRepository abstract interface and a concrete Excel workbook repository class that contains the implementation intended for that interface.

In this sample, the Excel client uses the User Profile Service framework to retrieve predefined user profile settings from an Excel workbook repository class object that are used for ODBC-based applications. The client's only function at this point is to create data source names (DSNs) in your operating system that can be referenced by ODBC-based applications. Careless programmers usually don't check for the existence of DSNs that are required for their ODBC-based applications to function. You can use this sample User Profile Service framework to guarantee that the DSNs required by your application do exist.

To run this sample,

1. Ensure that Excel 97 or later and Data Access Objects (DAO) 3.5 or higher are installed on your PC.

2. In the directory where the samples for this chapter have been copied to your PC (C:\VBDesign\Bridge by default), register UserProfileFx.dll by typing the following at a command prompt: *regsvr32 UserProfileFx.dll*.

3. Start Excel.

4. Open the UserProfile.xls sample file.

If all is well, a workbook will appear in Excel that resembles Figure 5-3.

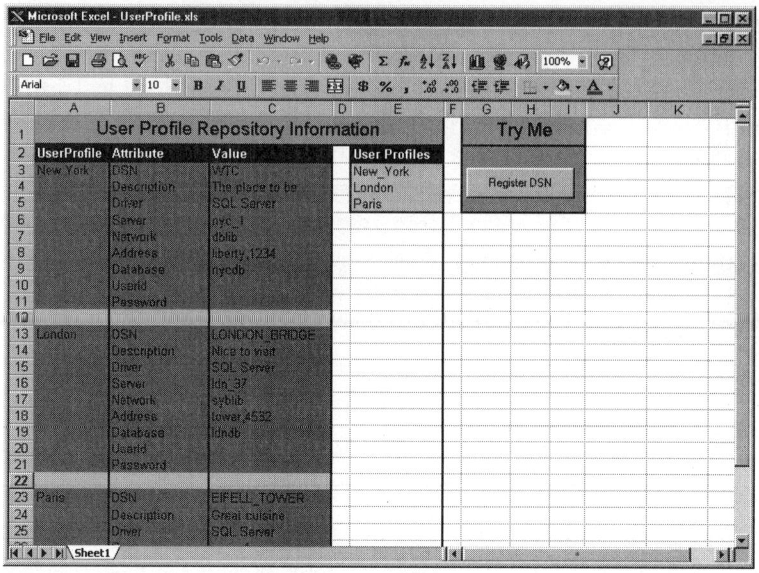

Figure 5-3.
An Excel workbook used as a user profile repository.

On the worksheet under the area labeled User Profile Repository Information, you will find the user profile settings. On the right side of the worksheet under the Try Me section, click the button labeled Register DSN, which brings up the User Profiles dialog box. (See Figure 5-4.)

Figure 5-4.
Dialog box containing user profile settings retrieved from the Excel workbook repository.

This dialog box uses the User Profile Service framework to display the various user profile settings by name that are located on the left side of the worksheet. Clicking the OK button will result in an attempt to create a DSN based on the currently selected user profile. You can see whether the attempt was successful in the User DSN tab of the ODBC Data Source Administrator dialog box. (You can invoke this dialog box by double-clicking the ODBC icon located in the Control Panel.) For instance, if you selected New_York, you would find a DSN entry in the dialog box labeled WTC. (See Figure 5-5.)

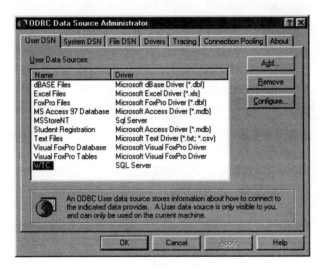

Figure 5-5.
*The ODBC Data Source Administrator dialog box serves as the user
interface to the ODBC administrator.*

This sample illustrates the advantages of a User Profile Service framework, but it is more important for us to understand how the framework is extended to support a repository workbook class created in Excel VBA by applying the Bridge design pattern. The following sections briefly describe all the Bridge design pattern participants that facilitate extensibility of the User Profile Service framework in this sample. Refer to the Bridge folder on the companion CD for a full disclosure of the source code.

The UserProfileRepository Interface

The UserProfileRepository (abstraction) class is an abstract interface that defines how to persist UserProfile objects to a repository. Because the interface is abstract, it contains no implementation of its own. Concrete classes inherit this interface, providing unique implementation to store, retrieve, and remove user profiles from a particular data source. In the UserProfileFx ActiveX DLL project, I took these steps:

1. Created a class module.

2. Changed the *Name* property value to UserProfileRepository.

3. Changed the *Instancing* property value to PublicNotCreatable.

4. Defined the interface methods without implementation, as follows:

```
' Class Name:    UserProfileRepository

Option Explicit

Public Function GetKeys(Keys() As String) As Long
End Function

Public Function GetUserProfile(Key As String) As UserProfile
End Function
    ⋮
```

The UserProfileRepBridge Class

The UserProfileRepBridge (bridge) class is a concrete class that inherits the UserProfileRepository abstract interface. The implementation of this class is special because, instead of persisting UserProfile objects to a particular data source, it delegates the task by publishing events to subscribing implementors. In the UserProfileFx ActiveX DLL project, I took these steps:

1. Created a class module.

2. Changed the *Name* property value to UserProfileRepBridge.

3. Changed the *Instancing* property value to PublicNotCreatable, permitting UserProfileRepBridge class objects to be created only via the UPFactory class object, which is discussed in Chapter 8, "Object Factory."

4. Inherited the UserProfileRepository interface by using the keyword *Implements*.

5. Defined corresponding events for each method in the UserProfile-Repository interface.

6. Published a specific event for each method implementation of the UserProfileRepository interface.

The resulting UserProfileRepBridge class looks like this:

```
' Class Name:    UserProfileRepBridge

Option Explicit

' Inherit the UserProfileRepository interface.
Implements UserProfileRepository

' Define an event that corresponds to each property and method of
' the UserProfileRepository interface.
Public Event GetKeys(Keys() As String, ByRef KeyCount As Long)
Public Event GetUserProfile(Key As String, ByRef UP As UserProfile)

    :


' Implement all properties and methods of the
' UserProfileRepository interface. In the implementation of each,
' publish the corresponding event.

Private Function UserProfileRepository_GetKeys(Keys() As String) _
    As Long
    RaiseEvent GetKeys(Keys, UserProfileRepository_GetKeys)
End Function

Private Function UserProfileRepository_GetUserProfile( _
    Key As String) As UserProfile
    RaiseEvent GetUserProfile(Key, _
                                UserProfileRepository_GetUserProfile)
End Function
    :
```

The WorkbookRepImpl Class

The WorkbookRepImpl (implementor) class is defined within Excel in VBA. The WorkbookRepImpl class is a concrete class that defines an Excel workbook repository implementation intended for the UserProfileRepository interface. WorkbookRepImpl subscribes to events published by a given UserProfileRep-Bridge class object. Event subscription is optional; therefore, as is the case in this sample, WorkbookRepImpl is subscribing to only two of the four events. Upon notification, its event handler is called automatically. Using the Visual Basic editor in the UserProfile Excel workbook project (UserProfile.xls), I took these steps:

1. Created a class module.

2. Changed the *Name* property value to WorkbookRepImpl.

3. Declared a member variable of type UserProfileRepBridge using the keyword *WithEvents*. Doing so implicitly enables WorkbookRepImpl objects to subscribe to any events published by a given UserProfile-RepBridge object they are referencing.

4. Defined event handler methods only for events of interest to Work-bookRepImpl.

5. Defined an *Attach* method, which allows WorkbookRepImpl objects to attach to any given UserProfileRepBridge object at run time. This action will invoke an implicit subscription for all events that have de-fined event handlers in WorkbookRepImpl.

6. Defined a *Detach* method, which allows a client to request that a WorkbookRepImpl object release its reference to a UserProfileRep-Bridge object. This action will result in an implicit unsubscribe of all events. In addition, subscription cancellation will occur if the *Attach* method is passed Nothing or when the WorkbookRepImpl object is destroyed. Keep in mind that you do not have to call the *Detach* method to unsubscribe from one UserProfileRepBridge object before subscribing to another. Simply calling the *Attach* method with a refer-ence to another UserProfileRepBridge object will implicitly cancel the previous subscription and subscribe to events from the new object.

Here is the resulting WorkbookRepImpl class:

```
' Class Name:   WorkbookRepImpl

Option Explicit

Private WithEvents RepBridge As UserProfileFx.UserProfileRepBridge

' Attach Implementor to Bridge. Doing so will allow the
' Implementor object to subscribe to events published by the Bridge
' object.
Public Sub Attach(upRepBridge As UserProfileFx.UserProfileRepBridge)
    Set RepBridge = upRepBridge
End Sub

' Detach Implementor from Bridge. This results in an implicit
' unsubscribe of all events published by the Bridge object.
Public Sub Detach()
    Set RepBridge = Nothing
End Sub
```

```
' Implicitly subscribe to events GetKeys and GetUserProfile
' published by the Bridge object by defining the following event
' handlers respectively.
'
Private Sub RepBridge_GetKeys(Keys() As String, KeyCount As Long)
    ' Excel implementation code located here.
    ⋮
End Sub

Private Sub RepBridge_GetUserProfile(Key As String, _
    UP As UserProfileFx.UserProfile)
    ' Excel implementation code located here
    ⋮
End Sub
⋮
```

COMments

The User Profile Services framework resides in an ActiveX DLL that supports the single-threaded apartment model (STA). When a client like Microsoft Internet Explorer—which supports the multithreaded apartment model (MTA)—creates an instance of a class defined in this component, COM will automatically do the following:

1. Spawn a new thread.

2. Create a single-threaded apartment in the new thread.

3. Construct an instance of this class within the apartment.

4. Return a proxy that references the class instance to the thread in the client that initiated the action.

All requests made to this User Profile Service framework object will be marshaled between threads. Consequently, if permitted, a client could possibly construct a UserProfileRepBridge (bridge) object in one thread and a UserProfileRepository implementation class (implementor) object in another. This results in a costly performance lag because the implementor and the bridge objects are bridging across threads. All client requests made to the bridge will be marshaled from the client's thread to the bridge's thread. All events published from the bridge will be marshaled from the bridge's thread to the implementor's thread. If the client expects a return value from a request, it must be marshaled back from the implementor's thread to the bridge's thread, and finally to the client's thread.

To avoid this dilemma, you want to create the bridge and the implementor in the same thread, which results in both objects residing in the same COM apartment. When objects live in the same apartment, they can access each other through a direct address pointer (no proxy required) and produce optimal performance. This is easier said than done, because implementors by nature do not exist in the same ActiveX component as the bridge. Implementors generally are created in other components to dynamically attach new behavior. Visual Basic does not support MTA; therefore, the Bridge design pattern is best suited for clients that support the same threading model as the framework DLL. When an STA client creates objects from an STA ActiveX DLL, the objects are created within the client's apartment. All requests to the object are therefore made through a direct address pointer.

To produce the best performance for the framework, however, I defined the UPFactory class (described in Chapter 8, "Object Factory") that will at least create all framework-defined class objects within the same apartment, if used by an MTA client. So, if other concrete repository classes were defined within the framework that inherited the UserProfileRepository interface, you could rest assured that requests to these objects would execute implementation within the same apartment.

Avoid using the Bridge design pattern in out-of-process servers (such as ActiveX EXE projects) because, regardless of the threading model, a client containing an implementor would have to link with a bridge object across process boundaries. This is even more costly than linking across threads, and the deficit increases dramatically when the processes are distributed on different nodes.

A possible complement to an out-of-process server is a Smart Proxy Bridge (described in Chapter 7, "Smart Proxy"), which allows you to implement the Bridge design pattern locally to the client process while still providing transparent access to remote objects.

Related Patterns

A Bridge design pattern closely resembles an Adapter design pattern, discussed in Chapter 4. Like the Adapter, the Bridge supports an interface expected by the client and delegates client requests to other objects that carry out the task. The Bridge and the Adapter differ in their intentions. The Adapter's purpose is to tie an interface expected by a client to an implementation that would otherwise be inaccessible because of incompatible interfaces. On the other hand, the Bridge's purpose is to loosen the bind between interface and implementation so that a change to one has no direct impact on the other.

CHAPTER SIX

Object By Value

A programmer new to object-oriented programming in Microsoft Visual Basic might assume that all that is required to pass an object by value is to include the *ByVal* reserved word in a function declaration. For example:

```
Public Sub Foo(ByVal br As Bar)
    br.color = GREEN
End Sub
```

One could mistakenly infer that if the function caller passed in a Bar object that the Visual Basic compiler would create a copy of the object. The function code block could then manipulate the copy without affecting the original. For example:

```
Dim myBar As Bar

Set myBar = New Bar
myBar.color = BLUE
Call Foo(myBar)

' Question: Does myBar.color = BLUE?
'
' Answer: No. The value of myBar.color is GREEN.
```

The value of *myBar.color* changes in the calling program because passing an object by value actually passes a reference to the object. For an explanation of this functionality, refer back to Chapter 2.

Another common misconception along the same lines is that if a class defines only a Property Get procedure to return an object and not a Property Set procedure, the class property is read-only. For example:

```
' ClassModule Foo
'
Private m_Bar As Bar
    ⋮
Public Property Get TheBar() As Bar
    Set TheBar = m_Bar
End Property
```

One might then assume that the Visual Basic compiler will return a copy of the Bar object when the *TheBar* Property Get procedure is called, and whatever the caller does to it has no effect on the original. For example:

```
Dim myFoo As Foo
Dim myColor As Color

Set myFoo = New Foo

' You can do this.
myColor = myFoo.TheBar.Color

' Question: Can you do this?
myFoo.TheBar.Color = PURPLE

' Answer: Yes, because a copy of the object reference to a Bar
'         object is returned to the TheBar Property Get procedure,
'         not a copy of the object itself.
```

In both of the previous source code examples, a copy of an object reference is returned—not a copy of an object. To review the explanation provided in Chapter 2, an object variable in Visual Basic contains a reference to an object, not the object itself. Therefore, when an object variable is passed by value, a copy of the object variable is created that references the same object. Hence actions performed on all copies of an object variable affect the same object.

The Object By Value design pattern described in this chapter enables you to pass an object by value—passing a copy of the object rather than the object reference—by writing the object's state to a data stream, passing the data stream to the recipient process that constructs a copy of the object, and updating the new object's state from the data stream. This will produce an exact copy of the original object in the recipient process's address space.

Purpose

The Object By Value design pattern passes or returns an object by value from one function process to another, resulting in the receiving process obtaining a copy of the object rather than a copy of an object reference.

Utilization

Use the Object By Value design pattern in the following circumstances:

■ **To pass or return a copy of an object to a caller**   This will protect the original object from unwanted state changes. For example, you can modify the property values of an object that is passed or returned by value without impacting the original object.

■ **To pass or return a copy of an object from one process to another**   This allows the recipient process to fully benefit from the services offered by an object without having to incur the performance cost usually associated with cross-process object interaction. When a COM object is created in the client process, the client directly references a memory address in its process space, resulting in immediate method invocation. COM objects created outside the client process suffer from significantly slower response times because a client process cannot reference the memory addresses of objects in other processes. Instead COM interposes and creates a proxy object in the client process that the client references directly in memory. When the client invokes a method on the object, a procedure known as marshaling occurs: The proxy object packages the request into a well-defined data packet and forwards the request to a stub object that unpackages the request and invokes the method on the real object. The reverse occurs if the method has a return value or has parameters that are passed by reference. To avoid the major performance hit involved in marshaling data across process boundaries you can create a copy of the object in the client process. All object method invocations will then happen directly on the local copy of the object.

■ **To pass or return a copy of an object between dissimilar object systems**   This task is difficult to accomplish without using the Object By Value design pattern. For example, you might want to create the original object in Visual Basic and then pass a copy of it to a Java application. Java and Visual Basic have different semantics and syntax for defining an object, but, providing both sides agree on how to interpret a data stream, it's possible to "re-hydrate" an object created in one language platform in another.

Scenario

In the process of developing a workflow application, you might find that instead of passing pure data from one process to another, it would be more efficient and scalable to pass around objects by value. Objects contain data, and methods that perform intelligent operations on that data. Passing the entire object is more efficient than requiring each process in the workflow to reimplement the behavior required to update a given data structure.

A point of sale system is an ideal candidate for the Object By Value design pattern. An order could be an object that contains data for the item—description, quantity, and price—but it would also contain the methods for adding and removing items from the order, calculating the total order value, changing the billing information, and so forth. For example, if a customer uses Microsoft Internet Explorer to place an order on line using your e-commerce system, both an ActiveX DLL class library that defines an Order class and an OCX ActiveX control that defines an order form are downloaded to the customer's computer. An instance of the order form control is created and embedded in an HTML document that is loaded in the customer's Web browser. In addition, an Order object is created to receive data from the order form control when a customer fills out the form. When the customer submits the order, the Order object is passed by value to the sales management process, which can then pass it by value to various other processes (for instance, credit card validation, inventory management, or accounts receivable) as part of the order fulfillment process. The sales management process might do the initial dispatching of the Order object to other processes, but some of the processes could also perform a set of actions on the Order object and pass it by value to other processes (for example, from warehouse to shipping and handling).

Passing the Order object by value rather than by reference offers some significant benefits. As mentioned earlier, each process is able to take advantage of the functionality provided by the Order object. Operations in a workflow system tend to occur serially among several processes distributed across a network, so passing the Order object by value is ideal because each process can invoke operations on an Order object that resides locally within the process, thus avoiding a high performance cost. Another benefit worth noting is that each process in the workflow can persist the state of the Order object with respect to the changes made in that process. If process B is ready to send the Order object to process C but process C is unavailable, process B can persist its Order object and resubmit the Order object by value to process C at a later time. When objects are passed by value rather than by reference, managing an object's state at different stages of the workflow process becomes an elegant design solution.

Although passing an object by value is not a language feature readily available in Visual Basic, implementing the Object By Value design pattern described in this chapter will effectively allow you to accomplish the desired results for your workflow application.

Object Model

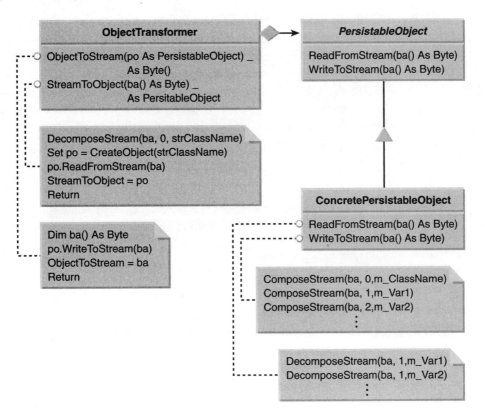

Roles

The roles and functions of the Object By Value design pattern are as follows:

- **PersistableObject**   Specifies an interface for reading and writing the state of an object to and from a data stream.

- **ConcretePersistableObject**   A class that implements behavior of the PersistableObject interface for reading and writing its state to a data stream.

- **ObjectTransformer**   A class that defines the behavior for facilitating the transformation of an original object's state to a data stream and a data stream back into a newly constructed copy of the original object in the same state.

Relationships

The relationship between all Object By Value design pattern participants is as follows:

- A sender process creates a PersistableObject object and maintains a reference to an ObjectTransformer object and a Conduit mechanism. Using the ObjectTransformer object, the sender process initiates the action to extract the state of its PersistableObject to a data stream and sends the stream on its way down the Conduit mechanism.

- A recipient process retrieves the data stream at the other end of the Conduit and, with the help of an ObjectTransformer object, converts the stream back into a copy of the original object.

NOTE: A Conduit mechanism is used to transport a data stream from point A to point B. This mechanism could be one of a number of technologies, such as COM, MSMQ, HTML, or MAPI.

Figure 6-1 illustrates the course of required events to pass or return an object by value.

Ramifications

Passing or returning an object by value results in the following consequences:

- **Prevents state changes to the original object** The recipient process can freely manipulate its copy of the object without impacting the original object's state.

- **Localizes object services, avoiding the performance overhead of cross-process object invocation** Because Visual Basic objects are synonymous with COM objects and COM objects are always passed by reference, the same holds true for Visual Basic. A major benefit of COM is location transparency. This means that the object reference can be pointing either to an object in a client process's address space or to a remote object located in the address space of another process running on the same workstation or across the network. The client remains oblivious to the object's location and continues to request object services as if the object were local to its address space. However, when the object being referenced is out of the client process's address space, requests and responses must be marshaled to and from the remote process. The overhead of such activity is tremendously higher than referencing an object within the same address space. (See Chapter 3, "COM Threading Models," and the books listed in the bibliography for a more in-depth coverage of COM.) Using the Object By Value design pattern to pass an object by value allows the remote recipient process to benefit from the services offered by an object without incurring the performance overhead cost of marshaling across process boundaries.

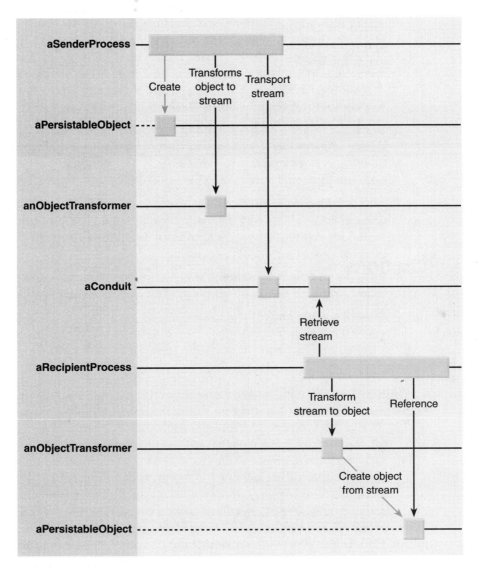

Figure 6-1.
Passing an object by value from sender to receiver.

■ **Supports sharing of object copies between systems using different types of objects**   A key participant of the Object By Value design pattern is the ObjectTransformer class. It would not be too difficult to envision using a Conduit mechanism (such as COM or MSMQ) that is supported by dissimilar object systems to transport a data stream. Once the data stream is accepted by the recipient process, a native object transformer could produce a copy of the original object by correctly implementing the object conversion specification you, as the designer, set forth. For example, a Visual Basic object transformer could convert a Visual Basic object to a data stream, and a Pascal object transformer could convert the stream into a Pascal object copy of the original Visual Basic object.

■ **Encapsulates the internal state of an object**   Because the data stream is a byte array, you are not forced to explicitly expose the state of an object by deprivatizing that object. The persistable object contains the inherent functionality for updating its state from a byte array.

■ **No compile-time type checking**   Because the data stream is a byte array, there is no type checking at compile time. Therefore the potential for sending a byte array of invalid data to a recipient process is possible, wasting valuable processing cycles.

■ **Passing an object by value is not a language feature**   Although not terribly difficult to implement, significant programmer intervention and cooperation is required to adhere to the specification defined for implementation of the Object By Value design pattern.

Implementation

Referring back to the Object Model section of this chapter, you will notice two core components in the class diagram that make up the Object By Value design pattern: PersistableObject and ObjectTransformer. A persistable object is an object that supports an interface (PersistableObject) that defines methods for reading and writing the object's state to a data stream. It is the responsibility of the class developer to implement the methods of this interface. This interface will permit different classes of objects to persist their state to a data stream with assistance from a single ObjectTransformer object. The ObjectTransformer object facilitates the transformation from stream to object and from object to stream. Here is one way to implement these components in Visual Basic.

Following verbatim the class diagram in the Object Model section of this chapter, you could define a persistable object interface (PersistableObject) with read and write methods for moving data into and out of a stream. You could then define a concrete class (ConcretePersistableObject) that implements that interface. If you adhere to the advice of this chapter, you would persist the state of the object to a byte array. As a result, you would have to create a class (ObjectTransformer) that would implement an algorithm for converting the data of dissimilar types of class member variables to a byte array stream. Keep in mind that because Visual Basic supports only interface inheritance (refer to Chapter 2 for in-depth coverage on this topic), new concrete classes will lack an elegant means by which to reuse this algorithm.

Fortunately for the Visual Basic development community, Microsoft added new class persistence features in Visual Basic 6 that allow you to implement the Object By Value design pattern with less effort than in previous versions. These features are usually associated with ActiveX controls that provide design-time properties, which can be set using the Properties window. Providing you save your work, whatever settings you make will be there the next time the project is loaded. (For details, refer to the section "Saving the Properties of Your Control" of the Component Tools Guide portion of the MSDN Library Visual Studio 6.0). The identical technology can be applied to classes defined in any type of ActiveX project. If you want a class in an ActiveX project to be persistable, you can implement this functionality without writing a single line of code. Select a ClassModule, and in the Properties window (see Figure 6-2) do the following:

1. Set its *Instancing* property to a value that makes it Public and Creatable. In an ActiveX DLL you do this by setting the property to MultiUse.

2. Set the *Persistable* property value to Persistable.

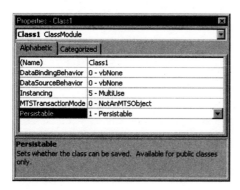

Figure 6-2.
Visual Basic 6 ActiveX project Properties window illustrates the property values required in a ClassModule to make the class's state persistable.

Now notice in the ClassModule editor that in addition to the Class events—Initialize and Terminate—there are now three new events: InitProperties, ReadProperties, and WriteProperties, as shown in Figure 6-3.

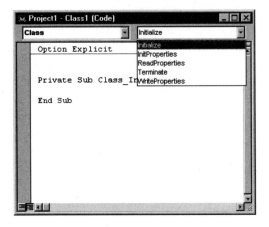

Figure 6-3.
ClassModule editor illustrates class events—InitProperties, ReadProperties, and WriteProperties—added as a result of making a class persistable.

To implement the Object By Value design, our only concern is the last two events: ReadProperties and WriteProperties. Both events accept a PropertyBag object parameter. The PropertyBag object stores data in the form of a byte array. To read and write a class object's state to and from a byte array stream, implement the ReadProperties and WriteProperties event handler procedures using the PropertyBag object, as shown in the following Employee class code extract.

```
' Class Employee
'
Private m_nEmpID As Long
Private m_strEmpName As String
⋮
Private Sub Class_ReadProperties(PropBag As PropertyBag)
' Read the data from the PropertyBag and update the
' state of the Employee accordingly.
    With PropBag
        m_nEmpID = .ReadProperty("EmployeeID")
        m_strEmpName = .ReadProperty("EmployeeName")
    End With
End Sub
```

```
Private Sub Class_WriteProperties(PropBag As PropertyBag)
' Write the state of the Employee into the PropertyBag.
    With PropBag
        .WriteProperty "EmployeeID", m_nEmpID
        .WriteProperty "EmployeeName", m_strEmpName
    End With
End Sub
```

It's clear from the code sample that when the *Class_ReadProperties* and *Class_WriteProperties* event handlers are invoked, the *PropertyBag.ReadProperty* and *PropertyBag.WriteProperty* methods respectively must be called to persist an object's state. The method prototype for *PropertyBag.ReadProperty* reads as follows:

PropertyBag.ReadProperty(*DataName*[, *DefaultValue*])

ReadProperty returns a property value stored in the byte array inside the PropertyBag. The *DataName* parameter contains a string expression associated with the value in the PropertyBag, and the *DefaultValue* parameter is an optional parameter that contains the value to be returned if nothing is stored in the PropertyBag's byte array under the given *DataName*.

The method prototype for *PropertyBag.WriteProperty* reads as follows:

PropertyBag.WriteProperty(*DataName*, *Value*[, *DefaultValue*])

The *WriteProperty* method stores the contents of the *Value* parameter in the PropertyBag, which it associates with the *DataName* string expression. *DefaultValue* is optional and is ignored by the class persistence features utilized in the Object By Value design pattern.

That's all that is required to make a class persistable. The persistent class developer doesn't need to be concerned with what initiates persistance but rather, once persistence is started, that the appropriate functionality is implemented. Nonetheless our job is not finished yet because as the design pattern implementers we need to answer two very important questions:

- How should the persistent process be initiated?

- How does the Object By Value design pattern make use of this technology?

The answer to both these questions lies in the implementation of the ObjectTransformer class. The ObjectTransformer class implements two methods: *ObjectToStream* and *StreamToObject*. The following example shows the source code you should expect to see as implementations of both these methods.

```
' Project:        ObjTransformLib
' File Name:      ObjectTransformer.cls
' Copyright:      5/99 Bill Stamatakis
' Class Name:     ObjectTransformer
' Note:           Defines the behavior that facilitates passing an
'                 object by value
Option Explicit

Public Function ObjectToStream(instanceTag As String, _
                               obj As Object) As Byte()
' Converts a persistable object to a byte array stream
    Dim pb As PropertyBag

    Set pb = New PropertyBag
    pb.WriteProperty instanceTag, obj

    ObjectToStream = pb.Contents
End Function

Public Function StreamToObject(instanceTag As String, _
                               byteArr() As Byte) As Object
' Creates an object from a byte array stream
    Dim pb As PropertyBag

    Set pb = New PropertyBag
    pb.Contents = byteArr

    ' Instantiate object from PropertyBag
    Set StreamToObject = pb.ReadProperty(instanceTag)
End Function
```

The *ObjectTransformer.ObjectToStream* method returns a byte array containing the state of the persistable object *obj*. The *instanceTag* variable contains a string expression that is stored with the persistable object's state and acts as the key association for reconstructing a new copy of the persistable object from the stream. Although this might seem strange, you'll notice that the PropertyBag object is not only utilized in the persistable class (as we saw earlier), but it's utilized here also. The WriteProperties event in the persistable class object is triggered by the following line of code.

```
pb.WriteProperty instanceTag, obj
```

If you think about it, the PropertyBag object must exist before and after the persistable object is destroyed because it's ultimately responsible for the state of an object. The PropertyBag object invokes the WriteProperties event in the persistable object and passes a reference to itself. The persistable object writes its state into this referenced PropertyBag as previously illustrated in the Employee class code sample. Once the PropertyBag object contains the state, it can then expose it as a byte array stream via its *Contents* property, which is then returned from the *ObjectToStream* method, as shown here.

```
ObjectToStream = pb.Contents
```

The *ObjectTransformer.StreamToObject* method constructs a persistable object from a byte array. The *instanceTag* parameter contains a string expression that is used to locate the correct point in the byte array data stream where the class name is stored. The *byteArr* parameter stores the byte array containing the state of the persistable object to be constructed. Here again a PropertyBag object is required. First the PropertyBag object must consume a byte array through its *Contents* property, and then it can construct a persistable object from the byte array via its *ReadProperty* method.

When the *ReadProperty* method is called, after the PropertyBag object creates a persistable object it then invokes the persistable object's ReadProperties event, passing it a reference to itself. The object then updates its state accordingly, as previously illustrated in the Employee class code sample.

A subtle but highly beneficial point of this implementation is that you will never have to reimplement the ObjectTransformer class. A persistable object of any type can reuse the ObjectTransformer class.

Sample Application

In order to demonstrate the applicability of the Object By Value design pattern, I have created a sample offline banking system called the BSTAM Banker. It effectively allows bank customers to perform various actions against their accounts off line without having to sacrifice functionality for performance. The user will receive an almost instant reply to all banking services for any type of request (e.g., deposit funds, withdraw funds). This application only permits downloading an account for offline use; in a complete system you could expect the capability to update your bank account by uploading changes back to the bank's computer system. The performance costs of the entire transaction would be significantly less than if the customer were making the transaction on line. With offline banking, all account changes are submitted in a single transmission, while with online banking, every service request results in a remote transmission in both directions—one for the request and the other for the reply from the object providing the service.

You might ask, "How is offline banking implemented in the BSTAM Banker?" Answer: using the Object By Value design pattern. BSTAM Banker contains four major components: BankSvr.EXE, BankClient.EXE, Account-Lib.DLL, and ObjTransformLib.DLL.

- BankSvr is an ActiveX EXE that you should think of as the bank's central computer system. It contains the original SavingsAccount objects that will be passed by value to BankClient.

- BankClient is the COM client (Standard EXE) software given to all bank customers to allow them to do offline banking from their home computer by means of a Windows graphical user interface (GUI). Under the hood, BankClient obtains a local copy of a Savings-Account object passed by value from BankSvr.

- AccountLib is an ActiveX DLL class library that defines the SavingsAccount class. The SavingsAccount class is persistable, thus making it possible to pass it by value.

- ObjTransformLib is an ActiveX DLL class library that defines the Transformer class used to facilitate a persistable object transformation to and from a byte array data stream.

When the bank customer clicks the Retrieve Account button in the BSTAM Banker GUI to download a savings account, the following sequence of events, illustrated in Figure 6-4, occurs to allow BankClient to obtain a SavingsAccount object by value from BankSvr.

- BankClient binds to a Teller object that resides in BankSvr. Since the object is outside BankClient's address space, COM intercedes by creating a Teller proxy object that resides in BankClient's address space and a Teller stub object in BankSvr's address space. Requests for service from the Teller object are transmitted across process boundaries by these components. This layer is inaccessible to and can be taken for granted by the Visual Basic programmer.

- BankClient makes a request to the Teller object to retrieve a Savings-Account object that is returned as a byte array:

```
Private Sub cmdRetrieveAcct_Click()
    Dim byteArr() As Byte
    Dim bRetCode As Boolean
    Dim strPrompt As String
```

```
strPrompt = "Enter one of the following accounts: " _
            & vbNewLine _
            & "orion0425, spencer0220, or matthew0316"

m_strAcctNo = InputBox(strPrompt, _
            "BSTAM Banker - Retrieve Account")
    ⋮
' Obtain a copy of a SavingsAccount object in the form
' of a byte array from the cross-process BankSvr COM
' server.
bRetCode = m_Teller.RetrieveAccount(m_strAcctNo, _
                                    byteArr)

    ⋮
```

■ The *RetrieveAccount* method of the BankSvr's Teller object re-
trieves the requested SavingsAccount object from its in-memory
database (which is really a Dictionary object). It then converts the
SavingsAccount object to a byte array data stream by invoking the
ObjectTransformer.ObjectToStream method and returns it to the
BankClient caller.

```
Public Function RetrieveAccount(AcctNo As String, _
   ByteArr() As Byte) As Boolean
' Locate and return SavingsAccount object by value to
' caller.
   Dim sa As AccountLib.SavingsAccount

   ' Locate a SavingsAccount object in the SavingsAccount
   ' Dictionary object (m_SavingsAccounts), and transform
   ' it to a byte array that is returned to the caller.
   If m_SavingsAccounts.Exists(AcctNo) Then
       Set sa = m_SavingsAccounts(AcctNo)
       ByteArr = m_Transformer.ObjectToStream(AcctNo, sa)
       RetrieveAccount = True
   Else
       ⋮
```

■ BankClient converts the byte array data stream into a local copy of a
SavingsAccount object by invoking the *StreamToObject* method of
the ObjectTransformer object.

```
Private Sub cmdRetrieveAcct_Click()
    ⋮

' Transform byte array into a local copy of the
' SavingsAccount from the out-process.
   Set m_SavingsAcct = m_Transformer.StreamToObject( _
                                     m_strAcctNo, byteArr)

    ⋮
```

119

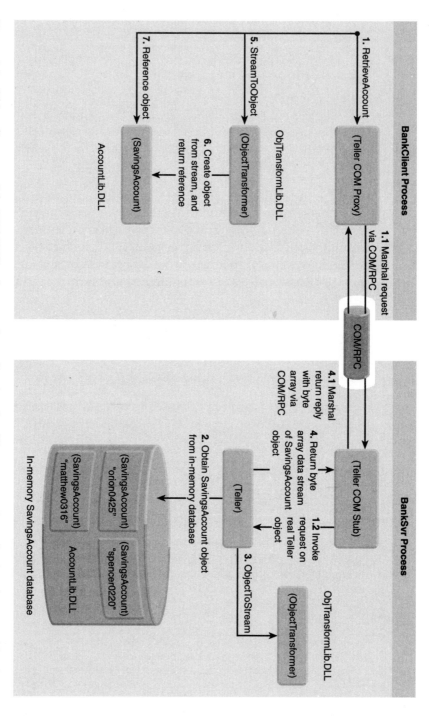

Figure 6-4. *Object diagram of the BSTAM Banker sample application that illustrates passing a SavingsAccount object by value from BankSvr to BankClient.*

The key participants of this sample application that make up the Object By Value design pattern include the following:

■ SavingAccount (ConcretePersistableObject). This class must be and is persistable because its *Persistable* property value is set as such and because it provides behavior to read and write its state to and from a byte array data stream by implementing *ClassReadProperties* and *ClassWriteProperties* event handlers as shown in the following code extract.

```
Private Sub Class_ReadProperties(PropBag As PropertyBag)
' Read in property values from a byte array via the
' PropertyBag object.
    With PropBag
        m_strAccountNo = .ReadProperty("AccountNumber")
        m_strAccountOwner = .ReadProperty("AccountOwner")
        m_dblInterestRate = .ReadProperty("InterestRate")
        m_dblBalance = .ReadProperty("AccountBalance")
    End With
End Sub

Private Sub Class_WriteProperties(PropBag As PropertyBag)
' Write out property values to a byte array via the
' PropertyBag object.
    With PropBag
        .WriteProperty "AccountNumber", m_strAccountNo
        .WriteProperty "AccountOwner", m_strAccountOwner
        .WriteProperty "InterestRate", m_dblInterestRate
        .WriteProperty "AccountBalance", m_dblBalance
    End With
End Sub
```

■ Transformer (ObjectTransformer). This class defines the behavior required to facilitate transformation of a persistable SavingsAccount object to and from a byte array data stream. The source for this class is identical to what was illustrated in the Implementation section of this chapter.

Refer to the companion CD for the complete source code.

COMments

As in Visual Basic, passing a COM object by value in C++ is not a built-in language feature but is a feature the majority of the COM programming community would like to see added to the Microsoft COM specification. I hope it will happen soon and, since Visual Basic object-oriented programming is deeply rooted in COM, the feature will eventually find its way into Visual Basic. In the interim, the Object By Value design pattern can allow you to implement this feature today.

Related Patterns

The Object By Value design pattern, similar to the Prototypical Object Factory (Chapter 9), permits an object to be cloned. However, the Object By Value design pattern can also pass the clone to a recipient across process boundaries. Similar to the Smart Proxy (Chapter 7), the recipient is then referencing an object in its own process address space, thus avoiding the overhead of cross-process invocation. Unlike the Smart Proxy, however, all object invocations are performed within the local copy, whereas a Smart Proxy can intelligently decide when to delegate requests back to the original object across process boundaries.

CHAPTER SEVEN

Smart Proxy

What can you surmise from this scenario?

> Ms. Smart Proxy says, "I accept this award on behalf of Bill Stamatakis, who could not be here tonight because he is on a business trip in Tokyo. Bill wanted me to relay his sincerest gratitude for this gesture and to thank the following people for their contributions that lead to this award…"

Based on this excerpt, you can guess that Ms. Smart Proxy represented Bill Stamatakis at an awards ceremony by accepting a prize intended for him, and communicated his appreciation to the audience. Hence, the expected outcome was satisfied when Bill's name was called to receive his award at the podium. If Bill knew he would be unavailable to attend the ceremony but chose not to ask someone to fill in for him or did not notify the members of the ceremony committee, the presenter would have been in an awkward predicament.

Ms. Smart Proxy's role was therefore important in keeping the award presentations flowing smoothly. One can easily imagine other scenarios in which a system would break down if the actions associated with a specific individual were not carried out by the individual, or by a representative of that individual, also known as a proxy. According to Dictionary.com, the definition of a proxy is "The person who is substituted or deputed to act or vote for another."

Replacing the word "person" with "object" allows us to view the concept of a proxy from the perspective of object-oriented software development.

Purpose

The Smart Proxy design pattern provides a reference to a surrogate object that represents a real object in a given context.

Utilization

The Smart Proxy design pattern is useful in the following circumstances:

- If you want to provide transparent access with the most optimal performance to the real object, which does not reside in the same address space as the client thread that initiated the request

- If you want to regulate access to the real object by requiring the client to have specific rights to invoke the properties and methods of the real object

- If you want to defer creation of the real object until it's needed

Scenario

To understand when to employ the Smart Proxy design pattern, consider an example of the first situation described in the "Utilization" section. An out-of-process COM server (ActiveX EXE) is running on a server connected to your company network. Microsoft Visual Basic clients running on workstations connected to the network bind to objects on this server through the COM layer. Because the client and server processes do not reside in the same process address space, a proxy to the real object on the server is automatically returned to the client. The proxy delegates the client's request across the network to the real object. The source code for the client remains the same whether the object being referenced is in-process (ActiveX DLL) or out-of-process (ActiveX EXE), but performance degradation will be evident in an out-of-process scenario. Therefore, the least amount of interaction with the server, the better.

Typically an object's state and behavior are represented as properties and methods in an interface. For example, this code extract illustrates the steps to construct and initialize a Person object.

```
Dim person1 As HRComponent.Person

' Construct a Person object and retain a reference to the person1
' object variable.
Set person1 = New Person

' Initialize the state of the Person object.
```

```
With person1
    .Name = "Smith"
    .Age = 32
    .Height  = "5-10"
End With
```

If HRComponent is an ActiveX DLL, the cost of setting each property is minimal because the Person object resides in the client process's address space. The interface of the Person object clearly is self-documenting because the properties distinctly define what the Person object supports. This is good programming style from the perspective of object-oriented design.

If HRComponent is an ActiveX EXE, however, the cost of setting each property value is considerably higher. The Person object does not reside in the client process's address space, so each property assignment is individually delegated across the network to the real object running on the ActiveX EXE server. The object variable *person1* has a reference to a proxy provided internally by Visual Basic. This proxy transparently packages and submits each request to the real object. Furthermore, if the code were to request a property value (such as *strName = person1.Name*), the proxy would forward this request across the network to the real object because the proxy is stateless by default. The proxy's sole purpose is to forward requests to the object that it represents.

You can solve this out-of-process performance problem in two ways: you can modify the interface to support setting a series of properties in one call, or you can employ the Smart Proxy design pattern. Let's examine both approaches.

A common and effective solution is to create an array of name-value pairs, which you can do by creating a two-dimensional array of type Variant, as shown in the following code extract. The first row of the array is the header containing the names. All the following rows contain the values for each name. Performance is superior to the individual property-setting approach, but this method of implementation doesn't provide a true object-oriented solution. The interface supported by the Person object is no longer self-documenting. Debugging and understanding the code becomes significantly more difficult.

```
Dim person1 As HRComponent.Person
Dim attribs(0 To 1, 0 To 2) As Variant

' Construct a Person object and return a reference to the person1
' object variable.
Set person1 = New Person
```

(continued)

125

```
' Set up attributes for submission to Person object:
'
' Initialize header of names.
attribs(0, 0) = "Name"
attribs(0, 1) = "Age"
attribs(0, 2) = "Height"

' Initialize values per name.
attribs(1, 0) = "Smith"
attribs(1, 1) = 32
attribs(1, 2) = "5-10"

' Send UpdateState request to Person object.
Call person1.UpdateState(attribs)
```

It might be worth sacrificing the principles of object orientation in order to increase performance. Implementing the Smart Proxy design pattern, however, allows you to stick to your principles and at the same time gain the much-needed performance.

A smart proxy is "smart" because, unlike a "dumb" proxy that just forwards all requests to the real object, the smart proxy can decide when it is necessary to contact the real object. For instance, the smart proxy can accumulate and package a series of requests into a compound structure that is submitted to the real object in one call across the wire. Also, a smart proxy can cache the real object's state locally in the client process. Requesting the property value of a smart proxy returns the results as quickly as if the client were accessing the real object in-process. A Smart Proxy design pattern is really a class that wraps the dumb proxy provided within Visual Basic. (See Chapter 4.) The Smart Proxy design pattern in essence implements the same Person interface that both the dumb proxy and real object implement. (See Figure 7-1.) The Smart Proxy design pattern therefore remains transparent to the client without compromising performance or object-oriented principles.

In the Smart Proxy design pattern implementation, you can choose to use a two-dimensional array of type Variant similar to the non–object-oriented solution described previously. Since it is an internal implementation, it would remain private to the class. Setting a property value would update the two-dimensional array defined internally. When you've updated the properties in the smart proxy, follow through with a call to a method that submits all property settings as a single request with an accompanying array. The SmartProxy-Person class submits requests to the dumb proxy that is automatically generated by Visual Basic. For simplicity, let's assume the SmartProxyPerson class is creating

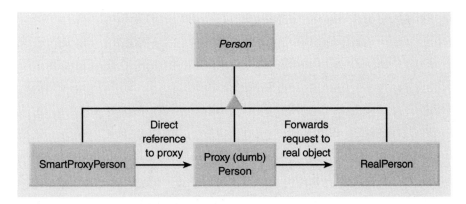

Figure 7-1.
Smart Proxy design pattern implementation of the Person class.

an instance and holding onto a reference to the dumb proxy in its *Class_Initialize* event handler, relieving the client of that task. (The "Implementation" section of this chapter covers the possible implementation options in more detail.) Let's also assume the state is cached locally. When the client requests a property value, it is returned from the SmartProxyPerson object that is in-process. The code extract below is a feasible scenario for updating multiple property values of the real Person object as a single request.

```
Dim person1 As HRComponent.SmartProxyPerson

' Construct a SmartProxyPerson object and return a reference to the
' person1 object variable.
'
' During initialization, SmartProxyPerson constructs a dumb proxy
' Person object to which it ultimately delegates all requests
' intended for the real Person object that resides outside the
' address space of the client initiating the request.
'
Set person1 = New SmartProxyPerson

' Set the property values.
person1.Name = "Smith"
person1.Age = 32
person1.Height  = "5-10"

' Update the state of the real person object.
person1.SetComplete
```

Object Model

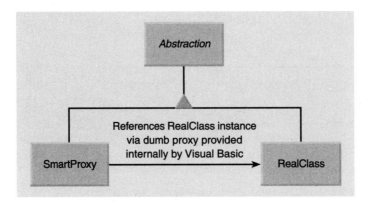

Roles

The roles and functions of the Smart Proxy design pattern are as follows:

- **Abstraction (Person)** The interface that is implemented by both the SmartProxy class and the RealClass class. Abstraction allows SmartProxy to represent the real object in any context where the real object might be required.

- **RealClass (RealPerson)** Defines the implementation for the real object.

- **SmartProxy (SmartProxyPerson)** Represents the real object in a given context. When the real object is remote to the client process's address space, the SmartProxy object can cache the state of the real object to provide optimal performance. It can also accumulate updates to the state and submit the updates as a single request to the real object.

  ❑ To manage the costly creation process and memory allocation of the real object, the SmartProxy object can delay instantiating the real object until specific functionality is requested by the client.

  ❑ The SmartProxy object can provide secure access to the real object. For example, one user might have rights to change the state of the real object, while another might have rights only to look at the state.

Relationships

A client, unaware of the difference between the SmartProxy object and the real object, obtains a reference to a SmartProxy object that supports the interface the client expects. The SmartProxy object maintains an internal reference to the real object that implements the state and behavior defined in the interface. When the client makes a request via the interface, the SmartProxy object carries out the request according to the intentions of the SmartProxy component designer, which might be performance, security, efficiency, or some combination of the three. The SmartProxy object will delegate work to the real object when necessary.

Ramifications

COM supports the concept of *local/remote transparency*. This means that when a client obtains a reference to a COM object that supports the interface the client expects, the client will receive a direct reference to the object in memory, providing the object resides in the client process's address space. If the COM object does not reside in the client process's address space, COM will interpose and create a proxy object in the client process's address space that supports the same interface as the real object residing out-of-process. The proxy object maintains an internal reference to the real object. All submissions to the proxy are packaged for out-of-process travel and forwarded to the real object. This marshaling feature of COM is transparent because it requires no programmer intervention. ActiveX component projects are deeply rooted in COM; hence this feature also applies to Visual Basic.

A proxy provided by COM is considered dumb because it does not intelligently decide how to handle each unique request to the real object—all requests are simply forwarded to the real object. This can have a severe impact on performance depending on the volume of submissions.

The use of a smart proxy is a solution that will alleviate the impact on performance without compromising the principles of object orientation. Keep in mind that a smart proxy might prove useful in other scenarios (as briefly stated in the "Utilization" section). The implementation of a smart proxy requires programmer intervention, however. The programmer must define a class that implements the same interface as the real object. Within the class implementation, the programmer must decide when to delegate requests to the real object. Furthermore, the programmer must ensure that the smart proxy object is loaded in the client process's address space.

Using the Smart Proxy design pattern can be advantageous, but don't ignore the price of maintenance.

Implementation

By definition, a smart proxy object must inherit the same interface as the real object it represents and should reside in the client process's address space to provide the best possible performance to the client. In that regard, a smart proxy class intended for reuse with different clients must be packaged in an ActiveX DLL component. (DLLs load in the client process's address space.) To implement the interface of the real object, the ActiveX DLL in which the smart proxy class is defined must reference the same type library that defines the interface implemented by the class that defines the real object.

In general, you don't need to make the client aware of whether it is referencing the smart proxy object or the real object. Providing this level of transparency can be the most challenging aspect of the design, but it will allow you to take advantage of the benefits (listed in the "Utilization" section of this chapter) without disruption to the client code. Providing this level of transparency will require the removal of explicit object creation from the client code.

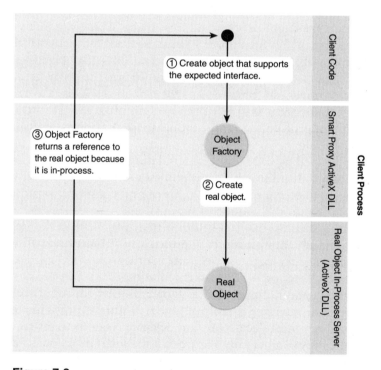

Figure 7-2.
The object factory adds local/remote transparency to the client code by determining that the object requested by the client can be created in the client's address space.

Implementing an Object Factory design pattern (Chapter 8) within the ActiveX DLL that defines the smart proxy is a suitable alternative to using the keyword *New* or the *CreateObject* function. The object factory can easily address the local/remote transparency issue by determining whether the object requested by the client can be constructed in the client's address space. If so, the object factory creates an instance of the real object and then returns a direct reference to the client. (See Figure 7-2.) Otherwise, the object factory creates an instance of the real object running in a separate process (ActiveX EXE), at which point COM will interpose and return a dumb proxy of the real object. The object factory then will create a smart proxy that maintains a reference to the dumb proxy created by COM. A direct reference to the smart proxy is returned to the client. (See Figure 7-3.) Eventually, all requests intended for the real object will be submitted by the smart proxy via the COM dumb proxy.

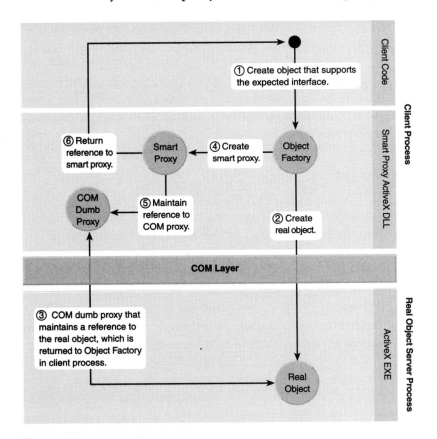

Figure 7-3.
The object factory adds local/remote transparency to the client code by determining that the object requested by the client must be created in the address space of another process.

Smart proxies can also serve as security guards for the real object by regulating access to the real object's properties and methods. Using an object factory will make the introduction of secured access to the real object nonintrusive to the client application. You cannot enforce security, however, if the client is permitted to create an instance of the real object by employing conventional language features (such as the keyword *New* or the *CreateObject* function). To enforce security, follow these steps:

1. Create an ActiveX DLL project.

2. Define the abstraction interface, real object, smart proxy, and object factory classes.

3. Set the *Instancing* property value of the object factory class to Multi-Use to enable clients to create instances of this class.

4. Set the *Instancing* property value of the abstraction class to Public-NotCreatable to enable clients to declare variables of this type, while at the same time preventing them from creating instances of it. The reason for this prevention is that the abstraction interface contains no implementation of its own and should be considered abstract. (Refer to Chapter 2 for more on the topic of abstract vs. concrete classes.)

5. At this point you have two choices, one of which is more secure than the other.

   ❑ To prevent the client from creating instances of the real object and smart proxy classes, set their *Instancing* property values to PublicNotCreatable. The client can still declare variables of both types, however, and can easily detect their existence either through IntelliSense technology or through the Visual Basic Object Browser.

   ❑ To make the client completely oblivious to the existence of the real object class and the smart proxy class, set both *Instancing* property values to Private. Private classes can implement public interfaces in ActiveX components. Only through the create method of an object factory can the client create an instance of a private concrete class (such as the real object or the smart proxy) that implements the abstraction interface. If security was not required initially but later became a critical need, using this approach allows the introduction of security via a smart proxy class with absolutely no disruption to the client code.

The client code that accesses the smart proxy and object factory combination can be as simple as the following code extract.

```
' Because the PersonFactory abstracts the explicit creation, it is
' not difficult to imagine that the PersonFactory could be enhanced
' to return a SmartProxyPerson instead of a RealPerson object
' without modification to the following client code.
    Dim personFact As PersonFactory
    Dim person1 As Person

    ' Create PersonFactory.
    Set personFact = New PersonFactory

    ' PersonFactory creates an object that supports the Person
    ' interface expected by the client. The client is oblivious
    ' to whether the object is the real person or the smart proxy.
    Set person1 = personFact.CreatePerson()
```

WARNING: Be extremely cautious when implementing public interfaces in private classes. Based on Visual Basic's implementation of COM, requests made through the public interface do not marshal across apartment boundaries, which include cross-thread and cross-process. Run-time errors will result. To avoid this scenario, make the private classes PublicNotCreatable. You can't prevent the client from being aware of the existence of these classes, but you can still prohibit the client from creating instances of them. This is not the ideal solution, but it is effective nonetheless. I suspect that someday this functionality in Visual Basic will be improved.

Sample Application

I have created a home security system, located on the companion CD, to illustrate the benefits of local/remote transparency coupled with optimal performance. The home security system allows the user to activate or deactivate particular features either from within the home through a direct link on a desktop computer or remotely with a laptop computer through a dial-up line. The remote access enables home owners to rest assured that their property is secure even when they are out of town. A great selling point of my system is that—unlike the competition—interfacing with the system through a dial-up line instead of the direct link has almost no noticeable performance difference. Hence, home owners have confidence in the system whether they are at home or away.

OK, my home security system doesn't really work, but it is a fully functioning simulation. Of course, the main focus here is how I used the Smart Proxy design pattern in my system architecture. Access to the system is transparent to the user whether or not she is at home, because the graphical user interface is the same, the process of connecting is the same, and the performance cost from dialing up is so small as to be unnoticeable. Implementing the Smart Proxy design pattern affords the same benefit from a software development standpoint, which is local/remote transparency without changing the interface to the real object or compromising performance. Table 7-1 lists the components that form the home security system.

Table 7-1. **Components of the Home Security System**

Components	Contents
SecurityLib.tlb (Type Library)	Interfaces SecurityGuard and DataStream are compiled here.
RealGuardLib.dll (ActiveX DLL)	RealGuard class is defined here.
SecurityProducerLib.dll (ActiveX DLL)	Classes SecurityGuardFactory and Smart-Guard are defined here.
RemSecureAdvisor.exe (ActiveX EXE)	Remote RealGuard instances reside here.
HomeSecure (Standard EXE)	Client of an object that supports the Security-Guard interface.

The home security system exhibits the applicability of the Smart Proxy design pattern; however, it might require the conglomeration of various design patterns to develop the architecture necessary for the system to function correctly.

Figure 7-4 on page 137 paints a clear picture of the home security system process using COM object notation. Following is a brief synopsis that emphasizes the use of the Smart Proxy design pattern, but that includes other dependent pieces that assist in defining the required behavior of the Smart Proxy design pattern. Refer to the sample code on the companion CD for the full disclosure.

- **SecurityGuard interface (Abstraction)** This is the interface expected by the client (HomeSecure). The client expects some behavior manifested by an object that supports this interface, more so when the client makes requests.

- **DataStream interface** This interface was designed with the intent to serve as a conduit for sending and receiving streams of instructions between the smart proxy (SmartGuard) and the real object (RealGuard). The client need not be aware of or concerned about the existence of this interface. This is purely an implementation detail agreed upon by SmartGuard and RealGuard.

- **RealGuard (RealClass)** This class implements the behavior for the SecurityGuard interface. To simulate the activation and deactivation of security features (such as engaging the electric fence or releasing the alligators into the pit), RealGuard persists its state in a security.ini file. The next time the user loads the client (HomeSecure), an instance of RealGuard will load its state from the INI file. RealGuard also implements the DataStream interface, for which it defines the behavior for sending and receiving a batch of instructions in one invocation.

- **SmartGuard (SmartProxy)** This class represents the real object (RealGuard) in the client (HomeSecure) process's address space when the real object is in a remote location (RemAdvisor). For optimal performance, the state of RealGuard is cached in SmartGuard, and requests to update the state or invoke behavior in RealGuard can be packaged as a compound instruction. The requests are then sent in a single invocation to the RealGuard object via DataStream interface operations.

■ **SecurityGuardFactory** This class provides local/remote transparency to the client (HomeSecure) by creating an instance of an object that supports the SecurityGuard interface. If the home owner is at home, SecurityGuardFactory will create an instance of RealGuard in the HomeSecure process's address space. If the home owner is away, SecurityGuardFactory creates an instance of SmartGuard in the HomeSecure process's address space that references a RealGuard object, which resides in the address space of a remote process (RemAdvisor). As the following code extract illustrates, the *CreateInstance* method of SecurityGuardFactory accepts an enumerated data type, Location, as a parameter to simulate the choice of the home owner using the home security system from a direct link at home (AT_HOME), or on a dial-up line away from home (ON_THE_ROAD).

```
' Project:      SecurityProducerLib
' File Name:    SecurityGuardFactory.cls
' Copyright:    1/99 Bill Stamatakis
' Class Name:   SecurityGuardFactory
⋮
Public Function CreateInstance(WhereAmI As Location) As _
                                SecurityLib.SecurityGuard
    Select Case WhereAmI
    Case AT_HOME
        Set CreateInstance = New RealGuardLib.RealGuard
    Case ON_THE_ROAD
        Set CreateInstance = New SmartGuard
    End Select
End Function
```

■ **HomeSecure (Client)** This application is a client that expects an object that supports the SecurityGuard interface through which the core functionality of the home security system is defined.

■ **RemAdvisor (Remote Process)** This ActiveX EXE serves as a residence for the RealGuard object from which a COM proxy is generated and returned to the HomeSecure client. A SmartGuard object encapsulates the reference to this proxy through which all requests intended for the RealGuard are ultimately submitted.

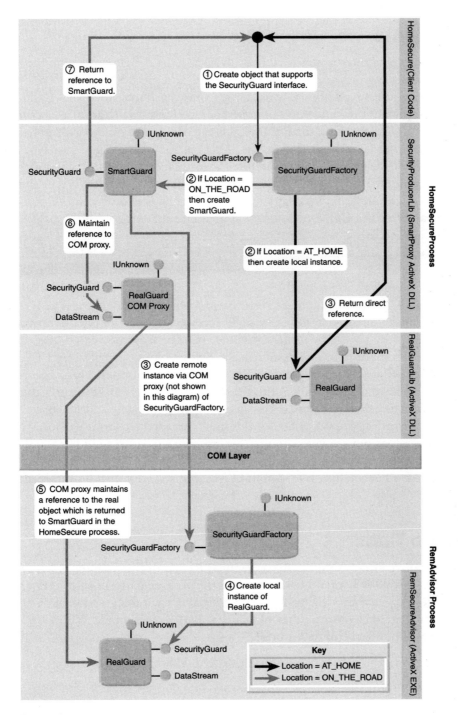

Figure 7-4.
Home Security system architecture diagram.

COMments

Notice that there is no Visual Basic project in the sample containing the Security-Guard class that stubs out the properties and methods—my intention was to create just a type library containing COM interfaces. In Visual Basic ActiveX component projects, you can generate type libraries in addition to component binaries by checking the Remote Server Files option on the Component tab of the Project Properties dialog box. There is no option to generate type libraries only, however. I decided to define the interfaces using the Microsoft Interface Definition Language (IDL) and compile the interfaces into a type library.

Throughout this chapter, I've mentioned the local/remote transparency feature of the COM technology that is an inherent part of Visual Basic. I've explained that when a client requests a reference to an interface of an object that doesn't reside within the client process's address space, COM will interpose and create a proxy in the client's address space that services requests across process boundaries to and from the real object. While this is true, you should be aware that COM proxies might also be created within the client process's address space when the client is a multithreaded application and the type of thread safety defined by the client is incompatible with the objects created in that client's address space. The end result might well be a proxy created by COM in one thread that services requests to the real object in another thread. (See Chapter 3 for more on this topic.) Proxies always perform less efficiently than direct references; there is a noticeable lag even within the same address space, so smart proxies are also appropriate for this multithreaded scenario. Version 6 of Visual Basic does not provide support for creating multithreaded clients, hence the reason that scenario was not previously mentioned. As discussed in Chapter 3—although generally it is inadvisable—you can roll your own multithreaded client application.

Related Patterns

A Smart Proxy design pattern is similar to that of the Adapter (Chapter 4) and the Bridge (Chapter 5) design patterns. All three patterns implement an interface expected by a client. By the same token, each design pattern delegates client requests to some other object that performs the task. Where each design pattern differs is in its purpose.

CHAPTER EIGHT

Object Factory

We can all appreciate the main benefit of being able to plug a product, anything from a rice steamer to a chain saw, into an electrical outlet. Despite the radical differences in behavior among such products, they all function without fail once they're plugged in (assuming you have a live power supply and an otherwise functioning product). This plug-and-play ability allows us to enjoy quite an extensive list of amenities. Product manufactures can develop new products that are guaranteed to function with any standard electrical outlet. Most of us can't imagine life without electricity, but a device that requires electricity to operate that doesn't plug into a standard electrical outlet is useless in the average household. You can infer from this that the concept of electric-powered products has been successful because of the standard interfaces designed for supplying and consuming electricity. Having a standard interface enables a manufacturer to produce products with varying behavior, which translates to various benefits experienced by the user. The system producing the electricity is oblivious to the behavior and the resulting benefits of these products. The system's only requirement is that any product needing electricity must support the interface expected by the electrical system.

This plug-and-play concept can also be applied to developing object-oriented software systems. A client application (the electrical system) can reference any class of object (the product) that supports the interface (the plug) it expects. Implementing plug-and-play functionality in a software system allows you to dynamically introduce new behavior into the system. For this implementation to be possible, the client application must be oblivious to the objects that support the interface it expects. The Object Factory design pattern is the means by which you accomplish this end.

Purpose

Define an interface for creating objects of a specific type. Object creation occurs in the concrete classes that implement this interface.

Utilization

The Object Factory design pattern is useful in the following circumstances:

- Keeps the client oblivious to the various classes of objects that support a particular interface expected by the client

- Controls the object creation process, which is impossible using conventional language features such as the *New* keyword or the *Create-Object* function

Scenario

Without a doubt, systems evolve. Evolution of a system is mainly due to the demand for new features or enhancements to existing ones. A good system design abstracts the roles of the various objects in the design such that the defined relationships between the objects remain static. These abstractions are manifested in the form of interfaces. Concrete examples of these interfaces are the classes that implement them. Dissimilar classes can implement a single interface differently. Unique system functionality results from the various implementations of the interfaces. This sort of system design is called a framework.

A *framework* dictates the roles and relationships of objects within a system and usually provides built-in behavior (known as the default feature set). Using the Object Factory design pattern, a framework allows you to introduce unanticipated new features or enhancements to a system in a nonintrusive manner. For example let's assume that you've built an application that interacts with a Sybase database server. Currently the users must physically connect to the network from their desktop computers to run the application. However, you have been getting numerous requests from users who want to run the system off-line on a laptop computer while commuting on lengthy train rides to and from the office. You decide that a Microsoft Access client database is the suitable candidate for off-line access. Because both databases support structured query language (SQL), interaction between your application and the database is identical. What isn't identical is the method by which communication on a more rudimentary level is carried out. For best performance, Data Access Objects (DAO) is the most appropriate choice for communication with Access, and Remote Data Objects (RDO) for Sybase. (This problem has been resolved by Microsoft's development of ActiveX Data Objects [ADO], which provides a single ideal solution for both worlds. For the sake of making a point, let's assume ADO doesn't exist and that DAO and RDO are the only two database object models developed by Microsoft.) In order for your application to provide the Access database off-line feature, or any other feature that requires accessing some other data source, you need to build a data acquisition framework that I will refer to as universal data objects (UDO). UDO will define interfaces that the client application can use to successfully manipulate data from any source. The details of how data manipulation instructions are transmitted to the data source are encapsulated in concrete classes that implement the interfaces provided by UDO. The Object Factory design pattern permits the development of various database implementations within a framework, as shown in Figure 8-1. A client application can use this framework in a plug-and-play fashion.

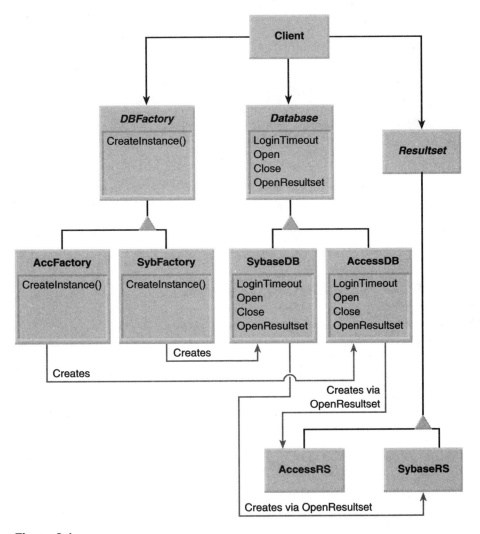

Figure 8-1.
The universal data objects (UDO) framework incorporates the Object Factory design pattern to permit plug-and-play of distinct database and resultset implementations.

Object Model

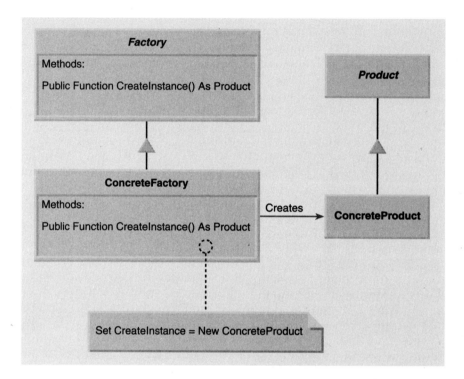

Roles

The roles and functions of the elements of the Object Factory design pattern are as follows:

- **Product**   The interface expected by the client
- **ConcreteProduct**   The concrete class that implements the Product interface
- **Factory**   The interface that defines a method for creating instances of concrete classes that support the Product interface
- **ConcreteFactory**   The concrete class that implements the Factory interface and provides the functionality to create instances of a corresponding ConcreteProduct class

Relationships

The client application doesn't declare variables of the concrete class type. Instead it declares variables that maintain references to objects that support the Product and Factory interfaces. How the client obtains a reference to a ConcreteFactory object can vary depending on the system design, but references to ConcreteProduct objects are always provided by the ConcreteFactory.

Ramifications

The Object Factory design pattern allows a client application to remain oblivious to the properties of concrete classes that implement the interface the client expects. As a result, the concrete classes can be modified to introduce new behavior into the client application without the client's knowledge. The client code remains frozen and rebuilding the client application is not required. Depending on the system design, you might not even need to restart the system to realize the new behavior. This capability is utopia for a software system.

Utilizing the Object Factory design pattern allows the component designer to regulate the creation process of concrete class instances. For example, you can prohibit creation of an object if the client doesn't have the required security clearance. Another situation worth considering is from a purist standpoint: an object should never be created in an invalid state. A client should be able to invoke all interface methods without the object raising an exception as the result of invalid state conditions. The Object Factory design pattern allows you to create an object in any of its possible states, or in some cases a single valid state, by permitting the client to pass parameter values to its interface creation methods.

The previous two points combined make the Object Factory design pattern a crucial ally and sometimes a required partner in implementing many of the other design patterns described in this book. For example, implementing the Singleton design pattern (Chapter 10) would be impossible. A local/remote transparent Smart Proxy design pattern (Chapter 7) would be very difficult to accomplish. The Repository design pattern (Chapter 11) would be less elegant.

Implementation

You can implement the Object Factory design pattern in Microsoft Visual Basic in various ways. Let's examine a few. First, adhering to the object model, you could design a Factory interface that defines a method for creating objects of a specific type. The Product interface in that diagram represents the type of object expected by the client. For each class that implements the Product interface, a corresponding class that implements the Factory interface is required. A parallel hierarchy of concrete factories and products must be maintained.

To lessen the number of factories, a hybrid of the functionality of the Factory and something else can be combined. For example, in the "Scenario" section, Figure 8-1 contains classes SybaseDB and AccessDB that implement the Database interface. As you might expect, the Database interface defines methods to open and close a database and a property for setting the login timeout threshold. (You can probably imagine other relevant database functionality that would be useful to define in this interface.) Notice, however, that in addition to this expected functionality the Database interface defines an *OpenResultset* method. This method is used to create concrete Resultset objects that correspond to the Database object implementation. The client uses this method to submit queries to the database that return results. It's only logical to have the Database implementation create and populate its associative Resultset object with the results from the database. As shown in Figure 8-1, there are three parallel class hiearchies: DBFactory, Database, and Resultset. Instead of having a fourth (RSFactory), the function of creating Resultset objects is consolidated with the function of retrieving the results from the database.

Combining the creation of related objects in one factory interface is yet another approach that not only lessens the number of factories required but also groups interdependent, compatible products. For example, to build an automobile you need an engine, a body, doors, windows, wheels, and so on. One can appreciate the fact that automobiles come in all shapes and sizes. Hence the components that make up a particular model are in most cases unique to that model. Moving the intelligence of identifying compatible components from the assembler (client) on the assembly line to the manufacturer (factory) in the department that is casting the parts in metal will make the process more efficient and dynamic. In more object-oriented terms, despite the fact that interfaces expected by the client remain static (you always need doors), the state and behavior of objects that implement these interfaces are dynamic (you need doors that fit) and can be the cause of incompatibilities that are enforceable only through intelligent processing (source code that validates implementation of an interface and the state of a given object).

Grouping the creation of compatible components under a single factory interface allows a concrete factory class instance to process intelligently by constructing and initializing objects with appropriate behavior and in a valid state relative to other components created by the factory. Figure 8-2 is a plausible representation of an Object Factory design pattern for the BSTAM automobile manufacturer. Depending on the StammerFactory, the assembler is either assembling a 576i or a 586i. The factory guarantees the assembler is working with compatible body and engine parts. True to the real specifications, both models share the same body but have different engines. To support the engine in the 586i, significant adjustments to the suspension are required. These adjustments are encapsulated in the body. Hence not only are the engines incompatible (which is obvious from looking at the diagram), but so are the bodies because the state of the body must be initialized to different values in order to reflect the required suspension adjustments (which is not obvious from looking at the diagram, but is handled by the appropriate *StammerFactory.CreateBody* method).

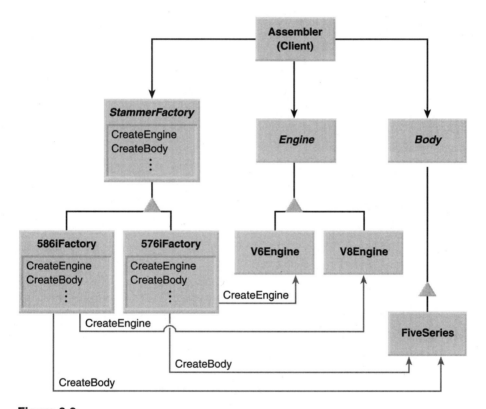

Figure 8-2.
Object Factory design pattern that illustrates manufacturing of related components in a single factory, as a result guaranteeing compatibility between interdependent objects and lessening the number of concrete factories required.

Another variation of the Object Factory design pattern, shown in Figure 8-3, that will further limit the number of factories required involves designing a parameterized object factory. The create method of the factory accepts a parameter that allows it to create an instance of a particular class that supports the expected interface. Referring back to the BSTAM automobile example illustrated in Figure 8-2, you will notice there are separate instances of the StammerFactory object factory for manufacturing parts for distinct models (576i and 586i). Although this approach might seem to be the most sensible, these factories can be consolidated into one FiveSeriesFactory object factory. The create method for each component created must be passed a parameter that contains the model type (576i or 586i). This design variation might be the best option for BSTAM since they produce other model lines such as the 6, 7, and 8 series. The advantage of this approach is that it's easier to deploy new implementations, such as a 566i. A simple change and redeployment of the ActiveX DLL containing the FiveSeriesFactory class is all that is needed to add the new implementation. Also,

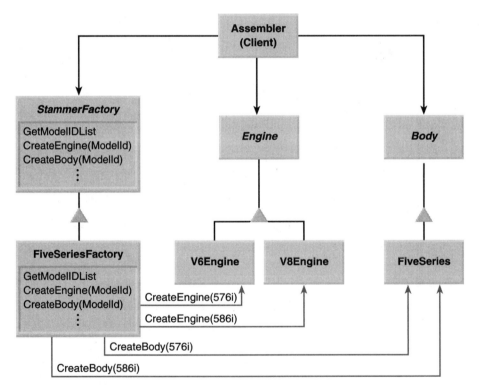

Figure 8-3.
Parameterized Object Factory that consolidates the number of factories used in Figures 8-1 and 8-2 by requiring a parameter to be passed to each create method.

because the object factory knows the list of supported parameters, you can provide a value-added feature to applications by including the ability to query the object factory for this list. Maybe this feature can appear in the form of menu options on a user interface, the number of which dynamically grows and shrinks depending on the currently registered ActiveX DLL.

Sample Application

To convey the benefits and applicability of the Object Factory design pattern, I have decided to build on the automobile example described in the Implementation section of this chapter by creating a virtual showroom application for BSTAM automobiles, shown in Figure 8-4. Customers who can't make it to the nearest dealer for a test drive can enter the virtual showroom where they can check out the latest models and go on a virtual test drive.

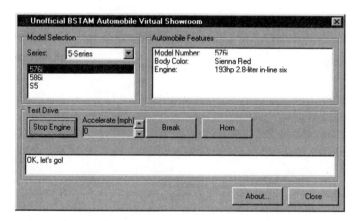

Figure 8-4.
The Unofficial BSTAM Automobile Virtual Showroom sample application demonstrates the use of the Object Factory design pattern.

In this sample application, the customer has a choice of test driving a BSTAM 576i, 586i, or S5. BSTAM manufactures an extensive line of models that continues to grow and change from year to year. In order to reflect these changes in the virtual showroom, the system is designed as shown in Figure 8-5. Notice that all components directly related to the Object Factory design pattern are defined in the ActiveX DLL project BSTAMPlant. To address changes to the product line, new concrete StammerFactory and Stammer classes are added to the BSTAMPlant project, which is then rebuilt and redeployed to the Microsoft Windows workstations running the BSTAMShowroom Standard EXE application. BSTAMShowroom is a client of BSTAMPlant. What follows is a brief depiction of the components that play a key role in this implementation of the Object Factory design pattern. Refer to the sample code on the companion CD for a full disclosure.

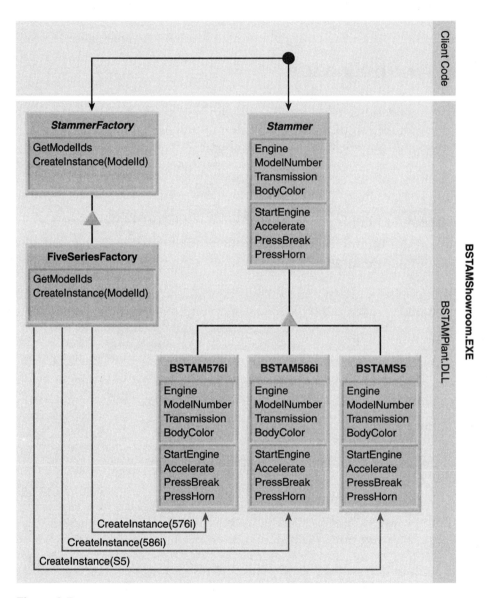

Figure 8-5.
Class diagram for the Object Factory design pattern as implemented by the sample application Unofficial BSTAM Automobile Virtual Showroom.

Key components defined in the BSTAMPlant ActiveX DLL project include:

■ **Stammer (Product)** This interface is an abstraction of the product expected by the client, BSTAMShowroom. The client will reference objects that support the Stammer interface.

```
' Project:      BSTAMPlant
' File Name:    Stammer.cls
' Copyright:    2/99 Bill Stamatakis
' Class Name:   Stammer

Public Property Get ModelNumber() As String
End Property

Public Property Get Engine() As String
End Property

Public Function Accelerate(ToMph As Long) As String
End Function

    ⋮
```

■ **BSTAM576i, BSTAM586i, and BSTAMS5 (ConcreteProduct)** These are concrete classes that implement the Stammer interface. Although all three classes are of type Stammer, they are clearly unique in implementation, which translates as different products in the client application (BSTAMShowroom).

```
' Project:      BSTAMPlant
' File Name:    BSTAM576i.cls
' Copyright:    2/99 Bill Stamatakis
' Class Name:   BSTAM576i

Implements Stammer

Private Property Get Stammer_ModelNumber() As String
    Stammer_ModelNumber = "576i"
End Property

Private Property Get Stammer_Engine() As String
    Stammer_Engine = "193hp 2.8-liter in-line six"
End Property
    ⋮

' File Name:    BSTAM586i.cls
' Class Name:   BSTAM586i

Implements Stammer
```

(continued)

149

```
Private Property Get Stammer_ModelNumber() As String
    Stammer_ModelNumber = "586i"
End Property

Private Property Get Stammer_Engine() As String
    Stammer_Engine = "282hp 4.4-liter 32-valve V8"
End Property
    ⋮
```

■ **StammerFactory (Factory)** This interface's most important functionality is that it defines the method for creating Stammer objects based on a *ModelId* parameter, making this a parameterized object factory interface. This interface also defines a method that returns a list of a valid model ids that the client application will depend on to dynamically update its user interface and to make requests back to a ConcreteFactory object to construct an instance of a particular model.

```
' Project:      BSTAMPlant
' File Name:    StammerFactory.cls
' Copyright:    2/99 Bill Stamatakis
' Class Name:   StammerFactory

Public Function GetModelIds() As String()
End Function

Public Function CreateInstance(ModelId As String) As Stammer
End Function
    ⋮
```

■ **FiveSeriesFactory (ConcreteFactory)** Concrete class that implements the StammerFactory interface. This class's most important feature is that it defines behavior for creating instances of the concrete classes BSTAM576i, BSTAM586i, and BSTAMS5, which support (implement) the Stammer interface. The class is obviously a factory that manufactures 5-Series sedan objects. As shown in the following code extract, the desired concrete class is instantiated based on the *ModelId* parameter it receives from a given client.

```
' Project:      BSTAMPlant
' Copyright:    2/99 Bill Stamatakis
' Class Name:   FiveSeriesFactory

Implements StammerFactory

    ⋮
```

```
Private Function StammerFactory_CreateInstance(ModelId As _
    String) As Stammer
' Construct the approriate Stammer based on the ModelId
' provided.
    Select Case ModelId
    Case "576i"
        Set StammerFactory_CreateInstance = New BSTAM576i
    Case "586i"
        Set StammerFactory_CreateInstance = New BSTAM586i
    Case "S5"
        Set StammerFactory_CreateInstance = New BSTAMS5
    Case Else
        Set StammerFactory_CreateInstance = Nothing
        ' Raising an exception in this case is advisable.
        ' Err.Raise ...
    End Select
End Function
```

Key components defined outside the BSTAMPlant ActiveX DLL project include the BSTAMShowroom (Client). This Standard EXE project contains the client code that defines the usage of the Stammer objects. It in essence provides a virtual exhibit of various BSTAM (Stammer) models, and lets the user take one on a test drive via a Windows user interface. The application is designed so that it can dynamically recognize the addition of new Stammer models and the removal of discontinued models from the virtual showroom without a single required code change to the client. This is possible because of the Object Factory design pattern implemented by the BSTAMPlant ActiveX DLL that serves up StammerFactory and Stammer objects. The client's only concern is to obtain a reference to an object that supports the StammerFactory interface through which it invokes the *CreateInstance* method, passing the method a unique model id to create and return a reference to a specific object that supports the Stammer interface. How does the client know what the valid model ids are? The client queries the StammerFactory object for the list of valid model ids, which it then stores in the *lstModels* list box control. When the user clicks on a model id in the list box control, the list box Click event is fired. As a result the corresponding *lstModels_Click* event handler is invoked. The event handler contains the code to retrieve the currently selected item in the list that contains a valid model id. It uses this id as a parameter to the *StammerFactory.CreateInstance* method.

```
Private Sub lstModels_Click()
    Dim strModelId As String

    ⋮
```

(continued)

```
' Get models from currently selected item in the
' lstModels list box control.
strModelId = lstModels.Text

⋮
Set m_Stammer = m_StammerFact.CreateInstance(strModelId)
⋮
```

COMments

In a multithread process, COM objects can potentially reside in different apartments. (Refer to Chapter 3 for in-depth coverage of COM threading apartment models.) A side benefit of implementing the Object Factory design pattern in Visual Basic is that it is a means by which to dictate in what apartment a COM object will reside. This has significant performance implications. An object factory that uses the keyword *New* will create objects in the same apartment in which the object factory resides.

COM objects can also reside in server processes external to the client process. Therefore keep in mind that an initial request from a client to create an object would require two remote calls: one to reference a Factory instance and another to create the desired object. However, if a client intends to create multiple instances of a class, it should then hold on to the Factory reference to avoid the performance hit of an extra unnecessary remote call.

Related Patterns

The Prototypical Object Factory (Chapter 9), Repository (Chapter 11), and Singleton (Chapter 10) design patterns are by-products of the Object Factory because they in essence are factories designed to solve specific recurring problems.

CHAPTER NINE

Prototypical Object Factory

When the term "clone" is used, we often think of a product that is an exact duplicate of an original. Cloned products in many cases are created by using information gathered through reverse engineering the original. However, in spite of the fact that we expect clones to be exact duplicates, we still often perceive that the quality is deprecated in a clone. Furthermore if you clone the clone, you might expect the quality to further diminish.

In software development, however, a clone and the original are identical in every respect. When you use the Prototypical Object Factory design pattern, the responsibility for producing a clone of an object resides with the object itself. No reverse engineering is required. This feature plays a key role in creating an application that permits plug-and-play of new functionality at run time.

Purpose

To determine the types of objects an object factory can create by registering prototypical class instances with the object factory. The object factory creates new instances by cloning the registered prototypes.

Utilization

Use the Prototypical Object Factory design pattern for the following reasons:

- For the same reasons you would use the Object Factory design pattern (Chapter 8), which are to keep the client oblivious to the potentially unlimited implementations of the interface it expects and to regulate the creation process.

- To minimize the parallel class hierarchies of factory to product as described in Chapter 8.

- To dynamically register at run time new classes of objects for the factory to create or to unregister existing classes of objects.

Scenario

You have developed an electronic financial trading system that executes orders on the New York Stock Exchange. Because the system has proven to be stable and reliable, your manager has laid out a plan to add a list of new destinations (such as London and Tokyo) for trade execution over the next few months. As the number of destinations increases to include exchanges around the world, the application evolves to a 24-hour trading system. No downtime is tolerable because, as we all know, time is money. If traders can't place orders on a given exchange because the system has to be shut down to bring new destinations on line, the company could lose a great deal of money.

Implementing the Object Factory design pattern (Chapter 8) in this situation might seem ideal because it uses an ActiveX DLL in which you can define the destination interface, various classes that implement the destination interface, and a factory class that creates a specific class instance of the destination interface expected by the client application. To add a new destination you would first define a new class within the ActiveX DLL and update the factory class implementation so that the factory class would know how to create an instance of the new class. Next you would rebuild the DLL (select Make DLL from the File menu in the Microsoft Visual Basic IDE) and redeploy the DLL to all desktop machines running your electronic trading system.

Unfortunately, there is a catch: If the trading system is running on a machine you're trying to copy the DLL to, the operating system will not allow you to replace the DLL because it is in use. You could copy the DLL, along with a copy of the trading system executable, to a different directory and run the trading system from this new location. However, you'll notice that the new destination is still not available, even to the new instance of the trading system, because Microsoft Windows defines the behavior of DLL usage such that when a client process attempts to load a DLL it looks first in memory. Because the original instance of the trading system application loaded the old DLL, the new instance of the application will grab that version of the DLL from memory. So you're still left with no choice but to restart the trading system application.

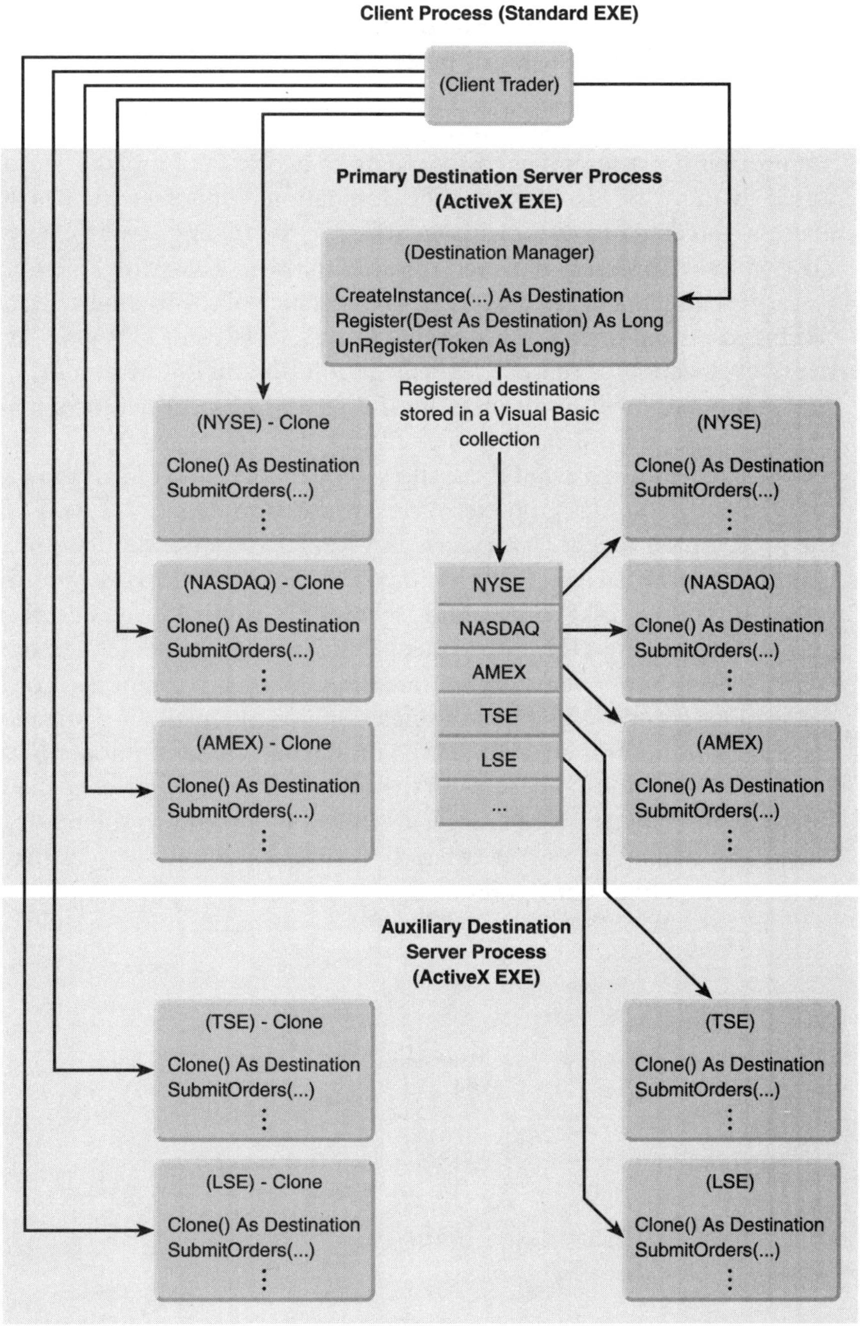

Client Process (Standard EXE)

(Client Trader)

Primary Destination Server Process (ActiveX EXE)

(Destination Manager)

CreateInstance(...) As Destination
Register(Dest As Destination) As Long
UnRegister(Token As Long)

Registered destinations stored in a Visual Basic collection

(NYSE) - Clone

Clone() As Destination
SubmitOrders(...)
⋮

(NYSE)

Clone() As Destination
SubmitOrders(...)
⋮

(NASDAQ) - Clone

Clone() As Destination
SubmitOrders(...)
⋮

(NASDAQ)

Clone() As Destination
SubmitOrders(...)
⋮

(AMEX) - Clone

Clone() As Destination
SubmitOrders(...)
⋮

| NYSE |
| NASDAQ |
| AMEX |
| TSE |
| LSE |
| ... |

(AMEX)

Clone() As Destination
SubmitOrders(...)
⋮

Auxiliary Destination Server Process (ActiveX EXE)

(TSE) - Clone

Clone() As Destination
SubmitOrders(...)
⋮

(TSE)

Clone() As Destination
SubmitOrders(...)
⋮

(LSE) - Clone

Clone() As Destination
SubmitOrders(...)
⋮

(LSE)

Clone() As Destination
SubmitOrders(...)
⋮

Figure 9-1.
The Prototypical Object Factory design pattern is implemented through primary and auxiliary server processes.

An alternative you might be thinking of at this point is to create the destination component as an out-of-process ActiveX EXE project rather than as an ActiveX DLL. This implementation leaves you with one central destination component being shared by several trading system clients, which makes deployment easier because you need to update only one file instead of a potentially unwieldy number. Also, because the destination component resides in its own process, you could restart it without affecting the trading system clients. You're now on the right track, but even this method won't work if a reference to the factory is being maintained by a running instance of the trading system and the destination component is registered as MultiUse. (Refer to Chapter 3 for an in-depth explanation of the various registration options.) Restarting the destination component will result in an invalid factory object reference, making the trading system on the client inoperable.

The best way to avoid these showstoppers is to implement the Prototypical Object Factory design pattern. As illustrated in Figure 9-1, you can define the prototypical object factory, which I'll refer to as the destination manager (DM), and an initial list of destinations in a single ActiveX EXE (primary destination server process). The trading system client would obtain references to destinations via the DM. Subsequent destinations can be defined in separate ActiveX EXE components, either one destination per component or multiple destinations grouped together in a single component (auxiliary destination server process), whichever is appropriate. Upon startup, these components must register their Destination objects with the DM. The DM then clones the Destination objects and returns references to them on demand to the trading system client. The trading system never has to be shut down, and new destinations can be brought on line at any point in time, even during the busiest trading hours.

Object Model

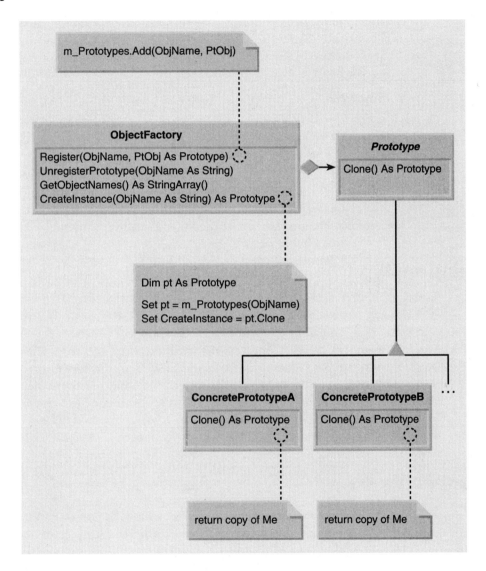

Roles

- **ObjectFactory** A concrete class that maintains a list of objects that support the Prototype interface. This class instructs these objects to clone themselves and returns references to the clones to the requesting client.

- **Prototype** The interface that defines a method for cloning instances of classes that implement this interface. This interface can be a hybrid, meaning that it not only defines the cloning method, but it defines other operations as well.

- **ConcretePrototype** A concrete class that implements the Prototype interface. When the *Clone* method of the Prototype interface is invoked, an instance of this class will create a copy of itself and a reference to the copy will be returned to the calling program.

Relationships

Unique ConcretePrototype classes inherit the Prototype interface and implement behavior for cloning themselves. The ObjectFactory object provides methods for adding and removing objects that support the Prototype interface (such as instances of the ConcretePrototype class) to and from the ObjectFactory's internal list. When a client invokes the *ObjectFactory.CreateInstance* method to create an instance of a specific object, the ObjectFactory object locates the requested object in its internal list and instructs that object to clone itself via its implementation of the *Prototype.Clone* interface method. The object creates a copy of itself and a reference to the copy is returned to the client.

Ramifications

- All the benefits realized by the Object Factory design pattern (Chapter 8) also hold true for the Prototypical Object Factory design pattern. The resounding theme is that you can easily create plug-and-play utopia in an application by allowing the addition and removal of objects in the factory at run time. From the end user's perspective, objects translate to system features, and the ability to change features dynamically is very useful and impressive to an end user.

■ Rather than defining separate classes for each distinct behavioral response to a particular interface operation, you can define a single class with behavior that varies depending on its state. The prototypical object factory can then facilitate a client's request by cloning a single object and setting its state accordingly.

■ If you use a framework library, you typically add new behavior to the framework by inheriting an interface the framework expects. You usually will not have access to the framework source code, so the framework needs some way to become aware of the fact that a new class exists that supports an interface it expects. If the framework is implemented using the Prototypical Object Factory design pattern, a client can register a new object that supports the interface expected by the framework with a prototypical object factory.

■ Cloning is not a built-in language feature of Visual Basic. Cloning requires an interface definition and implementation for all classes that inherit the interface.

Implementation

Depending on the system design, the Prototypical Object Factory design pattern can be implemented as an ActiveX EXE project, as I suggested in the "Scenario" section, or as an ActiveX DLL, as I alluded to in the third point of the "Ramifications" section.

Implementing the Prototypical Object Factory design pattern in an ActiveX EXE should be carried out as follows:

1. Define the Prototype interface ClassModule.

2. Set the Prototype's *Instancing* property value to PublicNotCreatable to permit clients of this component to only declare object variables of this type or define classes that implement this interface.

3. Define an ObjectFactory ClassModule.

4. Set the ObjectFactory's *Instancing* property value to MultiUse or SingleUse to allow clients to create instances of this class. (Refer to Chapter 3 of this book or to the *Microsoft Visual Basic 6.0 Programmer's Guide* for a complete explanation of the *Instancing* property values.)

5. Define a default set of ClassModules that implement the Prototype interface.

There are two rather important points to keep in mind when implementing the Prototypical Object Factory design pattern in an ActiveX EXE. First, if zero downtime tolerance is in place, subsequent requirements to create new ClassModules should be defined in new ActiveX EXE component projects, as illustrated in Figure 9-1. Second, the object factory must be implemented as a Singleton design pattern (Chapter 10) to ensure that all objects are registered with the same object factory.

Frameworks in many cases are implemented as DLLs that are loaded into a client process. The client typically extends the functionality of the framework by either inheriting framework interfaces or by trapping framework events. By implementing the Prototypical Object Factory design pattern, the framework can permit the dynamic extension of framework behavior.

Let's assume the client was developed as a Visual Basic Standard EXE project. In the References dialog box, you select the appropriate framework ActiveX DLL. This will give the client access to all the framework's interfaces, classes, enumerated data types, and user-defined types, which you can easily navigate through using the Object Browser in the Visual Basic development environment. In the client code you could then do the following:

1. Define ClassModules that implement the Prototype interface.

2. Set up a Singleton reference to the framework's object factory.

3. Create instances of the classes that support the Prototype interface and register these instances with the object factory using its registration method.

When operations are invoked in the framework that require the functionality defined in the Prototype interface, the behavior you defined in your Class-Modules will be available.

Sample Application

I have revised the Object Factory sample application discussed in Chapter 8 to create a framework that implements the Prototypical Object Factory design pattern. Like the Object Factory sample, this sample application is a BSTAM virtual automobile showroom that let's you take all available automobiles on a virtual test drive. In Chapter 8 the various models that appear in the list box on the user interface are retrieved by code that queries a specific factory for a list of model ids that correspond to the classes of objects that the factory can create.

The disadvantage of the Object Factory design pattern implementation is that the factory's knowledge of classes that support the interface that the factory expects is static. If you want to add other classes of automobiles to the application you must have access to the factory source code.

Let's assume the application was provided by BSTAM to its dealerships. Anytime BSTAM adds a new model to its product line, BSTAM sends out an updated application. No problem. Everything works as it should. However, let's also assume that a particular dealership does some after-market enhancements to the BSTAM automobiles and would like to make those vehicles available for test drives in the BSTAM virtual showroom application. In order to address this demand, BSTAM decides to enhance the application by implementing the Prototypical Object Factory design pattern to allow dealerships to add customized automobiles to the virtual showroom. What follows is a brief synopsis of the participants that form the Prototypical Object Factory design pattern. For a complete disclosure of the source code, refer to the companion CD.

The BSTAM virtual showroom application consists of a framework library that resides in the ActiveX DLL (BSTAMFx.DLL) and a Windows front end developed as a Standard EXE (BSTAMShowroom.EXE). Most of the application behavior originates from the framework library. The BSTAMShowroom is a thin client process that interacts with BSTAMFx, which is loaded in the client's address space. Custom Stammer automobile classes are defined in the BSTAMShowroom project. Instances of these classes are registered with specific factories in the framework, thus extending the framework behavior (or feature set). The following list describes the class modules contained in the BSTAM virtual showroom application that correspond to the classes and interfaces required by the Prototypical Object Factory design pattern.

- **Stammer (Prototype)**   Defined in the BSTAMFx.DLL project, this interface is an abstraction of the products manufactured by the framework object factories. Most notably, this interface defines a *Clone* method to permit classes that implement this interface to provide behavior for cloning instances of themselves.

```
' Project:      BSTAMFx
' File Name:    Stammer.cls
' Copyright:    2/99 Bill Stamatakis
' Class Name:   Stammer

Public Function Clone() As Stammer
End Function
  ⋮
```

■ **Stam5 (ConcretePrototype)**   Defined in the BSTAMShowroom.EXE project, this class implements the Stammer interface. As the following code extract illustrates, this class provides implementation for the *Clone* method that allows an instance of this class to clone itself.

```
' Project:     BSTAMShowroom
' File Name:   Stam5.cls
' Copyright:   2/99 Bill Stamatakis
' Class Name:  Stam5

Implements BSTAMFx.Stammer

Private Function Stammer_Clone() As BSTAMFx.Stammer
    Set Stammer_Clone = New Stam5
End Function
⋮
```

■ **StammerFactory (ObjectFactory)**   Defined in the BSTAMFx.DLL project, this interface defines methods that facilitate the implementation of the Prototypical Object Factory design pattern. As you can see from the object model for this design pattern (see the "Object Model" section of this chapter), defining a separate factory interface such as this is not required to make effective use of this design pattern. However, in the case of this application, defining an object factory interface allows the application to scale with less effort.

```
' Project:     BSTAMFx
' File Name:   StammerFactory.cls
' Copyright:   2/99 Bill Stamatakis
' Class Name:  StammerFactory

Public Function CreateInstance(ModelId As String) As Stammer
End Function

Public Function AddCustomStammer(ByVal Stammer As Stammer) _
  As Boolean
End Function

Public Function RemoveCustomStammer(ModelId As String) _
  As Boolean
End Function
⋮
```

■ **FiveSeriesFactory (ConcreteFactory)**   Defined in the BSTAMFx.DLL project, this class implements the StammerFactory interface, providing the behavior necessary to register prototypical instances of objects derived from the Stammer interface (such as Stam5, described previously). This class has implemented the *StammerFactory.CreateInstance* method to instruct these objects to create instances of themselves. (The objects create these instances of themselves by calling their implementations of the *Stammer.Clone* method.) The objects then return references to the clones to the calling procedure.

```
' Project:       BSTAMFx
' File Name:     FiveSeriesFactory.cls
' Copyright:     2/99 Bill Stamatakis
' Class Name:    FiveSeriesFactory

Implements StammerFactory
   ⋮

Private Function StammerFactory_CreateInstance(ModelId _
   As String) As Stammer
     Dim CustomStammer As Stammer

     ⋮
     ' If the prototypical Stammer object exists in the
     ' registered list, instruct the object to clone itself
     ' and return a reference to the clone; otherwise
     ' return Nothing and raise an error.
     If m_CustomStammers.Exists(ModelId) Then
         Set CustomStammer = m_CustomStammers(ModelId)
         Set StammerFactory_CreateInstance = _
             CustomStammer.Clone()
     Else
         Set StammerFactory_CreateInstance = Nothing
         ' Raising an exception in this case is advisable.
         ' Err.Raise ...
     End If
  ⋮
End Function

Private Function StammerFactory_AddCustomStammer _
   (ByVal Stammer As Stammer) As Boolean
     Dim strModelNum As String

     strModelNum = Stammer.ModelNumber
     ⋮
     ' Register prototypical objects.
     If Not m_CustomStammers.Exists(strModelNum) Then
         m_CustomStammers(strModelNum) = Stammer
         StammerFactory_AddCustomStammer = True
```

(continued)

```
        Else
            StammerFactory_AddCustomStammer = False
        End If
        ⋮
End Function

Private Function StammerFactory_RemoveCustomStammer _
    (ModelId As String) As Boolean
        ⋮
        ' Unregister prototypical objects.
        If m_CustomStammers.Exists(ModelId) Then
            m_CustomStammers.Remove ModelId
        End If
        StammerFactory_RemoveCustomStammer = True
End Function
    ⋮
```

COMments

This design pattern affords the same benefits and concerns described for the Object Factory design pattern in Chapter 8, which include regulating the apartment residence of COM objects, resulting in optimal performance scenarios, and providing multiple remote invocations in an out-of-process scenario to obtain a reference to the desired object. Read the "COMments" section in Chapter 8 for further elaboration.

Related Patterns

This design pattern, along with the Singleton (Chapter 10) and Repository (Chapter 11) design patterns, are by-products of the Object Factory (Chapter 8) design pattern because despite specific purposes that warrant the need to identify them as separate design patterns, they are all factories. They are designed to manufacture objects that support specific interfaces and return references to those objects.

CHAPTER TEN

Singleton

The average company has a mail department responsible for receiving and delivering packages at the company's address on your behalf. Many companies also have a main phone number through which questions, comments, and requests are communicated. Similarly, the average company uses a single printer installed on its network to serve a large number of workstations, avoiding the expense of attaching a printer to each workstation.

We can appreciate the benefits of these arrangements for numerous reasons. Consider the cost savings, for example. It's not very likely that all the workstations will submit print jobs nonstop throughout the day. It's also not likely that most employees require the services of the mail department or the central phone number on a consistent basis throughout the day. Having a single mail department, a central phone number, and a single printer is cost effective because the use of all these services per person is relatively low. You can apply the same reasoning to software development: software components in a given scenario might prove to be beneficial when designed to exist as a single instance.

Purpose

The purpose of the Singleton design pattern is to permit the creation of only a single instance of a class and to provide a global point of access.

Utilization

Use the Singleton design pattern when the service of a specific object is required by other objects in the system and when the service must be globally accessible. At the same time, the frequency with which clients use the service and the duration of processing the service must not be particularly long.

Scenario

You've designed an application that requires only a single connection to a database. Different components of the application run unique queries against tables in the database. The database object is globally accessible to all objects in the system. You could define a global database object, but there is no feature in the Microsoft Visual Basic language to prevent a client from creating another instance. Implementing a Singleton design pattern will allow you to control the number of database objects that can be created.

Object Model

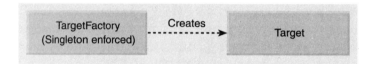

Roles

The roles and functions of the Singleton design pattern are as follows:

- **TargetFactory**   Defines a *CreateInstance* method to create a single unique instance of a Target object.
- **Target**   Defines the object expected by the client.

Relationships

A TargetFactory object creates a single instance of the Target class and retains a reference to that instance. The TargetFactory object then returns the reference to that Target object to the client. All subsequent *CreateInstance* requests will result in the TargetFactory object returning a reference to the same Target object that the TargetFactory object is referencing.

Ramifications

Sharing a single instance of a class is cost effective because a single instance doesn't depreciate the available memory, which is a finite resource. Also, the overhead of constructing an instance of the class occurs only when the initial request is made. The Singleton design pattern controls the instantiation of the target class, so the client can't violate its intent.

You can extend the Singleton design pattern to support multiple instances of the target class when this solution is warranted. For example, you can extend the Singleton design pattern so that instead of creating a single database connection object that connects to a particular database, the design pattern implementation will create unique database connection objects for several distinct databases. The only requirement is that you must modify the implementation of the *CreateInstance* method of the TargetFactory class. If you have scenarios that each require different behavior, you can design TargetFactory as an interface that concrete TargetFactory classes can implement, thus providing the benefit of polymorphism.

Implementation

Implementing a Singleton design pattern in Visual Basic is not possible with the current language features. You can, however, implement the Singleton design pattern by using the Object Factory design pattern (Chapter 8), as indicated by the TargetFactory class in the "Object Model" section of this chapter. This implementation in and of itself is not enough to prevent violation of the Singleton design pattern. Any member of the project, whether a form, a module, or a class, can define a method that creates any number of instances for a given class.

To enforce the Singleton design pattern for a target class, follow these steps in Visual Basic:

1. Create a Microsoft ActiveX component in which only the target class and the object factory for the target class exist. For the best possible performance, the ActiveX component should be an ActiveX DLL; this will be created with a single class module by default.

2. Rename the class module for your object factory to an appropriate name that represents your target class. You will return to this module to define its *CreateInstance* method.

3. Add a class module for the target class.

    ❑ Rename the target class with an appropriate name.

    ❑ Define its properties and methods.

    ❑ Set its *Instancing* property value to PublicNotCreatable. Doing so will prevent clients from creating instances of this target class.

4. Activate the object factory.

5. Ensure the object factory's *Instancing* property value is set to MultiUse. This will allow clients to create instances of the object factory class.

6. Now that the target class is defined, you can implement the *Create-Instance* method in the object factory class for creating instances of the target class. Calling the object factory's *CreateInstance* method is the only means by which a client can create an instance of the target class; hence, the Singleton design pattern is enforced. The target class object factory controls the number of target class instances permitted. But an important question should come to mind: If the user is allowed to create multiple instances of the object factory class, wouldn't each factory have its own unique target instance that it controls, which violates the intent of the Singleton design pattern? This would in fact be the case if a member of the object factory class were holding the reference to the target class instance.

As described in Chapter 2, classes defined in an ActiveX component project have global access to object variables publicly declared in other modules that reside in that same project. Storing a reference to the target class instance in a global object variable would prevent each object factory from holding its own reference to the target, thereby solving this problem. The following code extract depicts a possible implementation.

```
' Globals module
Public g_Target As Target
    :

' Possible implementation of the CreateInstance method in the
' TargetFactory class
Public Function CreateInstance() As Target
    If g_Target Is Nothing Then
        Set g_Target = New Target
    End If
    Set CreateInstance = g_Target
End Function
```

Regardless of the number of object factory class instances that reside in a client process, the one Singleton target class instance still remains, as shown in Figure 10-1.

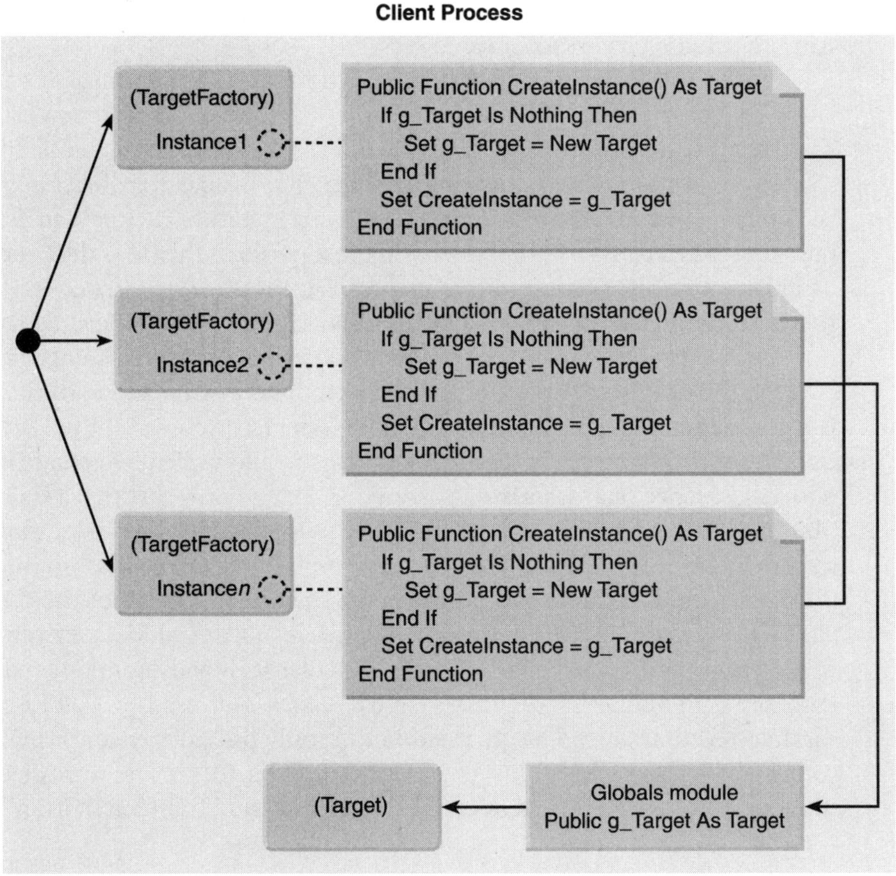

Client Process

Figure 10-1.
A client process with multiple TargetFactory class instances that share the same global object reference variable to a single Target class instance.

Sample Application

In this simple car loan calculator program, the user can view multiple calculators side by side so that he or she can easily compare the differences in monthly loan payments based on the loan amount and the loan interest rate. Even though the user can view multiple instances of the car loan calculator window, the program doesn't need to duplicate instances of the calculator engine. A single

169

Calculator object will be sufficient to serve any number of car loan calculator windows. Let's take a closer look.

Two projects have been created: AutoLoanCalcSvr and AutoLoanCalculator. To gain the full benefit of this section, load both projects into Visual Basic. The AutoLoanCalcSvr project is an ActiveX DLL that implements a Calculator class object as a Singleton design pattern. The Calculator object implements the functionality for calculating the monthly payments of the car loan. To implement the Singleton design pattern, you must perform the steps described in the "Implementation" section of this chapter. Set the *Instancing* property value of the Calculator class to PublicNotCreatable. Clients (AutoLoanCalculator) are now unable to create instances of this class. Notice that the CalcFactory class (see the Object Factory design pattern, described in Chapter 8) in this project is responsible for creating instances of the Calculator class. Set the CalcFactory class's *Instancing* property value to MultiUse to allow clients to create instances of it. An instance of a Calculator class can be created only through a CalcFactory object's *CreateInstance* method. In other words, the CalcFactory object controls the number of Calculator instances permitted. As the following code extract illustrates, the CalcFactory object permits only one instance of the Calculator class. All subsequent calls to *CreateInstance* result in CalcFactory returning a reference to that same instance of the Calculator. Finally, a minor but important step is to define the object variable *g_Calculator* used by CalcFactory as a module-level variable. This guarantees that only one reference to the Calculator object is shared by all instances of the CalcFactory class, regardless of the number of instances the client creates. (Refer to the "Implementation" section for a full explanation.)

```
' Class Name:   CalcFactory
Public Function CreateInstance() As Calculator
    If g_Calculator Is Nothing Then
        Set g_Calculator = New Calculator
    End If
    Set CreateInstance = g_Calculator
End Function
```

AutoLoanCalculator is a Standard EXE project. It is a client of the AutoLoanCalcSvr project. If you build this project, it will create an executable that, when run, displays an Auto Loan Calculator window. (See Figure 10-2.) From the File menu, select New Window to launch a new instance of the Auto Loan Calculator window. You can then make side-by-side calculations and compare the results. From a usage standpoint, it might seem that the application is launching another instance of itself: it is not. The one application instance is launching another instance of the window (Visual Basic form). Note that the form contains member object variables that maintain references to a CalcFactory object and a Calculator object. These member object variables are initialized in the form's *Form_Initialize* event handler function, as shown in the following code extract.

```
Private Sub Form_Initialize()
    Set m_CalcFact = New AutoLoanCalcSvr.CalcFactory
    Set m_Calculator = m_CalcFact.CreateInstance
End Sub
```

This event handler is called every time a new form is created. Each form instance maintains its own instances of the object variables *m_CalcFact* and *m_Calculator*. Because the Calculator object is a Singleton, you should recognize by looking at this client that each form instance has a unique instance of the CalcFactory class, but that they all share the same instance of the Calculator.

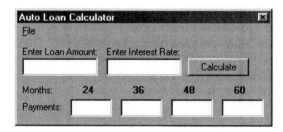

Figure 10-2.
The Auto Loan Calculator window.

COMments

The Singleton design pattern will always work between Visual Basic clients and servers. However, it has the potential to fail miserably when used with non–Visual Basic clients. COM threading apartment models are to blame for this failure. (See Chapter 3.) In short, publicly defined variables in Visual Basic modules are globally accessible to all instances of classes declared within the same project. Therefore, the Singleton is enforceable, or so it seems. It's more accurate to say that publicly defined variables in Visual Basic modules are globally accessible to all instances of classes declared within the same project that reside in the same COM apartment. It is therefore possible for two instances of CalcFactory to exist in different COM apartments, which results in unique instances of the Calculator class existing in each apartment.

To guarantee compliance of the Singleton implementation in a Visual Basic–generated ActiveX DLL, set the Threading Model option of the DLL to Single Threaded on the General tab of the Project Properties dialog box. (See Figure 10-3.) This forces all instances of classes defined in this DLL to exist in the same COM apartment. However, if the client is multithreaded, all requests to the Calculator object will be marshaled across thread boundaries via a proxy. The price you pay in this scenario is performance, and the price can be huge. If performance becomes an issue, avoid the Singleton implementation.

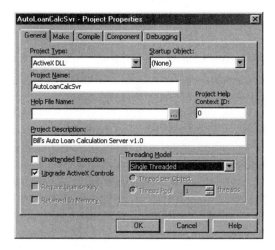

Figure 10-3.
Set the Threading Model option to Single Threaded.

Related Patterns

Based on the current constraints of the Visual Basic language, using an Object Factory design pattern (Chapter 8) to implement a Singleton design pattern has proven to be the most suitable approach.

CHAPTER ELEVEN

Repository

A repository is a place where you store stuff. In the context of design patterns, stuff is an object's state. When you switch from client/server to *n*-tier software development, it's evident that the applications you develop are no longer datacentric. Hence your system design and implementation are no longer constrained by how data needs to be manipulated; instead you think in terms of objects. To a certain extent, you produce software that mirrors the functional process of a business by defining classes that are named after industry-specific terminology. The classes would implement the functionality depicted in the business process. For example, if you were developing a financial equity trading system, you most likely would define a StockPortfolio class that implements methods for executing, canceling, and replacing orders. A benefit of object-oriented development is that it is self-describing. It allows the programmer to represent concepts in source code symbolically. People are able to associate symbols with what those symbols represent and the actions that surround them.

A stock portfolio is a collection of stocks owned by an individual (for example, Ethan Spencer) or an entity (for example, the New York City Fire Department Pension Fund). An order is an instruction to buy or sell stock at a specified price. The action of executing an order carries out that order, and the actions of canceling and replacing orders modify outstanding orders. Managing a stock portfolio by using a client application in the client/server development model would involve direct manipulation of the data stored in the database. A client in the *n*-tier model would only invoke methods on objects that represent the business process. This doesn't mean that databases have been discarded from the system. What actually has occurred is that the responsibility of maintaining the data has shifted from the client to the business objects.

In the typical object-oriented system, objects live in memory. Since memory is a finite and precious resource, objects generally have a life cycle. They are created when needed and destroyed when their services are no longer required, making room in memory for other objects. At some future time, when the object's services are in demand again, you might need to re-create the object in its prior state, as is the case in the financial trading system example. It's obvious that the state of a stock portfolio must be retained. The Repository design pattern facilitates a common means to retain the state of objects. This chapter will describe how to accomplish this in Microsoft Visual Basic.

Purpose

To define a common set of interfaces that allows an object's state to be stored and retrieved from a data store.

Utilization

Use the Repository design pattern for the following purposes:

- **To save the state of an object at a specific moment in time**   For example, whenever the state (the number of shares in the stocks held) of a StockPortfolio object has changed because of interface method invocations (*StockPortfolio.executeOrders*, *StockPortfolio.cancelOrders*, or *StockPortfolio.replaceOrders*), its state should be persisted to a repository.

- **To reestablish the state of an object from a specific moment in time**   For example, when a user logs off the stock portfolio management system, the StockPortfolio object that represents the user's portfolio is destroyed; however, the state is preserved in a repository. When the user decides to log on to the system again, a new StockPortfolio object must be created and the state reestablished, facilitated through a repository.

- **To abstract the varying implementations required to store and retrieve the state of an object from a specific data store**   For example, let's assume there are numerous classes in a stock portfolio management system that could individually define data manipulation routines implemented in a specific technology, such as Microsoft Data Access Objects (DAO). First, it would become increasingly difficult to maintain the various data manipulation routines. Second, if you decide to replace DAO with ADO (ActiveX Data Objects) technology, you would be required to change code in every class that references DAO. To avoid this predicament, the data manipulation routines for storing and retrieving data can be centralized and encapsulated in a repository class.

Scenario

Consider any stateful object system such as the equity trading system example mentioned previously. A StockPortfolio object must contain state, which reflects the value of the portfolio, the stocks it contains, the owner of the portfolio, and so on. The state of the StockPortfolio object must be retainable. For obvious reasons, such as to accommodate system crashes and to allow for efficient use of memory, it is rational to expect a stateful object to rehydrate its state from a data store when reincarnated. If the persistence to a data store resides in the implementation detail of each object, the data store becomes increasingly difficult to manage and maintain as the number of stateful objects in the system increases. Also, the business object developer would be required to have intimate knowledge of the data store. The Repository design pattern is an ideal solution for this type of scenario because it abstracts, in a separate object layer, the data manipulation of the data store that contains the state of a distinct type of object. As a result, the data store and the business objects are loosely coupled, so any constraints directly related to accommodating the data store are removed from the business object implementation. Changing data store technologies also becomes significantly less disruptive. Business objects can remain completely unaffected and oblivious to the change. Business object developers' hands are no longer tied by the data store technology or the learning curve associated with adopting a new data store technology.

Object Model

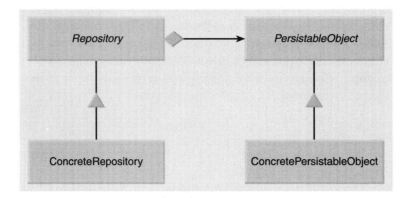

Roles

The roles and functions of the elements of the Repository design pattern are as follows:

- ■ **PersistableObject**   Specifies an interface for reading and writing the state of an object to and from a data stream

- ■ **ConcretePersistableObject**   A class that implements the behavior of the PersistableObject interface for reading and writing its state to a data stream

- ■ **Repository**   Specifies an interface for storing and retrieving the state of a PersistableObject object to and from a data store

- ■ **ConcreteRepository**   A class that implements functionality for storing and retrieving the state of a PersistableObject object to a specific type of data store

Relationships

To recover a persistable object from a repository, a concrete repository reconstructs a concrete persistable object by retrieving the persistable object's state from an underlying data store such as a flat file or a Microsoft SQL Server database. The concrete repository then creates an instance of the persistable object, initializing the persistable object's state with data from the data store by means of its PersistableObject interface's *WriteState* method, and returns a reference to the concrete persistable object to the requesting client. (See Figure 11-1.)

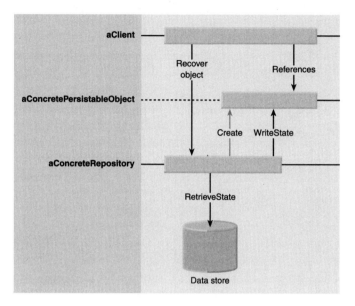

Figure 11-1.
This diagram depicts the steps taken to retrieve a persistable object from a repository.

To store a persistable object to a repository, a concrete persistable object (created by the client) is handed off to a concrete repository. The concrete repository extracts the state from the object by calling the object's Persistable-Object interface's *ReadState* method and writing the results to an underlying data store. (See Figure 11-2.)

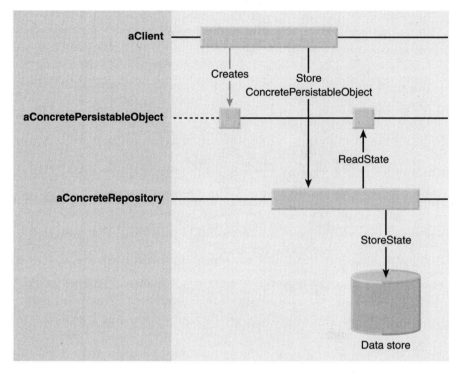

Figure 11-2.
This diagram depicts the steps taken to store a persistable object to a repository.

Ramifications

The Repository design pattern extracts the intricacies of data manipulation from the business object layer. As Figure 11-3 illustrates, in the typical client/server application, business rules and data manipulation are written in the client application. Switching to a three-tier architecture removes the business rules and data manipulation from the client and moves them to the business object layer. Consequently, the client code is leaner and simplified to a great extent. Also, via COM technology, the business objects are reusable and accessible to other client applications, which can utilize some or all of the business objects in a unique manner to produce a different implementation of the business process.

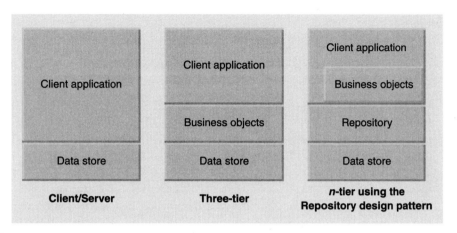

Figure 11-3.
Evolution diagram of advanced data-based Visual Basic development.

However, the business objects in a three-tier architecture are forced to manipulate data directly, hence moving the complexity out of the client and into the business object layer. Now the business object layer is constrained by the details surrounding the specific data store technology. The Repository design pattern abstracts the data manipulation process into a separate layer, minimizing the complexities and limitations associated with data manipulation in a data store.

Plug-and-play repository implementations for dissimilar data stores without a single code change are a built-in benefit of the Repository design pattern. Different concrete classes that implement the same Repository interface can provide behavior unique to persisting an object's state to its underlying data store.

The Repository design pattern produces a more efficient data manipulation scheme. A repository could, for example, maintain a database connection pool, avoiding the overhead of a one-to-one client connection. A repository could also maintain a cache, avoiding constant data requests to the underlying data store.

Object persistence is optional. By default, a class is not persistable. The programmer must make a conscious (but minimal) effort to make a class persistable, which is fully explained in the "Implementation" section of this chapter.

Implementation

As the class diagram in the "Object Model" section of this chapter clearly illustrates, the Repository design pattern comprises two components: a Repository and a PersistableObject. The PersistableObject interface defines the methods required for a class to read and write data into and out of some specified type of package (such as a byte array). A concrete class that implements the PersistableObject interface will use the properties and methods of the interface as the means by which to read and write its state into and out of the package defined by the interface. This in effect makes a class persistable. The Repository interface defines methods for storing stuff (an object's state) in a package to a data store, retrieving the stuff from a data store, reconstructing a persistable object, putting the stuff back into the specific type of package, and initiating the persistable object's read process on the package. Here's one possible implementation.

Within an ActiveX component project, instead of defining my own PersistableObject interface I've decided to take advantage of the class persistence features available in Visual Basic 6. This approach requires less code to be written, it's easy to implement, it's well documented in the online help, and since class persistence is an inherent part of the product, this approach is accessible to all Visual Basic programmers. To this end, you could build a single repository to persist all Visual Basic persistable objects.

Class persistence is available only to public creatable classes in an ActiveX component project. To turn class persistence on in an ActiveX component project set the *Instancing* property to a public creatable value (such as MultiUse in an ActiveX DLL) and set the *Persistable* property value to Persistable. Doing so will add three new class event handlers to the persistable class module: *Init-Properties*, *ReadProperties*, and *WriteProperties*. (See Figure 6-3 in Chapter 6.) In this implementation only the last two are used. Both the ReadProperties and WriteProperties events pass in a PropertyBag object parameter. As the name suggests, PropertyBag is conceptually a bag containing the property values of a persistable object. Property values are stored as a byte array inside the bag. The *ReadProperties* event handler implements the code to read the data out of the PropertyBag and into the persistable object's member variables that represent the properties (or state) of the object. The *WriteProperties* event handler implements the code to write a persistable object's property values (or state) into the

PropertyBag. The byte array that's in the PropertyBag is what's actually stored in the repository. When you implement both event handlers, your job is done as the persistable object designer. It isn't your concern how the persistent event handlers are invoked.

> **NOTE:** The Visual Basic class persistence features were also a major contributor to the Object By Value design pattern implementation. Refer to Chapter 6 for a more detailed explanation of that design pattern.

Next, add a class module to the project that defines a Repository interface. Set its *Instancing* property value to PublicNotCreatable since by definition an interface contains no implementation of its own. (Refer to Chapter 2 for in-depth coverage of interface implementations.) Finally, add a class module (ConcreteRepository) that implements the Repository interface. The concrete repository class will contain the code to invoke the *ReadProperties* and *WriteProperties* event handlers in a persistable object in order to store the object's state to a data store or to reincarnate an object with the state from a data store. The "Sample Application" section of this chapter includes code extracts that represent all participants of the Repository design pattern.

Sample Application

I have enhanced the off-line banking system sample application (BSTAM Banker) from the Object By Value design pattern (Chapter 6) to include the Repository design pattern. To summarize, the BSTAM Banker allows bank customers to perform an extensive list of banking services (such as depositing and withdrawing funds and checking the balance) against their accounts off-line. The benefits are mainly optimal system performance without the loss of functionality. Why shouldn't you have your cake and eat it too? In the Chapter 6 sample, customer savings accounts are maintained in a Scripting.Dictionary object by the BankSvr.Teller object. This requires the Teller object to have intimate knowledge about how to manipulate the Dictionary object. What if later you decide to store the accounts in a Sybase database? The Teller object's implementation would have to be rewritten using an appropriate Sybase database API.

Let's say, for example, you decide to use ADO. Manipulating data using ADO is not even remotely similar to using a Dictionary object. Sounds like a big change? Well it is. To remove from the business object layer the responsibility, complexity, and limitations associated with data manipulation in a specific type of data store, in this example I've replaced the Dictionary object with an implementation of the Repository design pattern. Since the SavingsAccount objects are persistable, half the design pattern is already implemented. All that is required is a Repository object. Hence this sample is an ideal fit. Finally, a new feature not found in the BSTAM Banker example in Chapter 6 has been added to allow a customer to update his or her account with the changes made offline. Account updates are ultimately stored in the Repository referenced by the Teller object. Since BSTAM Banker is already explained in great detail in Chapter 6, here I'll concentrate solely on the Repository design pattern implementation. For a complete source code disclosure, refer to the companion CD.

The key participants of the sample that make up the Repository design pattern include the following:

■ **SavingsAccount (resides in AccountLib.DLL)**   A concrete class that is persistable because its *Instancing* property value is set to MultiUse, its *Persistable* property value is set to Persistable, and it implements behavior for reading and writing its state to a byte array data stream by implementing the *ReadProperties* and *WriteProperties* class event handlers and by utilizing the PropertyBag object, as shown in the following code extract.

```
Private Sub Class_ReadProperties(PropBag As PropertyBag)
' Read in property values from a byte array via PropertyBag
' object.
    With PropBag
        m_strAccountNo = .ReadProperty("AccountNumber")
        m_strAccountOwner = .ReadProperty("AccountOwner")
        m_dblInterestRate = .ReadProperty("InterestRate")
        m_dblBalance = .ReadProperty("AccountBalance")
    End With
End Sub

Private Sub Class_WriteProperties(PropBag As PropertyBag)
' Write out property values to a byte array via PropertyBag
' object.
    With PropBag
        .WriteProperty "AccountNumber", m_strAccountNo
        .WriteProperty "AccountOwner", m_strAccountOwner
        .WriteProperty "InterestRate", m_dblInterestRate
        .WriteProperty "AccountBalance", m_dblBalance
    End With
End Sub
```

■ **Repository (resides in RepoLib.DLL)**   An interface that defines the methods for maintaining an object's state in a data store.

```
' Class Name:   Repository
' Note: Repository interface that defines the methods for
'        storing and retrieving a persistable object to and
'        from an underlying data store
'

Option Explicit

Public Function Add(PID As String, Obj As Object) As Boolean
End Function

Public Function Update(PID As String, Obj As Object) _
  As Boolean
End Function

Public Function Remove(PID As String) As Boolean
End Function

Public Function Retrieve(PID As String) As Object
End Function
```

■ **InMemRepository (resides in RepoLib.DLL)**   Concrete Repository class that implements the methods of the Repository interface for maintaining the state of persistable objects in an in-memory data store. A persistable object's state is stored in the form of a byte array inside a PropertyBag object. The repository must initiate the persistable object to read and write its state to and from a PropertyBag object. (Refer to the "Implementation" section of Chapter 6 for in-depth coverage on the PropertyBag.) The Transformer class defined in the Chapter 6 sample already provides this functionality, so instead of rewriting the code I've reused the Transformer. If a Transformer class wasn't already available, we would add the code shown in the comment directly above the calls to the Transformer object.

```
' Class Name:   InMemRepository
' Note: A concrete class that implements an in-memory data
'        store using a Scripting.Dictionary object
'

Implements Repository

Private m_ObjectStates As Scripting.Dictionary
```

(continued)

```
' Declared in the Globals.bas file.
' Transformer facilitates the persistence of an object's
' state to a byte array data stream stored in a PropertyBag
' object, which is explained in complete detail in the
' Implementation section of Chapter 6.
Public g_Transformer As ObjTransformLib.Transformer
    ⋮

Private Function Repository_Add(PID As String, _
    Obj As Object) As Boolean
' Adds a persistable object's state to the data store.
Dim byteArr() As Byte

    If Not m_ObjectStates.Exists(PID) Then
        ' This code must be implemented if you don't
        ' use the Transformer class from Chapter 6.
        '
        ' Dim pb As PropertyBag

        ' Set pb = New PropertyBag
        ' pb.WriteProperty PID, obj
        ' byteArr = pb.Contents

        byteArr = g_Transformer.ObjectToStream(PID, Obj)
        m_ObjectStates.Add PID, byteArr
        Repository_Add = True
    Else
        Repository_Add = False
    End If
End Function

    ⋮

Private Function Repository_Retrieve(PID As String) _
    As Object
' Creates a persistable object, reinitializes its state from
' the data store, and returns a reference to the object
    Dim vTemp As Variant
    Dim byteArr() As Byte

    If m_ObjectStates.Exists(PID) Then
        vTemp = m_ObjectStates(PID)
        byteArr = vTemp

        ' This code must be implemented if you don't
        ' use the Transformer class from Chapter 6.
```

```
                   '
                   ' Dim pb As PropertyBag

                   ' Set pb = New PropertyBag
                   ' pb.Contents = byteArr
                   ' Set Repository_Retrieve = pb.ReadProperty(PID)

                   Set Repository_Retrieve = g_Transformer _
                       .StreamToObject(PID, byteArr)
              Else
                   Set Repository_Retrieve = Nothing
              End If
        End Function

           ⋮
```

◾ **Teller (resides in BankSvr.EXE)**   The Repository design pattern is
put to use by the Teller object. SavingsAccount persistable objects
are added to the in-memory repository upon construction of the
Teller object via its *Class_Initialize* method:

```
' Teller.cls
'
Private Sub Class_Initialize()
    Dim sa As AccountLib.SavingsAccount
    Dim bRetcode As Boolean
    ' Declared as a member variable in Declarations section
    ' Private m_ObjectRep As RepoLib.Repository

    ' Construct in-memory repository
    Set m_ObjectRep = New RepoLib.InMemRepository

    ' Construct and initialize SavingsAccount objects, and
    ' store in in-memory repository.

    ' Maxwell Orion's account
    Set sa = New AccountLib.SavingsAccount
    With sa
        .AccountNumber = "orion0425"
        .AccountOwner = "Maxwell Orion"
        .InterestRate = 0.039
        .Deposit 30000#
    End With

    ' Add Maxwell's savings account object to in-memory
    ' repository.
    bRetcode = m_ObjectRep.Add(sa.AccountNumber, sa)
      ⋮
```

When a client requests a savings account, the Teller object retrieves the savings account object from the in-memory repository.

```
' Teller.cls
'
Public Function RetrieveAccount(AcctNo As String, ...) _
  As Boolean
    Dim sa As AccountLib.SavingsAccount
    ' Declared as a member variable in Declarations section
    ' Private m_ObjectRep As RepoLib.Repository

    ' Retrieve a SavingsAccount object from the
    ' SavingsAccount object repository (m_ObjectRep).
    Set sa = Nothing
    Set sa = m_ObjectRep.Retrieve(AcctNo)
    ⋮
```

When a client updates a savings account, the Teller object stores the state of the savings account object to the in-memory repository:

```
' Teller.cls
'
Public Function UpdateAccount(AcctNo As String, ...) _
  As Boolean
    Dim sa As AccountLib.SavingsAccount
    ' Declared as a member variable in Declarations section
    ' Private m_ObjectRep As RepoLib.Repository

    ⋮
    UpdateAccount = m_ObjectRep.Update(AcctNo, sa)
End Function
```

COMments

For best performance and reuse, define Repository classes in an ActiveX DLL. The underlying data store might be remote, so performance issues might already exist; there's no need to compound the problem by adding remote repository objects. Also remain cognizant of where the persistable objects reside. Ideally, persistence should be accomplished within the same COM apartment.

Related Patterns

The Repository design pattern, like the Object By Value design pattern (Chapter 6), requires the cooperation of persistable objects in order to be successful. However, unlike the Object By Value design pattern, the Repository design pattern doesn't require the client to have knowledge of how to produce a persisted data stream package. This is completely encapsulated by the repository. The Repository design pattern also shares attributes with the Object Factory design pattern (Chapter 8) because it abstracts the object creation process from the client code when retrieving an object from an underlying data store. You could define a repository interface for persisting a specific type of object. Each implementation can persist to a different type of data store, but the type of object to be created will remain static.

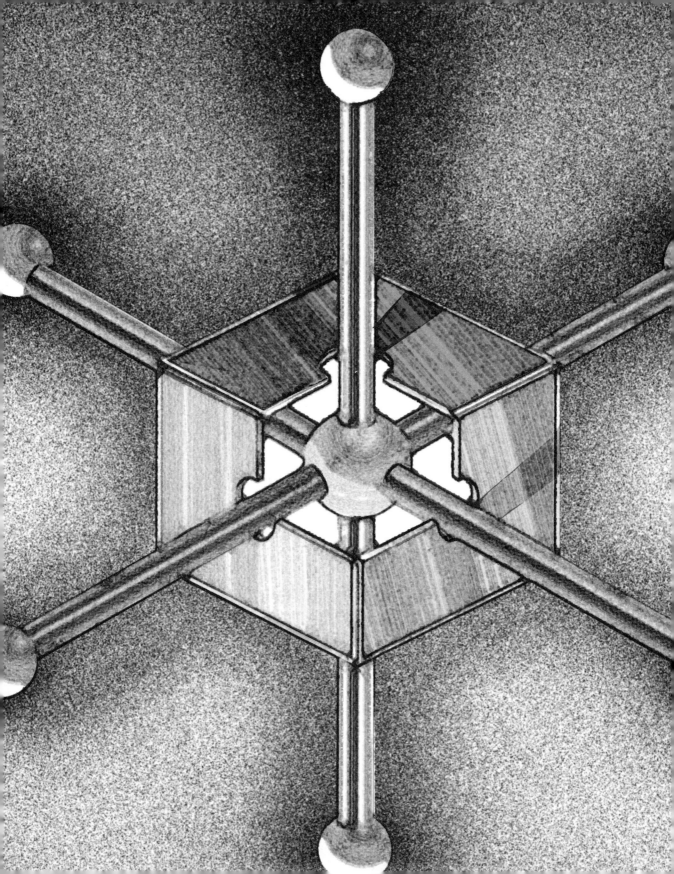

CHAPTER TWELVE

State

When multiple classes implement the same interface, each class defines distinct characteristics and behavior for the interface properties and methods. For example, both Golden Retrievers and Chihuahuas are distinct types of canines; from a software perspective, Canine is an interface that both the GoldenRetriever class and the Chihuahua class implement. Through the Canine interface, a client application could invoke the various methods that represent what canines do, such as bark, eat, run, and sleep. As you would expect, the behavior of these methods is unique between different classes—the amount of food a Chihuahua eats will normally be significantly different from the amount of food a Golden Retriever eats. Depending on the nature of the class, behavior within the same class might also be unique if the class is state sensitive. For example, canines, like most organic life forms, are sustained by a constant source of energy. Energy levels are maintained through a sufficient amount of food, exercise, rest, and so on. Level of energy is a state recognized by all classes of canine. Hunger is a substate of energy since it directly affects energy levels. When your pet Golden Retriever is hungry, possibly all behavioral patterns are altered. Moreover, the longer your Golden Retriever remains food deprived, the more apparent his change in behavior becomes. The same would be true for other canines such as Chihuahuas.

How do we account for such behavior changes in object-oriented development? The most common approach would be to use conditional language constructs within the interface method implementation of a class. These constructs determine the behavior to execute based on the state of the class implementation, which is represented by class member variables. Here's an example:

```
' Class Chihuahua
Implements Canine

Private m_iHungerLevel As Integer
    ⋮
```

(continued)

```
Private Sub Canine_Bark( )
    Select Case m_iHungerLevel
    Case 0 To 50
        MsgBox "Happy Bark"
    Case 51 To 100
        MsgBox "Agitated Bark"
    Case Is > 100
        MsgBox "Unhappy Bark"
    End Select
End Sub
```

As long as the class behavior isn't extremely sensitive to state changes, this approach is a sensible solution. The longer the list of accountable state conditions, the more complex and cumbersome this approach becomes. To avoid this complexity, consider using the State design pattern described in this chapter.

Purpose

Permit an object to change its behavior when its state changes by virtue of changing its class at run time.

Utilization

Use the State design pattern for the following purposes:

- To alter an object's behavior at run time based on changes to its internal state.

- To avoid compound conditional constructs based on an object's state. Instead define distinct classes that represent the specific behavior at a given state.

Scenario

NASA has hired you to build a spacecraft flight simulator that will be used to train astronauts how to maneuver in various atmospheric conditions. Learning to fly in the actual spacecraft would be impractical mainly because each spacecraft costs billions of dollars to manufacture and millions of dollars to maintain. Improper handling of the spacecraft could lead to structural damage, which could cost further millions of dollars to fix. A flight simulator is a cost-effective and practical alternative.

Environmental conditions such as weather patterns, temperature, and various forms of matter inside and outside the earth's atmosphere affect the state of the spacecraft. The maneuvering capabilities of the spacecraft change depending on its state. Because the factors affecting state and the variances in maneuverability are numerous, you decide to implement the State design pattern to manage all the possible changes in maneuvering behavior caused by state conditions. The class diagram in Figure 12-1 clearly depicts the design. The flight

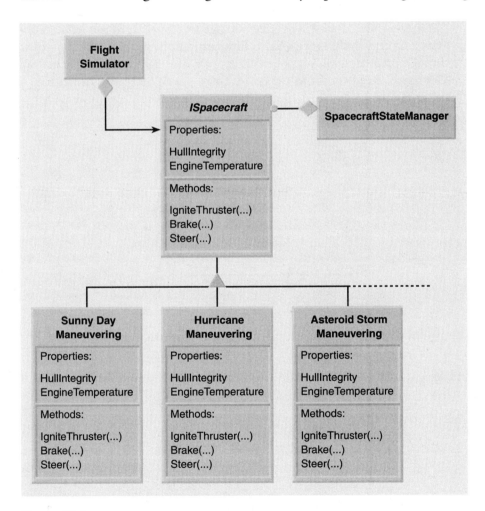

Figure 12-1.
The Flight Simulator application can effectively implement the State design pattern to create a scalable simulator that dynamically changes behavior based on external factors that affect its state.

simulator can start up in any initial state (such as Sunny Day Maneuvering or Hurricane Maneuvering). After startup, the simulator simulates an atmospheric change such as reentering the earth's atmosphere, which causes strong gravitational pull and ship contact with oxygen. These changes are manifested in the *HullIntegrity* property value, which affects the state of the spacecraft as determined by the SpacecraftStateManager object. As a result, the behavior of the methods *IgniteThruster*, *Break*, and *Steer* will dynamically change because of the intelligent state transition functionality implemented in the SpacecraftState-Manager object that will in effect change the ISpacecraft implementation at run time. In this design, the Flight Simulator application is oblivious to the State design pattern; it is simply referencing an object that supports the ISpacecraft interface. Read on for in-depth coverage of the State design pattern.

Object Model

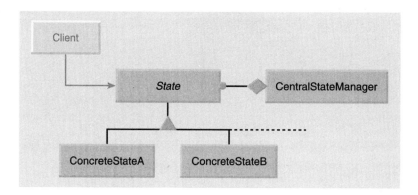

Roles

Here are the roles and functions of the State design pattern:

- **State** Specifies an interface expected by clients that encapsulates the behavior of a concrete State class instance. This interface is referred to as State because concrete classes that implement this interface are expected to be sensitive to state changes.

- **ConcreteState subclasses** Each subclass implements behavior associated with a specific state. The subclass doesn't maintain its state in local data-member variables. Instead it defers state management to the CentralStateManager object.

■ **CentralStateManager** A concrete class that performs the following actions:

❑ Serves as the single central repository for all state objects within a State design pattern instance. State is determined based on the values of data member variables.

❑ •Defines intelligent state transition behavior by returning a reference to the appropriate ConcreteState object based on the current state. This results in dynamic behavior changes.

Relationships

To obtain the dynamically changing behavior desired, a client must reference a ConcreteState object that in turn maintains a reference to a CentralStateManager object. Changes submitted by the client that affect state are forwarded to the CentralStateManager object.

The CentralStateManager object serves as the single central repository for state storage. It contains references to all available State objects. It performs the correct state transition behavior by returning a reference to the appropriate State object based on changes to its internal state.

When a client invokes behavior on a State object after a state change, this invocation will either be handled by the actual object or will be delegated to a different state object determined by the CentralStateManager. Figure 12-2 illustrates an object structure in which a client created a ConcreteStateA object. As a result, the ConcreteStateA object creates a CentralStateManager object that in turn creates all other State objects available. This diagram shows that without any state changes, invocations are handled internally by the original State object (ConcreteStateA) created by the client. Figure 12-3 illustrates the process that takes place when state changes that are sensitive to the CentralStateManager object occur. Those changes have caused the CentralStateManager object to return a reference to the ConcreteStateD object. Invocations to the Concrete-StateA object will now be delegated to the ConcreteStateD object until further changes to state occur that result in a state transition by the Central-StateManager.

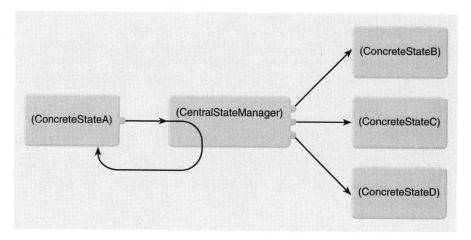

Figure 12-2.
Object structure of an initial state A determined by the ConcreteStateA object. Because no state changes have occurred yet, the CentralState-Manager object refers the ConcreteStateA object back to itself.

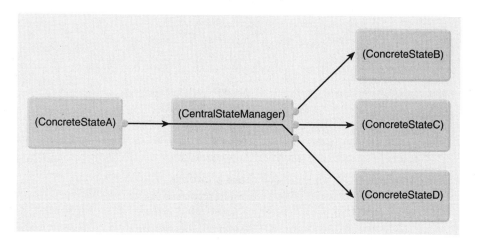

Figure 12-3.
Object structure of a State object that initially started out in state A (determined by the client's choice to create a ConcreteStateA object) that has been affected by state changes causing the CentralStateManager object to return a reference to ConcreteStateD. Client invocations on the ConcreteStateA object will be delegated to ConcreteStateD.

Ramifications

■ **Simplifies complex monolithic conditional constructs**   If you're developing a system in which new business rules (new behavior) are constantly being introduced based on changes in the state of business objects, a single method implementation that utilizes a *Select Case* or *If...Then...Else* construct will soon become unwieldy. Separating state-specific behavior into separate subclasses keeps the code manageable and readable.

■ **Permits the dynamic addition of new behavior at run time**   This solution is a perfect fit for systems in which business rules are constantly changing and the time to market is critical. A stock portfolio trading system that automatically trades stocks is an ideal candidate for this type of solution. Imagine changing the trading strategy of an auto-trading system by registering new ConcreteTradeState objects and unregistering existing ConcreteTradeState objects on the fly. This strategy would require the existing code to be recompiled and the system to be restarted to take advantage of the new system enhancements. The State design pattern allows you to avoid this situation. It also provides the benefit of enabling and disabling specific business rules with no recourse. The need to enable and disable specific business rules would be a severe handicap in a single compound conditional construct because it would require further modifications to the conditional checks. For unpredictable changes of events, such as dramatic market swings, an adjustment to the current set of business rules might be required for an immediate correction to a stock portfolio. Such an adjustment would be impossible with the single conditional construction approach.

■ **Concrete state objects are sharable**   Concrete state objects all by themselves are stateless. These classes of objects represent state-specific behavior within an applied context that is controlled by a central state manager object. Concrete state objects can be made sharable in any context by incorporating a generic central state manager that can be used with any kind of state object and disabling the use of the application-specific central state manager.

■ **Concrete state objects are self-reliant class objects**   The State design pattern allows a client to create an instance of any State subclass. Each subclass implements the behavior required to participate in the State design pattern. Each subclass also represents a unique initial state of an object when the object is first created.

■ **The State design pattern can increase the number of objects in memory** Replacing a monolithic conditional language construct with this design pattern will result in more objects residing in memory. To remedy this situation, objects can be created on demand and released when their reference counts hit zero, or the most frequently used objects can be maintained in a cache.

Implementation

You have a few options for designing and implementing the State design pattern. Your design will obviously influence your implementation. In the design we'll be discussing, all state concrete classes implement the same interface expected by a client application. A single central state manager class implements the state transition behavior that results in dynamic behavior changes at run time.

Implementing state subclasses is straightforward. In a class module, use the keyword *Implements* and implement all methods of the expected interface (State). Ensure that the class's *Instancing* property is of the public and creatable variety to allow reuse in different contexts. Next define a reference to a central state manager. All invocations to state interface methods that result in state changes should be forwarded to the central state manager. All method invocations that preempt behavior should be delegated to the appropriate state subclass object. A general rule of thumb is that class property settings (Property Let or Property Set procedures) should reflect state changes, and class method invocations should represent behavior. Here's a code extract of a BullishTrader class module that represents a state subclass implementation:

```
' BullishTrader.cls
Implements Trader

Private m_TradeSystem As TradeSystem
Private m_tsm As TraderStateManager
⋮

Private Property Let Trader_StockPrice(Stock As String, _
                                      RHS As Double)
    m_tsm.StockPrice(Stock) = RHS
End Property

Private Sub Trader_ExecOrder()
    Dim newTrader As Trader

    Set newTrader = m_tsm.getTraderObject(Me)
    If TypeName(newTrader) = TypeName(Me) Then
```

```
        Call m_TradeSystem.Buy(1000, Stock, m_tsm.StockPrice _
                        + ONE_UP_TICK)
    Else
        newTrader.ExecOrder
    End If
End Sub
    ⋮
```

Notice that setting the *StockPrice* property value is delegated to the Trader-StateManager (CentralStateManager) object. Depending on the stock price change, the state of the Trader object might or might not be affected. As the *Trader.ExecOrder* method implementation illustrates, first you call the *TraderStateManager.getTraderObject* method to determine the correct Trader object that needs to be created. If the price hasn't moved against whatever threshold is determined by the TradeStateManager object, the BullishTrader object will get a reference to itself back and will run through its implementation. Otherwise, the BullishTrader object will delegate to the object referenced by the *newTrader* object variable.

Implementing the CentralStateManager object requires a bit more work. It must maintain state and define state transition behavior based on state changes. To allow for the introduction of new behavior at run time based on state changes, the CentralStateManager object must have access to resources at run time that can be updated by some means external to it, such as a database. New conditions can also be introduced in the same manner. Building on the Trader theme from the last code extract, the following extract is a code sample of the TraderStateManager class. The TraderStateManager object maintains a Dictionary of Trader subclass objects that could have been populated either at class initialization time or on demand. When the *StockPrice* property value is updated, a property dirty flag is set to true to indicate to the *getTraderObject* method that it needs to evaluate the state prior to determining the correct Trader subclass object reference to return.

```
' TraderStateManager.cls

Private Property Let StockPrice(Stock As String, RHS As Double)
    m_Security.StockName = Stock
    m_Security.StockPrice = RHS
    m_bIsDirty = True
End Property

Public Function getTraderObject(currTrader As Trader) As Trader
    If m_bIsDirty Then
        ' Go through a set of rules to determine which Trader object
        ' reference to return.
```

(continued)

```
        If...Then
            Set Trader = m_Traders("BearishTrader")
        End If
        ⋮
        Else
            Set Trader = currTrader
        End If
End Sub
```

This TraderStateManager class implementation is obviously simplified, but the point is that it maintains the state and that a reference to the appropriate Trader object cached in a Dictionary is returned from *getTraderObject*. The sample application for this chapter covers in detail a full implementation of the State design pattern.

Sample Application

To demonstrate the effective use of the State design pattern, I've decided to resurrect a fad that died a few years ago—the virtual pet. To better appreciate the source code implementation, I recommend that you install and run the application (VPet.exe) off the companion CD.

This virtual pet is a Chihuahua. When you run the application, you will be presented with the dialog box shown in Figure 12-4, which lets you select one of four initial states for your Chihuahua: Happy, Content, Moderate, and Discontent. Select the state you want your Chihuahua to be initially created in, and click OK.

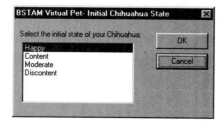

Figure 12-4.
Select the initial state for your virtual Chihuahua.

Your virtual Chihuahua window now appears, as shown in Figure 12-5. Notice the three progress bars on the right: Food Consumption, Bladder Control, and Affection Fulfillment. These progress bars represent the state of your

Chihuahua. The progress bars for food and affection at 100 percent and the progress bar for bladder at 0 percent indicate a happy Chihuahua. Varying percentages in the progress bars represent your Chihuahua at different states. On the left, you'll notice a face that looks nothing like a Chihuahua. Because of time constraints (and my lack of artistic abilities), I improvised by using the yellow face icons that ship with Microsoft Visual Basic to visually represent the expressions of a Chihuahua to help reflect the mood of your virtual pet based on its current state. In addition to the yellow face expressions, there is a Label control to the right of the face that displays the current Chihuahua class of object, in this case HappyChihuahua. Below that is a TextBox control that displays textual feedback from your pet about how it's feeling. By means of a timer control, every so often the food and affection levels deplete and the bladder level increases. If you continue to neglect your Chihuahua, it will eventually become an unhappy puppy. You take care of your Chihuahua by clicking on the three buttons located below the TextBox control. The Feed button returns Food Consumption to 100 percent. The Walk button allows your Chihuahua to empty its bladder, returning the Bladder Control level to 0 percent. The Throw Frisbee button returns the Affection Fulfillment level to 100 percent based on the fact that you're playing virtual Frisbee with your Chihuahua and giving it the attention it desperately requires.

Figure 12-5.
Monitor and control the health and happiness of your virtual Chihuahua.

Now that you've bonded with your new pet Chihuahua, let's take a look at the source code behind the application that makes it seem so real. Your virtual pet Chihuahua is an implementation of the State design pattern that spans a few components, as depicted in Table 12-1.

Table 12-1. **Components of the Virtual Pet**

Components	Contents
Dog.tlb	Type library that contains definitions for the following interfaces:
	IDog (State) interface is expected by the VPet application (Client).
	IDogFactory interface is used instead of the *New* keyword to gain more control of the object creation process.
	IDogStateRule interface is an abstraction of a rule used to determine state transitions.
ChihuahuaStSvr.DLL	Contains the IDog (State) concrete classes that represent a Chihuahua's behavior at different states.
ChihuahuaRuleSvr.DLL	Contains the IDogStateRule concrete classes that define the rules used in determining state transitions.
CSMSvr.DLL	Contains the DogStateManager (CentralStateManager) class that defines the Chihuahua state transition behavior.
DogState.mdb	Microsoft Access database that maintains a list of class names that support the interfaces IDog and IDogStateRule.
VPet.exe	Client application that references objects that support the IDog interface.

The State design pattern includes these key participants:

- **IDog (State)** Defines a dog interface expected by the VPet.exe application (Client). The classes that implement this interface are expected to be sensitive to state changes.

- **IDog implementation classes (ConcreteState subclasses)** Defined in ChihuahuaStSvr.DLL are classes HappyChihuahua, ContentChihuahua, ModerateChihuahua, and DiscontentChihuahua that implement the IDog interface. These classes provide behavior associated with a particular mood of the Chihuahua and supply the intelligence required to collaborate with the DogStateManager (DSM) when state changes occur. For instance, examine the next code listing, extracted from the HappyChihuahua class module.

```
' HappyChihuahua.cls
Implements DogLib.IDog

' Central State Manager
Private m_dsm As CSMSvr.DogStateManager
    ⋮

' IDog.Affection
Private Property Get IDog_Affection() As Integer
    IDog_Affection = m_dsm.Affection
End Property

Private Property Let IDog_Affection(RHS As Integer)
    m_dsm.Affection = RHS
End Property

' IDog.Bark()
Private Function IDog_Bark() As String
    Dim theDog As DogLib.IDog

    m_sNewClassName = m_dsm.getDogObject(m_sThisClassName, _
                                    m_DelegateDog)

    If m_sThisClassName <> m_sNewClassName Then
        IDog_Bark = m_DelegateDog.Bark
    Else
        If m_nIndex < 2 Then
            m_nIndex = m_nIndex + 1
        Else
            m_nIndex = 0
        End If
        IDog_Bark = m_Barks(m_nIndex)
    End If
End Function
```

Notice the HappyChihuahua class defers all read/write property value operations to the DSM referenced by *m_dsm*, as demonstrated in the Property Let and Property Get procedures for the *Affection* property. Property values represent the state. The effects of state changes are apparent when IDog methods are invoked, as illustrated in the HappyChihuahua implementation of the *IDog.Bark* method. To dynamically determine the appropriate bark behavior, the DSM is queried for a reference to the correct IDog implementation (object that implements IDog), which is returned in the *m_DelegateDog* argument. The DSM also returns the class name of the object that defines the behavior to be employed in the *m_sThisClassName* argument. If the class name is the same as the class that made the call to the DSM, the caller's implementation is executed; otherwise the implementation is delegated to the object reference returned by the DSM (*m_sNewClassName*). Regardless of the specific property or method implementation, you should consider the collaboration with the DSM as the State class implementation template and reapply it in all classes that support the IDog interface.

- **DogStateManager (CentralStateManager)** A class that serves as the central state repository for all IDog implementation classes. It also defines state transition behavior that involves returning the appropriate IDog implementation class object associated with the current state. To make for a more elegant solution, I decided to make not only the variety of IDog implementations but also the state transition rules dynamically configurable from a database. I accomplish this by defining the StateTrans table in the DogState Access database and including Rule and TrueOutcome fields that store IDogStateRule and IDogFactory implementation class names, respectively. (See Figure 12-6.) In the *DogStateManager.Init* method, a query is run against the StateTrans table to create IDogStateRule and IDogFactory objects. IDogStateRule objects and IDog objects created via IDogFactory objects are cached in arrays in the order in which the rules will be evaluated as determined by the EvalOrder field in the StateTrans table. In the *DogStateManager.getDogObject* method, the state transition algorithm, by means of a *For* loop, traverses the array of IDogStateRule objects from 0 to *n*. The first rule that evaluates to True results in exiting the *For* loop after setting the reference to the IDog implementation that corresponds to the rule. Implementing the DogStateManager is the most complex part of the State design pattern, but it has to be written only once. Adding new rules and state objects (IDog implementations) can be done without disruption to this code.

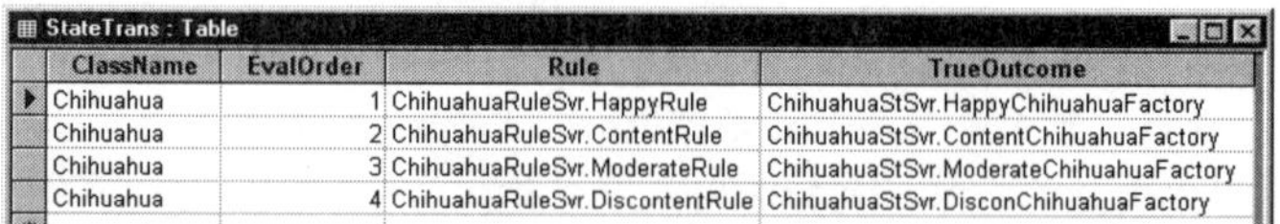

ClassName	EvalOrder	Rule	TrueOutcome
Chihuahua	1	ChihuahuaRuleSvr.HappyRule	ChihuahuaStSvr.HappyChihuahuaFactory
Chihuahua	2	ChihuahuaRuleSvr.ContentRule	ChihuahuaStSvr.ContentChihuahuaFactory
Chihuahua	3	ChihuahuaRuleSvr.ModerateRule	ChihuahuaStSvr.ModerateChihuahuaFactory
Chihuahua	4	ChihuahuaRuleSvr.DiscontentRule	ChihuahuaStSvr.DisconChihuahuaFactory

Figure 12-6.
StateTrans table that primarily stores the IDogStateRule and IDogFactory class names used by the DogStateManager to dynamically configure itself for participation in the State design pattern.

```
' DogStateManager.cls

Private m_sClassName As String
Private m_iAffection As Integer
:

Private m_bIsDirty As Boolean
Private m_rsDogClassInfo As ADODB.Recordset
Private m_Connection As ADODB.Connection
Private m_Rule() As IDogStateRule
Private m_Dog() As IDog

Public Function Init(ClassName As String) As Boolean
    Dim df As DogLib.IDogFactory
    Dim sConnect As String
    Dim sUID As String
    Dim sqlDogInfo As String
    Dim nRecCount As Integer
    Dim i As Integer

    sqlDogInfo = "SELECT Rule, TrueOutCome " & _
                 "FROM StateTrans " & _
                 "WHERE ClassName='Chihuahua' " & _
                 "ORDER BY EvalOrder;"
    sUID = "Admin"
    sConnect = "Provider=Microsoft.Jet.OLEDB.4.0; " & _
               "Data Source=" & App.Path & "\DogState.mdb"

    ' Establish connection.
    m_Connection.Open sConnect, sUID
    If m_Connection.State <> adStateOpen Then
        Init = False
        Exit Function
    End If

    ' Retrieve Rule and State class names from DogState
    ' Access database.
    m_rsDogClassInfo.Open sqlDogInfo, m_Connection, _
                          adOpenStatic
    nRecCount = m_rsDogClassInfo.RecordCount
    If nRecCount = 0 Then
        m_rsDogClassInfo.Close
        Init = False
        Exit Function
    End If

    ' Cache Rule objects and Dog (State) objects in arrays.
    ReDim m_Rule(0 To nRecCount - 1) As IDogStateRule
```

(continued)

```
      ReDim m_Dog(0 To nRecCount - 1) As IDog
      i = 0
      m_rsDogClassInfo.MoveFirst
      Do While Not m_rsDogClassInfo.EOF
          Set m_Rule(i) = _
              CreateObject(m_rsDogClassInfo("Rule"))
          Set df = _
              CreateObject(m_rsDogClassInfo("TrueOutcome"))
          Set m_Dog(i) = df.CreateInstance(False)
          m_rsDogClassInfo.MoveNext
          i = i + 1
      Loop
      m_rsDogClassInfo.Close

      Init = True
  End Function

  Public Property Get Affection() As Integer
      Affection = m_iAffection
  End Property

  Public Property Let Affection(RHS As Integer)
  ' Store property value and set dirty flag to true to
  ' indicate to the state transition algorithm that it needs
  ' to reevaluate.
  ⋮
          m_iAffection = RHS
          m_bIsDirty = True
  ⋮
  End Property

  Public Function getDogObject(inCurrentDogClass As String, _
      outDogObject As IDog) As String
  ' Employs state transition algorithm to determine the
  ' reference to the appropriate IDog object to return to the
  ' outDogObject object variable.

      Dim i As Integer

      ' Perform state transition algorithm only if any
      ' property values have been changed.
      If m_bIsDirty = True Then
          For i = 0 To UBound(m_Rule)
              If m_Rule(i).Evaluate(m_iAffection, _
                          m_iBladderLevel, _
                          m_iFoodConsumption) = True Then
```

```
                    m_sClassName = TypeName(m_Dog(i))
                    If m_sClassName <> inCurrentDogClass Then
                        Set outDogObject = m_Dog(i)
                    End If
                    Exit For
                End If
            Next i
            m_bIsDirty = False
        End If

        If Len(m_sClassName) = 0 Then
            getDogObject = inCurrentDogClass
        Else
            getDogObject = m_sClassName
        End If
    End Function
```

Related Patterns

The State design pattern could be considered a state-sensitive Smart Proxy (Chapter 7). It evaluates the state it's in and determines whether the current object is suitable to perform the requested operations. If not, it delegates the requests to the qualified object. All the while, the client remains incognizant. As far as the client is concerned, the object it is referencing is doing all the work.

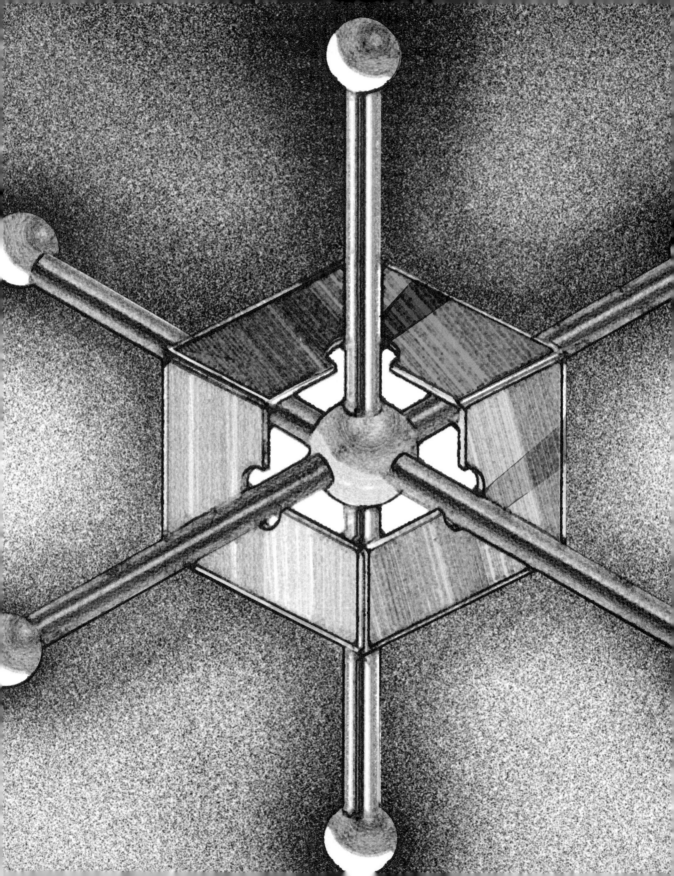

CHAPTER THIRTEEN

Event Service

Objects interact with one another through the interfaces they support. For example, if object A wants to request a service from object B, it must invoke an interface method implemented in object B. Standard invocations require object B to be available at the time of the request; if it isn't, an error is raised. Method invocations are usually synchronous: that is, object A will have to wait for object B to finish processing the request before continuing.

Interfaces permit polymorphic behavior, allowing different class objects that support the same interface to be referenced by a client application at run time. The interfaces themselves are static, however, so the roles and relationships among objects are statically defined in terms of the interfaces they support. For example, in the following code, Client App Module 1 defines an *InvokeBark* method that expects an object that supports the ICanine interface. Client App Module 2 calls the *InvokeBark* method and passes it a German-Shepherd object. This approach is dynamic in that the *InvokeBark* method can accept any class of object that supports the ICanine interface, not just a GermanShepherd object. Through this one invocation, different classes of objects would produce different behavior for the same *ICanine.Bark* method call. This approach is static in that the *InvokeBark* method expects the interface ICanine. If the GermanShepherd object doesn't support the ICanine interface, the Microsoft Visual Basic compiler will raise a "Type Mismatch" error. If no object is passed, the Visual Basic compiler will raise an error pertaining to an attempt to use a null object reference.

```
' Client App Module 1
Public Sub InvokeBark(Dog As ICanine)
    Dog.Bark
End Sub

' Client App Module 2
Dim myDog As GermanShepherd

Set myDog = New GermanShepherd
Call InvokeBark(myDog)
```

Static roles and relationships compel you to assemble your software system in a specific way. This requirement inherently forces dependencies between components, which can result in a monolithic object-based system. One way to minimize dependency is to make your interfaces as generic as possible. An example on the extreme end would be the equivalent of the Microsoft Windows SendMessage API. If you define an interface method that takes a Long as the first parameter to indicate the action to perform, followed by a varying set of parameters (*ParamArray*) for inputs and outputs as shown in the following code, this single interface could literally be used by all classes of objects to fulfill any role and by a designer to establish any type of relationship.

```
' All-purpose interface class module
Public Sub Invoke(Action As Long, ParamArray Params())
End Sub
```

However, this freedom eliminates the benefit of self-describing interfaces that are intuitive for the programmer developing the system. Another drawback is that the compiler can do only minimal compile-time strong type checking. As a result, the onus of enforcing a contract between the object requesting a service (client) and the object providing the service (server) moves out of the compiler and into the objects' implementations. The client and the server must agree on parameter inputs and outputs for successful collaboration. Taking this approach is obviously too drastic. The Event Service design pattern described in this chapter is a better alternative because it allows you to design a system in which a client requesting a service is decoupled from the server providing it. You can therefore establish dynamic roles and relationships without sacrificing the benefits of static interfaces.

Purpose

Decouple the direct communication between objects to minimize the interdependent relationships that constrain the ability to change or extend a system.

Utilization

Use the Event Service design pattern for the following purposes:

- To extend a system's functionality in a plug-and-play fashion
- To dynamically assemble relationships between objects

Scenario

A common approach to improving the debugging process of an application is to include logging functionality. Let's assume you're concerned about logging errors that the application raises or captures. You want the flexibility of logging the errors to any medium, such as a text file, a window, e-mail, the Microsoft Windows 2000 Event Viewer log, or any imaginable media that become available. Programming support for various media directly into the application is definitely not a scalable solution. You can solve this problem by using the Event Service design pattern to incorporate a logging mechanism into the application. This mechanism decouples the application that publishes the message from the subscriber—in this case, the various media that receive the message. Figure 13-1 illustrates a plausible object diagram of such an application.

Notice the reference to a LogEventService object, which facilitates the existence of a LogEventChannel object. The application also maintains a reference to the LogPublisher object, which is provided by the LogEventService

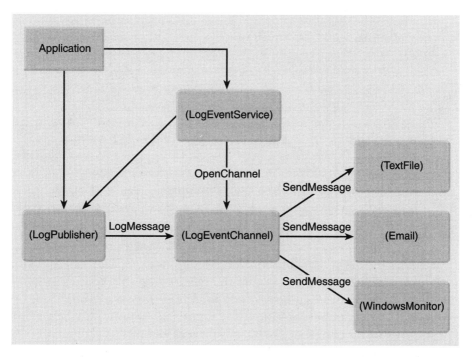

Figure 13-1.
Application log event service object model.

object. Additionally, the TextFile, Email, and WindowsMonitor objects are registered subscribers to the LogEventChannel object for the application, and the application is oblivious to their existence. The LogEventChannel object determines the registration policy. Your application simply logs messages by invoking the LogPublisher object's *LogMessage* method. The LogPublisher object in turn submits the message to the LogEventChannel object that ultimately notifies the subscribers (TextFile, Email, and WindowsMonitor).

Object Model

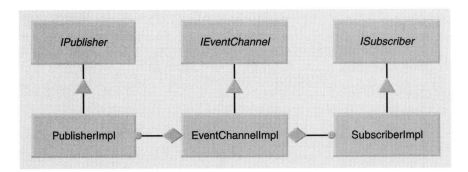

Roles

The roles and functions of the Event Service design pattern are as follows:

- **IEventChannel** An interface that serves as the intermediary between publishers and subscribers of events.

- **EventChannelImpl** A concrete implementation class of IEvent-Channel. The process of event flow is defined in the EventChannel-Impl class. For example, the EventChannelImpl class dictates whether events are synchronous or asynchronous, determines the priority of delivery, and determines the relationships between events, publishers, and subscribers. A common implementation might include a single publisher submitting events but many subscribers responding to the arrival of events in the event channel.

- **IPublisher** An interface that defines methods for publishing events on an EventChannelImpl instance.

- **PublisherImpl**   A concrete implementation class of IPublisher. Because the EventChannelImpl class determines how published events are handled, it is typical for the PublisherImpl class to have an intimate relationship with the event channel. Typically, the event channel programmer would also develop the publisher.

- **ISubscriber**   An interface that defines unique events (method signatures).

- **SubscriberImpl**   A concrete class that implements the ISubscriber interface. This class represents a unique class of subscriber. Implementing the ISubscriber interface and registering an instance of this class with the event channel makes this class responsive to events published on the event channel. Refer to the "Implementation" section of this chapter for further details.

Relationships

An application that wants to publish events must obtain a reference to an object that supports an IPublisher interface. An event is published when an IPublisher method implementation is invoked. The implementation of IPublisher must collaborate with an event channel to submit the event. An event channel is an object that supports the IEventChannel interface. The event channel decouples the publisher from the subscriber. When a publisher submits its event, the event channel routes the event to its subscribers by means of an ISubscriber interface. Subscribers are objects that support the ISubscriber interface and are registered to be called by an event channel. Your application design determines how a subscriber is registered. The "Implementation" section of this chapter will explore a few possible alternatives.

Ramifications

- **Decouples direct communication between objects**   As a result, there are no direct dependencies between objects in the relationship. Both publishers and subscribers can change autonomously.

- **Enables an extensible behavioral application environment**   New behavior can be introduced via the registration of a new subscriber.

■ **Centralizes invocation response behavior** A change in process requires defining a new event channel implementation rather than changing application code. For example, prioritizing the order of subscriber notification or whether notification should be asynchronous or synchronous can be defined in different event channel implementations.

■ **Minimizes explicit object interaction** An Event Service design pattern lessens the need for various APIs to be referenced in a client application to enlist new services. A client application publishes a single event to an event channel. New services are enlisted by means of newly registered subscribers.

Implementation

Visual Basic offers three different language features to facilitate the creation of an event service: *AddressOf*, Class events, and interface-based programming.

AddressOf

Registering a function to handle a specific event is a feature that has always existed in low-level languages such as C and C++. This feature is commonly referred to as a *callback function*. Typically, the program registering the callback function doesn't invoke it directly; a callback function is registered with a run-time service that invokes it when a particular event occurs. The address in memory of the callback function is registered with the run-time service, which gives the service the ability to locate and call the function. An ideal example of a run-time service is the Windows operating system. The Windows API contains a set of DLLs that in turn contain functions. Some of these functions enable you to subscribe to run-time service events via a callback registration.

Registering callback functions in Microsoft Visual Basic is possible, but not without limitations. Using the Visual Basic *AddressOf* unary operator followed by the function name will return the address of a Visual Basic function that can be passed to a Windows API function for callback registration. The Visual Basic callback function can be defined only in a standard module. Furthermore, Visual Basic doesn't support function pointers; therefore, it can't be the run-time service invoking the callback by means of the *AddressOf* operator. But despite these drawbacks, *AddressOf* is an incredibly useful language feature that permits

Visual Basic programmers to tap into some sophisticated run-time services such as those provided by Windows. For example, in the following code extract, a call is made to the Windows API *CreateThread* function by passing the address of the *CallMe* Visual Basic user-defined function. The Windows operating system run-time service will hand this address to the newly created thread to execute the function at that address.

```
hThread = CreateThread(0, 0, AddressOf CallMe, 0, 0, m_lThreadId)
' Do some work.
⋮

' The CallMe function is defined in a standard module.
Public Sub CallMe()
    ' Do some work.
    ⋮
End Sub
```

The *CreateThread* function executes asynchronously, so the code following it will immediately continue to execute. When the spawning of the new thread event occurs, the run-time service will invoke the *CallMe* function. Visual Basic doesn't have native language support for spawning threads in a process, but because it provides the *AddressOf* operator you can still take advantage of this most critical operating-system feature. Callbacks might have different semantics than the Event Service design pattern described in this chapter, but the concept is the same. The callback function signature is equivalent to the ISubscriber interface. *CallMe* is equivalent to a concrete class implementation of ISubscriber. A conceptual publisher and event channel exist inside the run-time service. Callbacks are therefore a valid Event Service design pattern implementation.

Class Events

Visual Basic allows you to declare, raise (publish), and handle (subscribe) events within Class and Form class modules. These abilities are all that's required to implement the constituents of the Event Service design pattern, which include the event channel, publisher, and subscriber. Events are declared and raised within the same class. By definition, this makes a class with declared events an event channel. Depending on your design, the publisher can be implicit or explicit. An implicit publisher exists when there is no explicit publisher interface but rather events are raised in the class methods wherever the programmer decides it is necessary. This is a good approach when you need to provide hooks for extending specific components within a system. The following code extract defines a TravelAgent class module that declares OnBookReservation and OnPurchaseTicket events. These events are raised during the booking and ticket purchasing processes.

```
' TravelAgent.cls

Option Explicit

Public Event OnBookReservation(ByVal Res As Reservation)
Public Event OnPurchaseTicket(ByVal Tick As Ticket)

Public Function BookReservation() As Reservation
    Dim theRes As Reservation
    ' The booking code...
    RaiseEvent OnBookReservation(theRes)
    BookReservation = theRes
End Function

Public Function PurchaseTicket() As Ticket
    Dim theTicket As Ticket
    ' The purchase ticket code...
    RaiseEvent OnPurchaseTicket(theTicket)
    PurchaseTicket = theTicket
End Function
```

Events are declared Public and the declaration includes the keyword *Event* followed by a method prototype similar to a subroutine. Events are raised within class methods using the keyword *RaiseEvent* followed by one of the declared events. In Visual Basic and COM–speak, an object such as TravelAgent that raises events is called an *event source*. Refer to the Visual Basic documentation for a complete explanation of how to implement an event source class.

Let's assume that TravelAgent objects are created within an electronic travel reservation system exclusively to facilitate the booking and purchasing of airline tickets. However, you want to make it convenient for the customer to book hotel accommodations and car rental reservations along with air travel. Because the TravelAgent object raises events, you don't have to make enhancements to the existing code base. New class modules compiled in a different project (DLL or EXE) can plug into the system by subscribing to the events raised by the TravelAgent object. Event subscribers are class modules that declare module-level object variables of an event source object's class using the keyword *WithEvents*. The following code extract reflects the definitions you would expect to find in a HotelAgent class and a CarAgent class that are subscribing to (or handling) events raised by a TravelAgent object.

```
Option Explicit

Private WithEvents aTravelAgent As TravelAgent

Public Sub Attach(ta As TravelAgent)
    Set aTravelAgent = ta
End Sub

Public Sub Detach()
    Set aTravelAgent = Nothing
End Sub

Private Sub aTravelAgent_OnBookReservation(ByVal Res As Reservation)
    ' Add event handler code here.
End sub

Private Sub aTravelAgent_OnPurchaseTicket(ByVal Tick As Ticket)
    ' Add event handler code here.
End Sub
```

Notice that the object variable *aTravelAgent* is declared as a type of TravelAgent event source class using the keyword *WithEvents*. Consequently in the Visual Basic class module editor, *aTravelAgent* will appear in the Object drop-down list box. Selecting it will result in the OnBookReservation and OnPurchaseTicket events appearing in the Procedure drop-down list box. To add an event handler for a given event, simply select the event from the Procedure drop-down list box. Event handlers are defined as private subroutines. They are named based on the name of the event prefixed with the name of the object variable that was declared *WithEvents* and an underscore (*aTravelAgent_OnBookReservation*). To receive events from a particular Travel-Agent object, a reference to the object must be maintained. The *Attach* and *Detach* methods facilitate the acquisition and release of a TravelAgent object reference. Declaring an event source object variable using *WithEvents*, defining event handler subroutines, and obtaining a reference to an associated event source object, together allow you to subscribe to events raised by a referenced event source object.

Interface-Based Programming

Interface-based programming is by far the most effective means of implementing the Event Service design pattern. Visual Basic includes the language features required to fully support this concept. In interface-based programming, clients program to an interface and server objects expose and support interfaces expected by clients. (Refer to Chapter 2 for in-depth coverage of interfaces.) For maximum effectiveness, an event service should be publicly accessible to publishers and subscribers in a different space (DLLs and EXEs running local or remote). To achieve this effectiveness, you are required to create an ActiveX type of project.

In an ActiveX project, define a class module for each interface in the Event Service design pattern. Interfaces have no implementation and can't be instantiated. Therefore these class modules should only have public properties and methods defined with no implementation. Also the class *Instancing* property value should be set to PublicNotCreatable to prohibit instantiation from a client. The following code extract illustrates plausible partial IEventChannel and ISubscriber interface definitions.

```
' IEventChannel.cls

Option Explicit

Public Function Advise(Context As String, _
   Subscriber As ISubscriber) As Long
End Sub

Public Sub Unadvise(Context As String, Cookie As Long)
End Sub
    ⋮

' ISubscriber.cls

Option Explicit

Public Sub Push(ByVal Context As String, ByVal vData As Variant)
End Sub
    ⋮
```

Within the same project you would typically define a concrete class that implements the IEventChannel interface, similar to the following partial code extract.

```
' EventChannelImpl.cls

Option Explicit

Implements IEventChannel

Private m_ctxList As Scripting.Dictionary
Private m_nCookie As Long

Private Function IEventChannel_Advise(Context As String, _
                        Subscriber As ISubscriber) As Long
    Dim ctx As Scripting.Dictionary

    ' Obtain Dictionary object for Context.
    ' If one doesn't exist, create it.
    If m_ctxList.Exists(Context) Then
        Set ctx = m_ctxList(Context)
    Else
        Set ctx = New Scripting.Dictionary
        Call m_ctxList.Add(Context, ctx)
    End If

    ' Create new cookie.
    m_nCookie = m_nCookie + 1

    ' Add Subscriber to context object with new associated cookie.
    Call ctx.Add(CStr(m_nCookie), Subscriber)

    ' Return cookie to client.
    ' Client must use cookie to unadvise.
    IEventChannel_Advise = m_nCookie
End Function
```

In general, subscriber implementations are defined in a separate ActiveX project so that they can be registered for events at run time. One possible alternative could be to create an ActiveX DLL project that defines subscriber classes. To define a subscriber class, perform the following steps.

1. Add a project reference to the ISubscriber interface data type (via the References option of the Project menu in the Visual Basic IDE). The location of this information will be in a COM type library. Depending on the packaging, the type library can be a stand-alone .tlb file or it can be embedded in an ActiveX server binary (DLL or EXE).

2. Add a new class module to the project.

3. Implement the ISubscriber interface using the keyword *Implements*. A subscriber implementation should look similar to the following code extract:

```
' SubscriberImpl.cls
Option Explicit

Implements ISubscriber

Private Sub ISubscriber_Push(ByVal Context As String, _
                             ByVal vData As Variant)

    ' Add subscriber-specific implementation code here.

End Sub
```

4. The final step involves code that resembles the following code extract to register subscriber objects on an event channel.

```
' Client stitch-in code for subscribing to "someevent" on
' an event channel referenced by m_EventChannel
m_nCookie = m_EventChannel.Advise("someevent", _
                                  New SubscriberImpl)
```

As you saw in the EventChannelImpl class code extract on the previous page, subscribers register for notification on a specified context that can be generated on the fly. It's important to recognize that the event channel determines the behavior of the event service infrastructure. The event channel in this case expects to register objects at run time under a context. The client provides both the object and the context at run time, as shown in the previous client code extract. In another scenario, the event channel could just as easily create subscriber instances and register to a context based on subscriber class information stored in a relational database.

Sample Application

A form in Visual Basic is represented as a special type of class that includes hooks into the Windows graphical user interface (GUI) technology. The gory details of the hooks remain suppressed within the Visual Basic run-time library. What the Visual Basic programmer has access to is a special type of class module officially referred to as a Form module. A Form module is associated with a particular window that can contain controls (children) such as buttons and list boxes. Both the window and its controls raise events in response to user inter-action. Visual Basic auto-magically subscribes to events simply by allowing the programmer to stub out event handler subroutines made readily available in the Object drop-down list box in the Form class module editor. This means of event handling, which by the way should be considered an implementation of an Event Service design pattern, has been the cornerstone technology advantage of pro-gramming Windows GUI applications in Visual Basic.

The purpose of this sample is to create a localized Windows application. The typical approach to localizing an application calls for replacing string lit-erals with variable references to strings that are obtained from a table. The form that would display the text usually follows one of two approaches: It incor-porates some auto-proportioning algorithm to resize the form and its controls, and makes font changes appropriately to accommodate the language text; or it determines a static proportion that can accommodate all anticipated languages the application must display. Both approaches eventually fall short of an ideal solution mainly because there is such a great disparity between the number of characters required to represent the words that form a given phrase. For example, a phrase in German that requires 100 characters might require only one char-acter in Japanese.

A third, less practiced alternative exists, which would be to maintain a completely separate form for each language. By using this approach, you can customize the display to the exact dimensions required. The important issue with this alternative is that you must figure out how to get all forms to publish iden-tical events that a single subscriber can handle. Hence the behavior is written once and remains consistent across multiple language implementations that can be provided at any point. You would also want to package each language version in its own satellite DLL that is interchangeable in the Windows application.

What better way to implement this third alternative than by taking advan-tage of the ActiveX DLL technology available in Visual Basic? Unfortunately, Form classes must be private in an ActiveX project, making them inaccessible from a client application. My solution to this problem is to create a public ActiveX class that encapsulates a Form object and delegates through appropri-ate method calls such as *IForm.Show* and *IForm.Hide*. In addition, this class must be able to notify a subscriber of events that would normally be handled in the Form class. This is accomplished by creating the interface-based implementa-tion solution of the Event Service design pattern that publishes the events cap-tured in the private Form object defined in the ActiveX DLL.

To clearly demonstrate the benefits of this approach, I've created a simulated online banking window that allows you to proceed in English or in Spanish by the click of a button. Based on your selection, you get the Security form in English or in Spanish. (See Figure 13-2.) Notice that despite the difference in language, pressing the OK and Cancel buttons produces identical behavior in both windows. Under the hood, this application consists of the following components.

- **FormsEnglish.DLL and FormsSpanish.DLL** Each ActiveX DLL defines the language-specific Security form for logging into the system.

- **Banker.exe** A Standard EXE that defines the initial Welcome form. Banker.exe creates an IForm object that either privately references an English or a Spanish Form object.

- **FormLib.tlb** A type library containing interfaces IForm and IForm-Events shared by the Banker EXE and the FormsEnglish and Forms-Spanish DLLs.

The code in the following discussion highlights the participants of the Event Service design pattern that contribute to the successful implementation of a localized satellite Forms DLL. For a full source code disclosure, refer to the companion CD.

The following components are compiled in FormLib.tlb and defined using IDL rather than Visual Basic. (Appendix B explains how to define interfaces in IDL directly and the reasons for doing so.)

Figure 13-2.
Sample application localized Security login window.

■ **IForm (Implicit IPublisher and explicit IEventChannel)** This interface defines the methods that invoke the encapsulated Form object and that register a subscriber interested in Form events. But it also provides *Advise* and *UnAdvise* methods for subscribing and unsubscribing, respectively, to events published by a concrete class of object that implements this interface. The events published in this case will coincide with the events initially captured in the encapsulated Form object.

```
interface IForm : IDispatch {
        [id(0x60030000)]
        HRESULT Show(
                [in, optional, defaultvalue(0)]
                        FormModalityConstants Modal,
                [in, optional] VARIANT OwnerForm);
        [id(0x60030001)]
        HRESULT Hide();
        [id(0x60030002)]
        HRESULT Advise(
                        [in] IFormEvents* frmEvt,
                        [in, optional] BSTR Notify,
                        [out, retval] long* );
        [id(0x60030003)]
        HRESULT UnAdvise([in] long Cookie);
    };
```

■ **IFormEvents** Defines event signatures published by concrete implementations of IForm, which in this case is the FormLogin class.

```
interface IFormEvents : IDispatch {
        [id(0x60030000), vararg]
        HRESULT OnEvent(
                [in] BSTR Evt,
                [in, out] SAFEARRAY(VARIANT)* Params);
    };
```

This next component is defined in both FormsEnglish.DLL and FormsSpanish.DLL:

■ **FormLogin (hybrid of PublisherImpl and EventChannelImpl classes)** Concrete class that implements the IForm interface. Its sole purpose is to delegate invocations to an associated private Form object and to publish events initially captured by the private Form object. Publishing is implicit because there isn't a separate IPublisher interface. Publishing occurs within the code, as the following code illustrates. Each satellite language ActiveX DLL must contain this class definition.

```
' FormLogin Class
Implements FormLib.IForm

' Form frmLogin related variables
Private m_frmLogin As frmLogin
Private WithEvents cmdOK As CommandButton
Private WithEvents cmdCancel As CommandButton

' IFormEvents
Private m_FormEvents As IFormEvents
    ⋮
' IForm interface implementation
Private Function IForm_Advise(ByVal frmEvt As _
                              FormLib.IFormEvents, _
                              Optional ByVal Notify _
                              As String) As Long
    Set m_FormEvents = frmEvt
End Function

' Form frmLogin event handlers that publish Form events to
' an IFormEvents object via its OnEvent method
'
Private Sub cmdCancel_Click()
    ' Publish cmdCancel button click event
    If Not m_FormEvents Is Nothing Then
        Call m_FormEvents.OnEvent("cmdCancel.Click")
    End If
End Sub

Private Sub cmdOK_Click()
    ' Publish cmdOK button click event
    If Not m_FormEvents Is Nothing Then
        Call m_FormEvents.OnEvent("cmdOK.Click", _
                              m_frmLogin.txtUserName, _
                              m_frmLogin.txtPassword)
    End If
End Sub
```

This final component is defined in Banker.exe:

■ **FormEventsImpl**   Concrete class that implements the IFormEvents interface. It implements event handlers to event signatures defined in the IFormEvents interface. In this particular sample application, this class is the only implemented subscriber. Hence consistent behavior is maintained across multiple satellite DLLs.

```
' FormEventsImpl Class

Implements FormLib.IFormEvents

' Implementation of IFormEvents.OnEvent
Private Sub IFormEvents_OnEvent(ByVal Evt As String, _
                                ParamArray Params() _
                                As Variant)
    If Evt = "cmdOK.Click" Then
        MsgBox "Ok button clicked" & vbLf & _
               "UserId = " & Params(0) & vbLf & _
               "Password = " & Params(1)
    Else
        MsgBox "Cancel button clicked"
    End If

End Sub
```

COMments

Using the Class Events technique is the native language support solution for an Event Service design pattern implementation in Visual Basic. It's definitely one of those features that lives up to the Visual Basic reputation of being unbelievably easy to implement while providing extremely powerful results. There is one huge disclaimer however. You must be aware of the underlying technology implemented by Visual Basic. Under the hood, this design pattern is implemented using Microsoft's COM connectable object technology. (Full documentation of this technology is available in the Microsoft Developer Network (MSDN) library.) Registering a subscriber requires a minimum of three interface method calls. Using *WithEvents* in-process and in the same threading apartment (see Chapter 3 for a complete discussion on threading) has negligible performance implications. Referencing objects out-of-process using *WithEvents* is costly, however, and should be avoided by all means.

Another subtle but important aspect of the Class Events approach is that the notification process is opaque. The only action that the event source class object can perform in Visual Basic is to raise an event by invoking the reserved word *RaiseEvent* and specifying the name of the event. When multiple subscriber class objects are registered to receive events via the *WithEvents* reserved word, controlling or determining the order of notification is impossible. You therefore can't set priority notifications. Also, there is no way to break the successive calls to all subscriber class objects. For example, you might want an event to bubble up through a list of ordered subscribers. Each subscriber can be empowered to cancel the event and prevent it from traveling to other subscribers. Finally, event publication is synchronous in COM connectable object technology. An event can easily get hung up in a subscriber, preventing the event channel from carrying out the publication to other subscribers.

A better alternative to using the Class Events method is the interface-based approach. With this approach, you build your own event channel, thereby avoiding the use of the COM connectable object technology. To this end, subscriber registration can be accomplished with a single interface method call; you're in complete control of the notification order; and your event channel can notify subscribers asynchronously. You are limited only by your design decisions.

It wouldn't be fair if I didn't mention the fact that Microsoft has realized that the COM connectable object technology is not a truly robust event service. In response, Microsoft has developed a whole new event service running as an operating system service in Windows 2000 as part of the Microsoft COM+ technology package. Consider the service to be an event channel that now supports most of the features you would have to build yourself using the interface-based technique.

Related Patterns

In general, the Event Service design pattern complements all other patterns because it provides a nonintrusive means of dynamically extending a system's behavior.

APPENDIXES

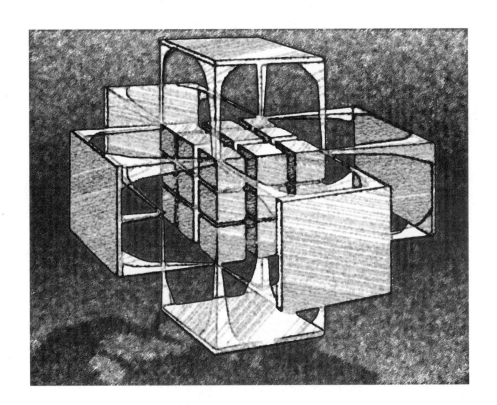

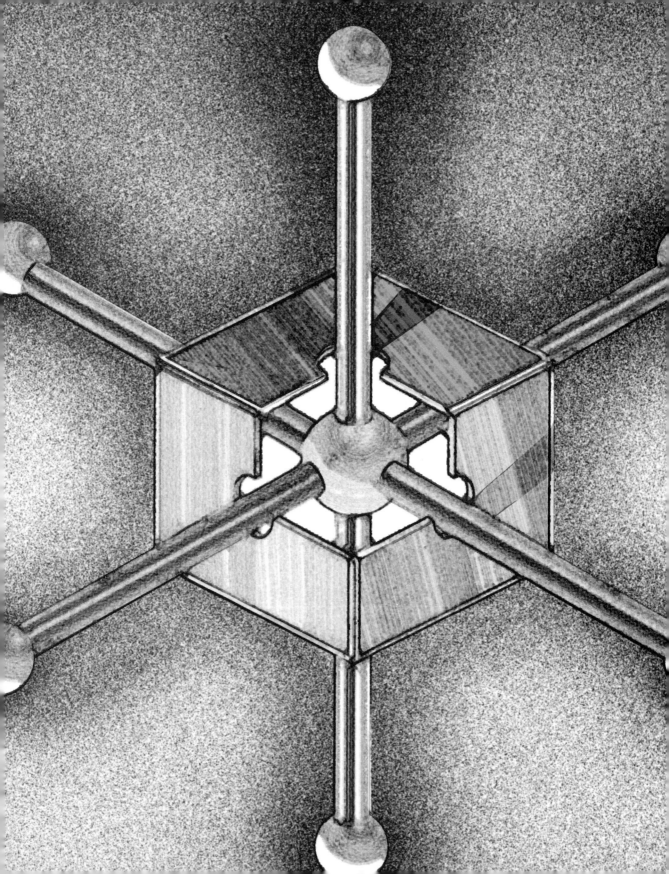

Object Notation

To illustrate concepts in this book, I used industry standard object modeling diagrams to visually depict interfaces, classes, objects, and the relationships that exist between them within a given context. The diagrams you'll find in this book include OMT class diagrams, OMT object diagrams, COM object diagrams, and UML interaction diagrams. What follows is a brief explanation of each type of diagram.

OMT Class Diagrams

Every "Object Model" section in Part II of this book contains a class diagram in Object Modeling Technique (OMT) notation that describes in pictorial form the design pattern covered in the chapter. The following discussion provides a brief summary of a subset of the basic class diagram notation used in this book. Refer to the book *Object-Oriented Modeling and Design* by James Rumbaugh et al. (Prentice-Hall, 1991) for more information.

In OMT notation, classes are represented as rectangles. Classes can be either abstract or concrete. Showing the class name in an italic font indicates abstract classes (interfaces). Concrete classes show their class names in a roman font. In this book, I illustrate both abstract and concrete classes with and without attributes, as shown in Figure A-1.

An abstract class is equivalent to an interface in COM. It is not creatable, but it can be inherited by another interface. This type of interface inheritance is not supported as of version 6 of Microsoft Visual Basic, but it is supported in other COM-enabled languages such as Microsoft Visual J++ and Microsoft Visual C++. Concrete classes can also inherit interfaces, and Visual Basic does

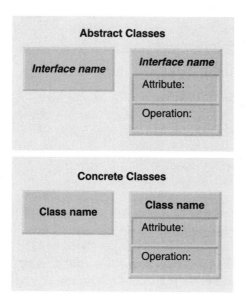

Figure A-1.
Class and interface entities depicted in an OMT diagram.

support this functionality. Furthermore, a concrete class defined in Visual Basic can inherit multiple interfaces. (See Figure A-2.)

A concrete class is creatable and is considered a named implementation of an interface. Interfaces represent a type, whereas concrete classes represent a unique implementation of a type. When a concrete class inherits multiple interfaces, it must provide implementations for all properties and methods in each interface. An instance of a concrete class can therefore support multiple types. Conversely, multiple concrete classes can implement a single interface, resulting in unique classes of objects that support the same type. Consequently, you gain the benefit of polymorphism.

Unlike Visual J++ and Visual C++, Visual Basic doesn't support implementation inheritance, which is the ability for one concrete class to inherit the implementation of another. In general, two types of implementation inheritance exist: public and private. Public inheritance is when a concrete class inherits the interfaces supported by another concrete class and their implementation. Private inheritance is when a concrete class inherits only the implementation of another concrete class, not the interfaces. Even though it's not supported directly, public and private inheritance can be accomplished in Visual Basic with a combination

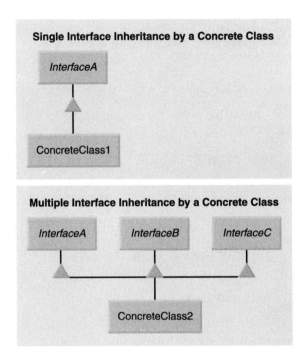

Figure A-2.
OMT diagram depicting Visual Basic support of interface inheritance.

of interface inheritance and composition. Composition is when a class defines a reference to another class. Implementation reuse is therefore possible without inheritance. Defining a reference from one class to another in OMT is referred to as an association. A solid line represents an association. (See Figure A-3.)

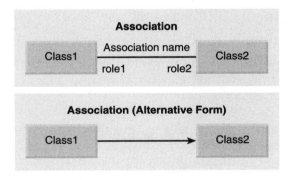

Figure A-3.
Association depicted in OMT.

A class can also define multiple associations between other classes. This multiplicity is represented by various line endings, as illustrated in Figure A-4.

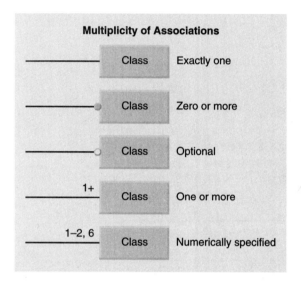

Figure A-4.
Multiplicity of associations depicted in OMT.

Another type of association depicted in OMT is aggregation, shown in Figure A-5. Aggregation is represented by a diamond on the end of the association line that touches the class that contains the references to another

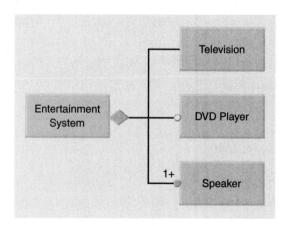

Figure A-5.
Aggregation depicted in OMT.

class. The difference between normal association and aggregation is subtle but important to distinguish. If the class containing the references tightly defines itself in terms of the classes it references, aggregation is appropriate. For example, an entertainment system is an aggregation of a television, a DVD player, speakers, and so on.

OMT Object Diagrams

In some chapters, I've used OMT object diagrams to further illuminate a concept. Object diagrams illustrate a particular instance of a class, as shown in Figure A-6. Objects are represented as rectangles with round edges. The object naming convention is usually to include the name of the class, prefixed by the letter "a" or the word "an," within parentheses. For example, if the class name is "Apple," the object name is "anApple."

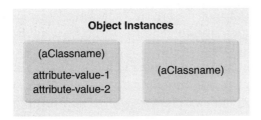

Figure A-6.
Object instances depicted in OMT.

COM Object Diagrams

Because Visual Basic is deeply rooted in COM, and most samples that I've included are based on ActiveX projects, I occasionally provide a COM object diagram to further explain a sample application. COM objects are represented as rectangles with round edges. COM interfaces are illustrated as a line with a circle at one end (affectionately referred to as a lollipop). The noncircle end touches the rectangle. The de facto interface naming convention is to prefix an interface name with a capital letter "I." For an object to be considered a COM object, it must support the IUnknown interface. IUnknown is normally rooted at the top of the rectangle. (See Figure A-7.)

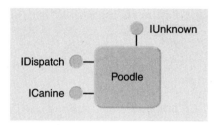

Figure A-7.
COM object diagram.

UML Interaction Diagrams

An alternative approach to listing the steps required to produce an end result is to illustrate the steps in an interaction diagram. For example, in the Object By Value design pattern chapter (Chapter 6), I use a Unified Modeling Language (UML) interaction diagram to describe copying an object by value from one process to another. This particular type of interaction diagram is also called a sequence diagram because it emphasizes the time ordering of object requests. Time flows down the *y*-axis, and the objects are listed on the *x*-axis. Objects follow the same naming convention described for OMT object diagrams (prefixed with the letter "a" or the word "an"). Solid vertical lines underneath the object represent the object's lifetime. Dashed vertical lines indicate that the object hasn't been created yet. Vertical rectangle regions indicate that the object is currently active. A horizontal line with an arrowhead on one end specifies an object request made to a target object. The request name is directly above the line. Requests flow in both directions. A request to create an object is a dashed horizontal line with an arrowhead. See Figure A-8 for an example of an interaction diagram.

> NOTE: Some of the diagrams you see in this book might initially appear as if the *x* and *y* axes are reversed, but in reality they've simply been turned on their sides so that the diagram will fit on a single book page.

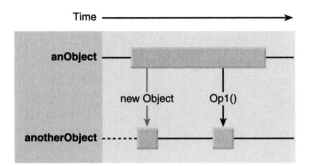

Figure A-8.
UML interaction sequence diagram (shown on its side, a style you'll see used throughout this book).

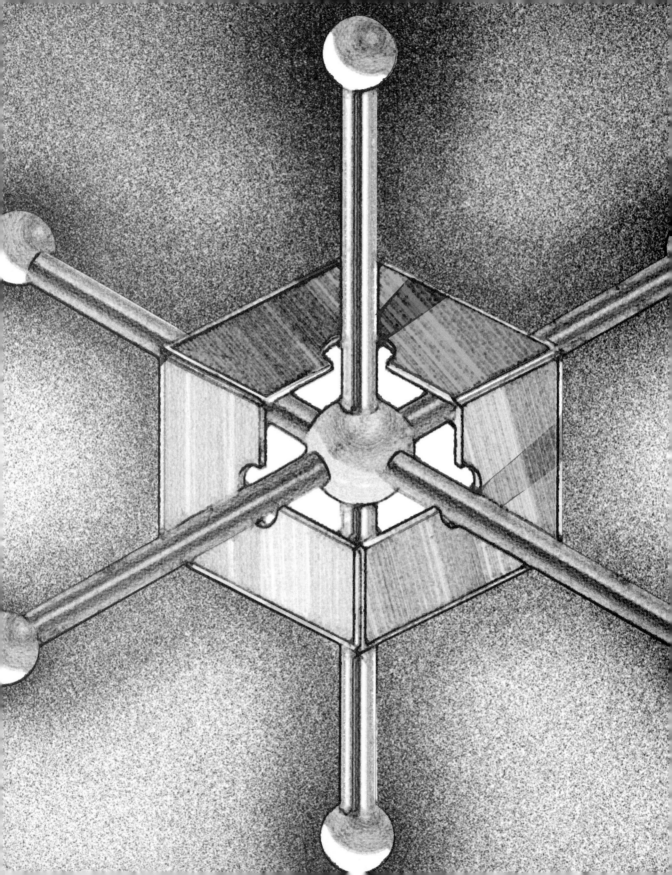

Working with Interfaces and Classes

Interfaces are the essence of most design patterns described in this book. Interfaces define the roles and determine the relationships of design pattern object participants. The design patterns featured in this book are implemented using Microsoft Visual Basic, which is possible only because the object-oriented language features in Visual Basic depend on COM and ActiveX. That said, interfaces are a cornerstone of the COM specification, which requires a formal abstraction of interface from implementation. It is therefore crucial to understand and appreciate how interfaces impact a system. This appendix briefly explains the following topics:

- Defining COM interfaces and classes in Visual Basic

- Freezing an interface contract using features provided in the Visual Basic integrated development environment (IDE) and using COM Interface Definition Language (IDL)

- Supporting Automation in ActiveX components created in Visual Basic for the benefit of scripting languages, such as Microsoft Visual Basic, Scripting Edition (VBScript) and Microsoft JScript, which are utilized by other technologies such as Active Server Pages (ASP)—Microsoft's scripting solution for a Web application that provides dynamic Web content

For more information on these topics, refer to Ted Pattison's book *Programming Distributed Applications with COM and Microsoft Visual Basic 6.0* and the article "Visual Basic Design Time Techniques to Prevent Runtime Version Conflicts," both of which are cited in the bibliography on page 249.

Defining COM Interfaces and Classes in Visual Basic

COM classes are named implementations of COM interfaces. A COM class can implement multiple interfaces and must implement at least one. A client obtains a reference to an instance of a COM class (an object) that implements an interface that the client expects.

A public creatable Visual Basic class is a COM class that has, at minimum, a single interface, which is referred to as its default interface. The default interface is provided internally by Visual Basic and serves two main purposes. First, it provides Automation support, which I'll go over in more detail later in this appendix. Second, it simplifies the formality of COM by making the distinction between the default interface and the implementation (the COM class) implicit. This implicit distinction allows class properties and methods defined as Public, such as those in the following code fragment, to automatically become part of the default interface.

```
' Class BankAccount
'
Public Property Get Balance() As Double
    ' Return the bank account balance.
End Property

Public Function Deposit(Amount As Double) As Double
    ' Deposit funds in the bank account.
End Function
```

This implicit use of the default interface also allows a Visual Basic client to declare object variables as types that appear to be class names, not distinguishable interface names, as shown in the following code fragment.

```
' Visual Basic Client
'
Dim myBankAccount As BankAccount
Dim dblBalance As Double

Set myBankAccount = New BankAccount

dblBalance = myBankAccount.Deposit(1000)
```

To me, declaring variables in this way seems to cloud the COM rule of separating the interface from the implementation and only leads to confusion. But the default interface exists, and *myBankAccount* is in reality typed as an interface, not as a class.

As illustrated throughout Part II of this book, defining and implementing interfaces in Visual Basic is straightforward. To define an interface, perform the following steps.

1. Add a class module to an ActiveX project.

2. Change the class module's *Instancing* property value to PublicNotCreatable.

3. Declare public properties and methods with no implementation code, as shown in the following code fragment.

```
' Interface IBankAccount
'
Public Property Get Balance() As Double
End Property

Public Function Deposit(Amount As Double) As Double
End Function
```

4. Implement additional interfaces in a Visual Basic class via the keyword *Implements*, as shown in the following code fragment.

```
' Class BankAccountImpl
'
Implements IBankAccount

Private Property Get IBankAccount_Balance() As Double
    ' Return the bank account balance.
End Property

Private Function IBankAccount_Deposit(Amount As Double) _
  As Double
    ' Deposit funds in the bank account.
End Function
```

You can see that implementing additional interfaces in a class is explicit. Notice that the implementation functions are declared as Private. Public declarations always apply to the default interface, which in the previous code fragment would be BankAccountImpl. Also, as the next code fragment illustrates, the client must explicitly declare a variable of type IBankAccount to reference the IBankAccount interface.

```
' Visual Basic Client
'
Dim myBankAccount As IBankAccount
Dim dblBalance As Double

Set myBankAccount = New BankAccountImpl
dblBalance  = MyBankAccount.Deposit(1000)
```

Providing that the code has no bugs, when you make the ActiveX project Visual Basic will create a type library that contains COM interface and class definitions as originally defined using only Visual Basic language features. (A type library is a COM artifact that consists of COM interface and class definitions in a binary package.) The type library is embedded into the ActiveX compiled file (DLL, OCX, or EXE). When the ActiveX component is registered on a computer, information about the interfaces and classes contained in the type library are added to the Windows Registry on that computer (more on this subject later).

Freezing Interface Contracts

If you're following best practices, once you've published an interface it should remain static because an interface should be considered a binding contract between the client that references it and the class that implements it. Without conscious care, run-time error 429, "ActiveX component can't create object," will occur. This error is raised when a client attempts to reference an interface that doesn't exist. Three main problems generate this error: COM can't find the ActiveX component; the type library of interfaces and classes isn't registered; or an interface contract has been broken. The first two reasons can be chalked up to easily resolvable configuration errors. The third, however, requires our utmost attention.

Problems involving broken interface contracts become significantly amplified in two common scenarios: naive ActiveX component developers deploy their components, which are then used by clients built elsewhere; and component team development environments. In the first scenario, the inexperienced component developer will typically deploy subsequent releases of a component that contains broken interface contracts to computers running the client application, thereby breaking clients that functioned properly with the previous version.

In the second scenario, incompatibilities occur in the development environments of the team members when each member does independent builds on his or her own machine based on the most current source files checked into the source control system. When a team works with a source control system, it's reasonable to adhere to a premise based on best efforts, which states that only proven, successfully built and tested source code should be checked into the source control database. You might think adhering to this premise would prevent any problems, but when the team is working with COM components an additional stipulation must be followed: before a team can co-develop an ActiveX component, interfaces must be defined and frozen.

COM identifies unique interfaces and classes not by the name you give them in Visual Basic but rather by globally unique identifiers (GUIDs). A GUID is 128-bit value that is guaranteed to be unique across time and space. GUIDs can be generated via the COM API function *CoCreateGuid*. A simple alternative is to generate GUIDs using Guidgen.exe, a utility that ships with Microsoft Visual Studio and with the Microsoft Platform SDK. By means of its simple user interface, as illustrated in Figure B-1, you can generate new GUIDs in four different formats and cut and paste them into your application. GUIDs that identify interfaces and classes are often referred to as IIDs (interface identifiers) and CLSIDs (class identifiers), respectively. GUIDs predate COM, where they're used in remote procedure calls (RPCs) and referred to as UUIDs (universally unique identifiers). All these types of IDs are synonymous. COM users prefer the term GUID.

> NOTE: Guidgen.exe is installed as part of the Visual Studio product suite and is by default located in the \Program Files\Microsoft Visual Studio\Common\Tools directory.

During the ActiveX component project Make process, Visual Basic internally calls *CoCreateGuid* to generate GUIDs for all interfaces and classes you defined within the project. To enable you to control GUID generation, I'll first explain how Visual Basic handles it, and then I'll describe the ideal solution for handling it by using a combination of Visual Basic features and COM IDL.

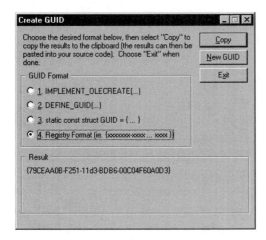

Figure B-1.
Guidgen.exe is a simple and easy way to obtain new GUIDs.

Controlling Interface Compatibility with Visual Basic

Visual Basic allows you to select one of three compatibility options. Select Project Properties from the Project menu, select the Component tab, and then select an option in the Version Compatibility frame. As you can see in Figure B-2, the options are No Compatibility, Project Compatibility, and Binary Compatibility.

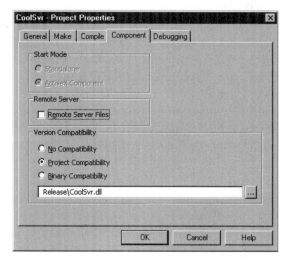

Figure B-2.
Set the compatibility option in the Project Properties dialog box.

Selecting the No Compatibility option will cause Visual Basic to generate new GUIDs for all interfaces, classes, and the embedded type library every time you build the component. Both the Project Compatibility and Binary Compatibility options use a previously registered type library to determine interface compatibility. The results generated by selecting the Project Compatibility option differ depending on the version of Visual Basic you're running. Visual Basic 5 will retain the GUID that identifies the type library but will generate new IIDs and CLSIDs. Visual Basic 6 will only generate new IIDs. It retains CLSIDs across builds with the intention of supporting scripting clients that reference objects via CLSIDs. In other words, every time you build the project clients that bind to interfaces using the IIDs will fail, but scripting clients will continue to work. Project Compatibility mode also allows you to extend an interface by adding new properties and methods. To support this feature, Visual Basic generates a new IID that identifies the interface with the additions, and it adds an IID substitution entry that maps the old IID to the new IID in the Registry. Clients compiled with the older version therefore continue to work by binding to the new interface. New clients bind directly to the new interface.

Binary Compatibility provides the same features as Project Compatibility, with one addition. If you build your project with binary compatibility and then change an existing method, Visual Basic will alert you of a binary incompatibility prior to building the component. (See Figure B-3.) Clicking OK will result in breaking interface compatibility on older clients. New clients will obviously work. GUIDs that identify user-defined types (UDTs) and enumerations are also regenerated.

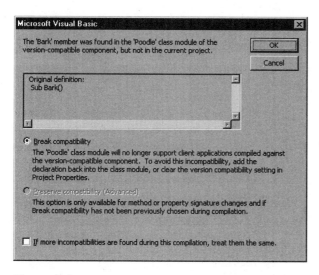

Figure B-3.
Interface incompatibility alert dialog box.

Controlling Interface Compatibility with Visual Basic and COM IDL

None of the available interface compatibility options provided in Visual Basic alone enforces interface uniqueness and freezes interface contracts in the most appropriate and efficient way. Any action that results in changing an interface, including adding new methods, should be considered the creation of a new interface, not an extension to an existing one. To gain full control of this issue, you should do the following.

- Avoid defining any properties and methods in the default interface (public method definitions in a public creatable class), with the exception of interface accessor methods for scripting language purposes. This point is explained in detail in the "Defining Automation Support" section.

- Define interfaces using COM IDL.

- Compile the IDL file into a type library using the Microsoft IDL (MIDL) compiler (midl.exe), which is included in the Visual C++ install.

- Register the type library using the Microsoft Type Library Registration Tool (regtlib.exe), which is located in the %SystemRoot% directory (\Windows in Windows 98 and Windows 95, \Winnt in Windows NT and Windows 2000).

- Servers that define classes that implement the interfaces and clients that bind to the interfaces supported by the classes must reference the same type library. Select References from the Project menu to open the References dialog box and set the appropriate references for a project. (See Figure B-4.)

- Once you've defined all classes that implement the interfaces packaged in the type library, select Binary Compatibility in the Project Properties dialog box to ensure that scripting clients continue to work across component builds.

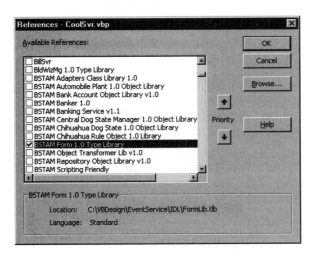

Figure B-4.
Project References dialog box.

To keep code fragments simple and straightforward throughout this book, you'll see in the "Implementation" section of many of the chapters in Part II that I illustrate how to create interfaces using only Visual Basic. However, if you've looked at the sample applications on the companion CD you've notice that in many instances I use a combination of Visual Basic and COM IDL to address the issue of enforcing interface compatibility. So it's only fair that I explain the two undisclosed tasks at this point: defining interfaces in COM IDL and compiling the IDL file into a type library.

Defining Interfaces in COM IDL

IDL, which stands for Interface Definition Language, is a C-like language used mainly for defining COM interfaces. Interface definitions are typically kept in .IDL text files that are eventually compiled into type libraries. The following code fragment of DogLib.idl (taken from the Chapter 12 sample application) illustrates the structure of an IDL file that is compatible with Visual Basic. (I stripped out some of the code to highlight the most important parts that we'll focus on.)

```
// File Name:    DogLib.idl

[
  uuid(F6378500-526F-11D3-BD77-00C04F60A0D3),
  helpstring("BSTAM Dog 1.0 Type Library")
]
library DogLib
{
    // TLib :  // TLib : OLE Automation :
    {00020430-0000-0000-C000-000000000046}
    importlib("STDOLE2.TLB");

    [
      uuid(F6378503-526F-11D3-BD77-00C04F60A0D3),
      dual,
      nonextensible,
      oleautomation
    ]
    interface IDog : IDispatch {
        :
        HRESULT Bark([out, retval] BSTR* );
    };
```

The following is a description of some of the elements in the IDL file.

- ■ **uuid(F6378500-526F-11D3-BD77-00C04F60A0D3)**   This line (in square brackets above the library statement) is the GUID associated with the DogLib type library that will be added to the Registry.

- ■ **library DogLib**   Defines the DogLib type library. In addition, all interfaces to be exposed in a type library must be defined within the *library* statement block.

- ■ **importlib("STDOLE2.TLB");**   This line is an instruction to import interfaces defined in type library STDOLE2.TLB. The IDispatch interface that is inherited by the IDog interface is obtained from the imported type library. To import interfaces from an IDL file, use the keyword *import*.

- ■ **uuid(F6378503-526F-11D3-BD77-00C04F60A0D3)**   This IID identifies the IDog interface.

- ■ **dual**   Attribute of interface IDog that indicates to the MIDL (Microsoft Interface Definition Language) compiler that IDog is both a custom v-table bound interface attribute and an Automation interface because it derives from interface IDispatch. Scripting language clients can then reference the IDog interface.

- ■ **nonextensible**   The IDispatch implementation includes only properties and methods defined in the IDog interface and can't be extended at run time with additional methods not defined in the interface.

- ■ **oleautomation**   Indicates to the MIDL compiler that you'll only use types in interface IDog that are supported by Visual Basic. You'll get a compiler warning when you don't adhere to those types. This attribute can also be used with pure custom interfaces (interfaces that don't derive from IDispatch).

- ■ **interface IDog : IDispatch**   Specifics an interface IDog that derives from interface IDispatch, thereby making it a dual interface. Methods are defined within the interface.

Compiling IDL into a Type Library

Once you've defined your interfaces in an IDL file, similar to the previous code fragment, run the file through the MIDL compiler to generate a type library (.TLB file). MIDL is a command-line compiler, meaning you must execute it from a command line as follows:

```
midl DogLib.idl
```

Defining interfaces using IDL might seem a little strange at first, but you eventually get used to it. You're probably thinking it must be difficult to get the IDL code right, especially as the project grows in size. To avoid these worries, you can use the best IDL code generator for Visual Basic available on the market— Visual Basic. To generate an IDL file in Visual Basic, perform the following steps.

1. Create and save an ActiveX DLL project, suffixing the name of the project with IDLGen. Visual Basic requires you to have at least one public creatable class in your project, but you don't have to put anything in it.

2. For each interface you want to define in the IDL file, you must add a class module and change its *Instancing* property value to PublicNotCreatable and define public properties and methods for the interface.

3. Make the DLL.

4. Using the OLE/COM Object Viewer utility that ships with Visual Studio, locate the type library embedded in the DLL. With a little house cleaning, you can reverse engineer the IDL into an .IDL text file. (To start the OLE/COM Object Viewer, select it from the Tools menu in Visual C++ or run the oleview.exe file directly.)

5. Unregister the IDLGen DLL.

6. Compile the cleaned up IDL using the MIDL compiler.

Defining Automation Support

You can define all interfaces, with the exception of the default interface, in a COM IDL file and compile the file into a type library using the MIDL compiler. Visual Basic doesn't allow you to change the default interface. The default interface is a dual interface, meaning it's a custom interface that derives from IDispatch. IDispatch is the only interface that a scripting language client can reference. For example, this type of reference occurs in VBScript when a variable is declared as Object, which is illustrated in the following code fragment.

```
Dim d As Object

Set d = CreateObject("CanineSvr.DogImpl")
d.bark
```

The call to the *bark* method translates to a call to the *IDispatch.Invoke* method, which invokes the default interface *bark* method call. If the *bark* method is defined in another interface implemented by the DogImpl class, Visual Basic will raise run-time error 438: "Object doesn't support this property or method." The reason this error is raised is that because the scripting language doesn't support custom interface referencing, it has no means by which to query for an interface. To address this problem, Visual Basic defines a default dual interface that the scripting language can reference. According to the rules of Automation implemented in Visual Basic, IDispatch can invoke methods only on its custom interface counterpart. This limitation can be overcome in other languages, such as C++ and Visual J++, but unfortunately not in Visual Basic. Hence, most Visual Basic programmers consider dual interfaces evil.

Nonetheless, with a conscious architecture decision, you can make dual interfaces work for you in Visual Basic to provide scripting support for all interfaces implemented in a Visual Basic COM class. This support can be accomplished by using the default interface only to define interface accessor methods for all other dual interfaces implemented by the class. The following code fragment is an example of such an implementation.

```
' Class FooBar defined in project FBLib

Option Explicit

Implements IFoo
Implements IBar

' Define interface accessor methods in the implicit default
' interface FooBar in class FooBar to access interfaces IFoo
' and IBar.
Public Function getIFoo() As IFoo
    Set getIFoo = Me
End Function

Public Function getIBar() As IBar
    Set getIBar = Me
End Function

' IBar interface implementation
Private Sub IBar_doBar()
    MsgBox "Doing IBar"
End Sub
```

```
' IFoo interface implementation
Private Sub IFoo_doFoo()
    MsgBox "Doing IFoo"
End Sub

Private Function IFoo_doFoo2(A As Integer, B As Integer) As Integer
    IFoo_doFoo2 = A * B
End Function
```

A scripting language client will now be able to access the nondefault interfaces IFoo and IBar because of the interface accessor methods defined in the default FooBar interface and because IFoo and IBar are also dual interfaces. The following code fragment illustrates a scripting client accessing the IFoo and IBar interfaces.

```
' Visual Basic Scripting Client

Dim myFoo As Object
Dim myBar As Object
Dim myFooBar As Object
Dim iAnswer As Integer

Set myFooBar = CreateObject("FBLib.FooBar")

Set myFoo = myFooBar.getIFoo()
myFoo.doFoo
iAnswer = myFoo.doFoo2(5, 2)

Set myBar = myFooBar.getBar()
myBar.doBar
```

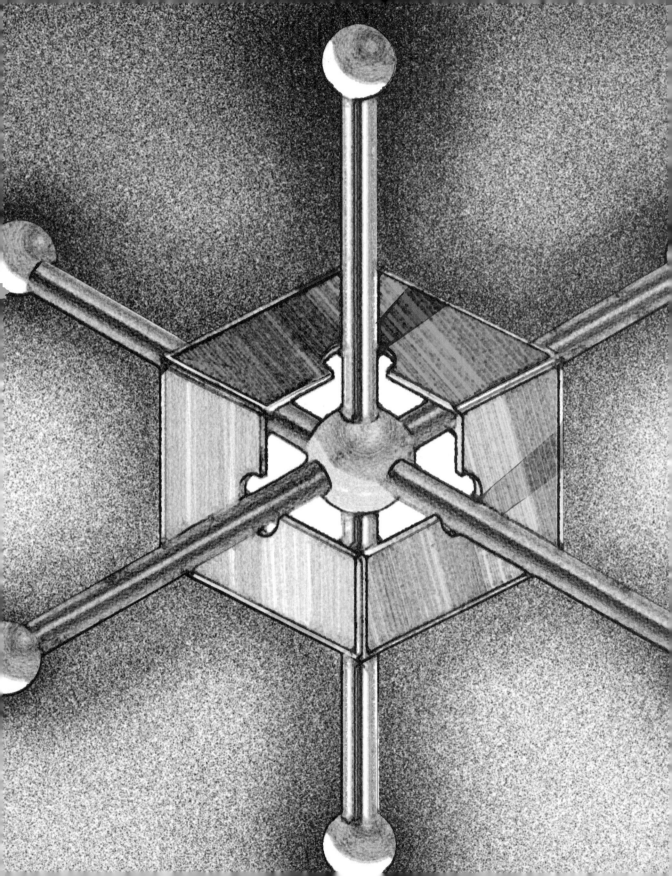

Bibliography

Booch, Grady, James Rumbaugh, and Ivar Jacobson. *The Unified Modeling Language User Guide*. Reading, Mass.: Addison-Wesley, 1999. (ISBN 0-201-57168-4)

Box, Don. *Essential COM*. Reading, Mass.: Addison-Wesley, 1998. (ISBN 0-201-63446-5)

Chappell, David. *Understanding ActiveX and OLE*. Redmond, Wash.: Microsoft Press, 1996. (ISBN 1-57231-216-5)

Gamma, Erich, Richard Helm, Ralph Johnson, and John Vlissides. *Design Patterns*. Reading, Mass.: Addison-Wesley, 1995. (ISBN 0-201-63361-2)

Lippman, Stanley B., and Josee Lajoie. *C++ Primer*. 3d ed. Reading, Mass.: Addison-Wesley, 1998. (ISBN 0-201-82470-1)

McKinney, Bruce. *Hardcore Visual Basic*. 2d ed. Redmond, Wash.: Microsoft Press, 1997. (ISBN 1-57231-422-2)

Pattison, Ted. *Programming Distributed Applications with COM and Microsoft Visual Basic 6.0*. Redmond, Wash.: Microsoft Press, 1998. (ISBN 1-57231-961-5)

Randell, Brian A., and Ted Pattison. "Visual Basic Design Time Techniques to Prevent Runtime Version Conflicts." *Microsoft Systems Journal* (January 2000): 35–49.

Richter, Jeffrey. *Advanced Windows*. 3d ed. Redmond, Wash.: Microsoft Press, 1997. (ISBN 1-57231-548-2)

————. *Programming Applications for Microsoft Windows*. 4th ed. Redmond, Wash.: Microsoft Press, 1999. (1-57231-996-8)

Rogerson, Dale. *Inside COM*. Redmond, Wash.: Microsoft Press, 1997. (ISBN 1-57231-349-8)

Rumbaugh, James, Michael Blaha, William Premerlani, Frederick Eddy, and William Lorensen. *Object-Oriented Modeling and Design*. Englewood Cliffs, N.J.: Prentice-Hall, 1991. (ISBN 0-13-629841-9)

INDEX

Page numbers appearing in italics refer to figures and tables.

William Stamatakis

William Stamatakis is a vice president at Morgan Stanley Dean Witter in New York City, where he designs and develops solutions for the Equities Sales and Trading Division. Fluent in Microsoft Visual Basic, Microsoft Visual C++, COM, and other development tools and technologies, he has taught classes on Visual C++ and the Microsoft Foundation Class (MFC) library for the Learning Tree. He has also contributed articles to *Visual C++ Developers Journal, Dr. Dobb's Journal,* and other publications. In addition to his demanding work schedule, Bill spends countless late night hours doing research and development on technology areas of interest.

Despite his deep-rooted passion for technology, what Bill enjoys most in life is spending quality time with his wife, Elva (taking the picture), and sons, Maxwell (on the tricycle) and Ethan (in the stroller).

The manuscript for this book was prepared and submitted to Microsoft Press in electronic form. Text files were prepared using Microsoft Word 97. Pages were composed by Microsoft Press using Adobe PageMaker 6.52 for Windows, with text in Galliard and display type in Helvetica bold. Composed pages were delivered to the printer as electronic prepress files.

Cover Graphic Designer
Girvin | Strategic Branding & Design

Cover Illustrator
Glenn Mitsui

Interior Graphic Artist
Rob Nance

Principal Compositor
Barb Runyan

Principal Proofreader/Copy Editor
Crystal Thomas

Indexer
Julie Kawabata

MICROSOFT LICENSE AGREEMENT
Book Companion CD

IMPORTANT—READ CAREFULLY: This Microsoft End-User License Agreement ("EULA") is a legal agreement between you (either an individual or an entity) and Microsoft Corporation for the Microsoft product identified above, which includes computer software and may include associated media, printed materials, and "online" or electronic documentation ("SOFTWARE PRODUCT"). Any component included within the SOFTWARE PRODUCT that is accompanied by a separate End-User License Agreement shall be governed by such agreement and not the terms set forth below. By installing, copying, or otherwise using the SOFTWARE PRODUCT, you agree to be bound by the terms of this EULA. If you do not agree to the terms of this EULA, you are not authorized to install, copy, or otherwise use the SOFTWARE PRODUCT; you may, however, return the SOFTWARE PRODUCT, along with all printed materials and other items that form a part of the Microsoft product that includes the SOFTWARE PRODUCT, to the place you obtained them for a full refund.

SOFTWARE PRODUCT LICENSE

The SOFTWARE PRODUCT is protected by United States copyright laws and international copyright treaties, as well as other intellectual property laws and treaties. The SOFTWARE PRODUCT is licensed, not sold.

1. GRANT OF LICENSE. This EULA grants you the following rights:

    a. Software Product. You may install and use one copy of the SOFTWARE PRODUCT on a single computer. The primary user of the computer on which the SOFTWARE PRODUCT is installed may make a second copy for his or her exclusive use on a portable computer.

    b. Storage/Network Use. You may also store or install a copy of the SOFTWARE PRODUCT on a storage device, such as a network server, used only to install or run the SOFTWARE PRODUCT on your other computers over an internal network; however, you must acquire and dedicate a license for each separate computer on which the SOFTWARE PRODUCT is installed or run from the storage device. A license for the SOFTWARE PRODUCT may not be shared or used concurrently on different computers.

    c. License Pak. If you have acquired this EULA in a Microsoft License Pak, you may make the number of additional copies of the computer software portion of the SOFTWARE PRODUCT authorized on the printed copy of this EULA, and you may use each copy in the manner specified above. You are also entitled to make a corresponding number of secondary copies for portable computer use as specified above.

    d. Sample Code. Solely with respect to portions, if any, of the SOFTWARE PRODUCT that are identified within the SOFTWARE PRODUCT as sample code (the "SAMPLE CODE"):

        i. Use and Modification. Microsoft grants you the right to use and modify the source code version of the SAMPLE CODE, *provided* you comply with subsection (d)(iii) below. You may not distribute the SAMPLE CODE, or any modified version of the SAMPLE CODE, in source code form.

        ii. Redistributable Files. Provided you comply with subsection (d)(iii) below, Microsoft grants you a nonexclusive, royalty-free right to reproduce and distribute the object code version of the SAMPLE CODE and of any modified SAMPLE CODE, other than SAMPLE CODE, or any modified version thereof, designated as not redistributable in the Readme file that forms a part of the SOFTWARE PRODUCT (the "Non-Redistributable Sample Code"). All SAMPLE CODE other than the Non-Redistributable Sample Code is collectively referred to as the "REDISTRIBUTABLES."

        iii. Redistribution Requirements. If you redistribute the REDISTRIBUTABLES, you agree to: (i) distribute the REDISTRIBUTABLES in object code form only in conjunction with and as a part of your software application product; (ii) not use Microsoft's name, logo, or trademarks to market your software application product; (iii) include a valid copyright notice on your software application product; (iv) indemnify, hold harmless, and defend Microsoft from and against any claims or lawsuits, including attorney's fees, that arise or result from the use or distribution of your software application product; and (v) not permit further distribution of the REDISTRIBUTABLES by your end user. Contact Microsoft for the applicable royalties due and other licensing terms for all other uses and/or distribution of the REDISTRIBUTABLES.

2. DESCRIPTION OF OTHER RIGHTS AND LIMITATIONS.

    • **Limitations on Reverse Engineering, Decompilation, and Disassembly.** You may not reverse engineer, decompile, or disassemble the SOFTWARE PRODUCT, except and only to the extent that such activity is expressly permitted by applicable law notwithstanding this limitation.

    • **Separation of Components.** The SOFTWARE PRODUCT is licensed as a single product. Its component parts may not be separated for use on more than one computer.

    • **Rental.** You may not rent, lease, or lend the SOFTWARE PRODUCT.

    • **Support Services.** Microsoft may, but is not obligated to, provide you with support services related to the SOFTWARE PRODUCT ("Support Services"). Use of Support Services is governed by the Microsoft policies and programs described in the user manual, in "online" documentation, and/or in other Microsoft-provided materials. Any supplemental software code provided to you as part of the Support Services shall be considered part of the SOFTWARE PRODUCT and subject to the terms and conditions of this EULA. With respect to technical information you provide to Microsoft as part of the Support Services, Microsoft may use such information for its business purposes, including for product support and development. Microsoft will not utilize such technical information in a form that personally identifies you.

- **Software Transfer.** You may permanently transfer all of your rights under this EULA, provided you retain no copies, you transfer all of the SOFTWARE PRODUCT (including all component parts, the media and printed materials, any upgrades, this EULA, and, if applicable, the Certificate of Authenticity), **and** the recipient agrees to the terms of this EULA.

- **Termination.** Without prejudice to any other rights, Microsoft may terminate this EULA if you fail to comply with the terms and conditions of this EULA. In such event, you must destroy all copies of the SOFTWARE PRODUCT and all of its component parts.

3. **COPYRIGHT.** All title and copyrights in and to the SOFTWARE PRODUCT (including but not limited to any images, photographs, animations, video, audio, music, text, SAMPLE CODE, REDISTRIBUTABLES, and "applets" incorporated into the SOFTWARE PRODUCT) and any copies of the SOFTWARE PRODUCT are owned by Microsoft or its suppliers. The SOFTWARE PRODUCT is protected by copyright laws and international treaty provisions. Therefore, you must treat the SOFTWARE PRODUCT like any other copyrighted material **except** that you may install the SOFTWARE PRODUCT on a single computer provided you keep the original solely for backup or archival purposes. You may not copy the printed materials accompanying the SOFTWARE PRODUCT.

4. **U.S. GOVERNMENT RESTRICTED RIGHTS.** The SOFTWARE PRODUCT and documentation are provided with RESTRICTED RIGHTS. Use, duplication, or disclosure by the Government is subject to restrictions as set forth in subparagraph (c)(1)(ii) of the Rights in Technical Data and Computer Software clause at DFARS 252.227-7013 or subparagraphs (c)(1) and (2) of the Commercial Computer Software—Restricted Rights at 48 CFR 52.227-19, as applicable. Manufacturer is Microsoft Corporation/One Microsoft Way/Redmond, WA 98052-6399.

5. **EXPORT RESTRICTIONS.** You agree that you will not export or re-export the SOFTWARE PRODUCT, any part thereof, or any process or service that is the direct product of the SOFTWARE PRODUCT (the foregoing collectively referred to as the "Restricted Components"), to any country, person, entity, or end user subject to U.S. export restrictions. You specifically agree not to export or re-export any of the Restricted Components (i) to any country to which the U.S. has embargoed or restricted the export of goods or services, which currently include, but are not necessarily limited to, Cuba, Iran, Iraq, Libya, North Korea, Sudan, and Syria, or to any national of any such country, wherever located, who intends to transmit or transport the Restricted Components back to such country; (ii) to any end user who you know or have reason to know will utilize the Restricted Components in the design, development, or production of nuclear, chemical, or biological weapons; or (iii) to any end user who has been prohibited from participating in U.S. export transactions by any federal agency of the U.S. government. You warrant and represent that neither the BXA nor any other U.S. federal agency has suspended, revoked, or denied your export privileges.

DISCLAIMER OF WARRANTY

NO WARRANTIES OR CONDITIONS. MICROSOFT EXPRESSLY DISCLAIMS ANY WARRANTY OR CONDITION FOR THE SOFTWARE PRODUCT. THE SOFTWARE PRODUCT AND ANY RELATED DOCUMENTATION ARE PROVIDED "AS IS" WITHOUT WARRANTY OR CONDITION OF ANY KIND, EITHER EXPRESS OR IMPLIED, INCLUDING, WITHOUT LIMITATION, THE IMPLIED WARRANTIES OF MERCHANTABILITY, FITNESS FOR A PARTICULAR PURPOSE, OR NONINFRINGEMENT. THE ENTIRE RISK ARISING OUT OF USE OR PERFORMANCE OF THE SOFTWARE PRODUCT REMAINS WITH YOU.

LIMITATION OF LIABILITY. TO THE MAXIMUM EXTENT PERMITTED BY APPLICABLE LAW, IN NO EVENT SHALL MICROSOFT OR ITS SUPPLIERS BE LIABLE FOR ANY SPECIAL, INCIDENTAL, INDIRECT, OR CONSEQUENTIAL DAMAGES WHATSOEVER (INCLUDING, WITHOUT LIMITATION, DAMAGES FOR LOSS OF BUSINESS PROFITS, BUSINESS INTERRUPTION, LOSS OF BUSINESS INFORMATION, OR ANY OTHER PECUNIARY LOSS) ARISING OUT OF THE USE OF OR INABILITY TO USE THE SOFTWARE PRODUCT OR THE PROVISION OF OR FAILURE TO PROVIDE SUPPORT SERVICES, EVEN IF MICROSOFT HAS BEEN ADVISED OF THE POSSIBILITY OF SUCH DAMAGES. IN ANY CASE, MICROSOFT'S ENTIRE LIABILITY UNDER ANY PROVISION OF THIS EULA SHALL BE LIMITED TO THE GREATER OF THE AMOUNT ACTUALLY PAID BY YOU FOR THE SOFTWARE PRODUCT OR US$5.00; PROVIDED, HOWEVER, IF YOU HAVE ENTERED INTO A MICROSOFT SUPPORT SERVICES AGREEMENT, MICROSOFT'S ENTIRE LIABILITY REGARDING SUPPORT SERVICES SHALL BE GOVERNED BY THE TERMS OF THAT AGREEMENT. BECAUSE SOME STATES AND JURISDICTIONS DO NOT ALLOW THE EXCLUSION OR LIMITATION OF LIABILITY, THE ABOVE LIMITATION MAY NOT APPLY TO YOU.

MISCELLANEOUS

This EULA is governed by the laws of the State of Washington USA, except and only to the extent that applicable law mandates governing law of a different jurisdiction.

Should you have any questions concerning this EULA, or if you desire to contact Microsoft for any reason, please contact the Microsoft subsidiary serving your country, or write: Microsoft Sales Information Center/One Microsoft Way/Redmond, WA 98052-6399.

OWNER REGISTRATION CARD   **Register Today!**   1-57231-957-7

Return the bottom portion of this card to register today.

Microsoft® Visual Basic® Design Patterns

FIRST NAME   MIDDLE INITIAL   LAST NAME

INSTITUTION OR COMPANY NAME

ADDRESS

CITY   STATE   ZIP

(   )

E-MAIL ADDRESS   PHONE NUMBER

U.S. and Canada addresses only. Fill in information above and mail postage-free.
Please mail only the bottom half of this page.

For information about Microsoft Press®
products, visit our Web site at
mspress.microsoft.com

Microsoft®